PALESTINIANS BETWEEN NA1

Palestinians Between Nationalism and Islam

RAPHAEL ISRAELI

Hebrew University, Jerusalem

VALLENTINE MITCHELL
LONDON • PORTLAND, OR

First published in 2008 by Vallentine Mitchell

Suite 314, Premier House,
112–114 Station Road,
Edgware, Middlesex HA8 7BJ

920 NE 58th Avenue, Suite 300
Portland, Oregon,
97213-3786

www.vmbooks.com

Copyright © 2008

British Library Cataloguing in Publication Data
A catalogue record has been applied for

ISBN 978 0 85303 731 6 (cloth)
ISBN 978 0 85303 732 3 (paper)

Library of Congress Cataloging-in-Publication Data
A catalog record has been applied for

Printed by Biddles Ltd., King's Lynn, Norfolk

Contents

PART IV: SUMMING UP

To Ellis Joffe

My comrade-in-arms in our youth
My colleague in adulthood
And my friend on rainy days

On his retirement from academe

Acknowledgements

This book is the brainchild of Mr Frank Cass, who thought that a thematic collection of already published articles by this author might provide a retrospective on the development of the same theme over the years. I enthusiastically embarked upon putting the volume together when I saw the benefits of that approach, especially after he published in 2003 a similar collection on the theme War, Peace and Terror in the Middle East. I am grateful to him and for its prompt implementation.

When venturing into an initiative of this sort, one may always run the risk of repetitiveness and of vain attempts to lend a new life to stale ideas whose time had revolved. But if done with sensitivity, this may hopefully end up not in ruminating on things past that have no relevance to the new state of affairs, but in illuminating the dynamics of a rapidly changing situation, with each already published article gaining its new place in the thematic whole and exemplifying a specific phase in the development of the theme. Some essays that had not been published before will hopefully add something innovative to the book and rescue the readers from the boredom of the trodden path and the familiarity of the déjà vu.

As always, I owe gratitude to my wife Margalit for her forbearance, and my home base at the Truman Institute of Hebrew University for the facilities, the library and the collegial advice that I have been continually enjoying. But, as always, all errors and responsibility for them remain exclusively with me.

Raphael Israeli
Jerusalem, Spring 2007

Introduction: Palestinian Affairs in World Perspective

For years, the West in general, and Europe in particular, has cultivated among its citizenry the notion of Palestinism, which took over from the other disappointing ideologies of the post-war era and was raised to the degree of unassailable truth, as Bat Ye'or has brilliantly demonstrated in her epoch-making *Eurabia*, released in Europe and America in 2005. The idea of Palestinism, which was upheld by European intellectuals of the left, soon won currency in the restive Muslim youth of Europe and found there its most vitriolic and hostile channels of expression. The idea was that the Israel of the pre-1967 War was a democratic and pioneering state, besieged by an Arab world which threatened its existence and which therefore won the sympathy of the West. After 1967, however, the large formula of the Arab–Israeli conflict, in which Israel had been by definition the underdog, was superseded by the small formula of the 'Israeli–Palestinian conflict', as if all the other threats against Israel had vanished, and in this new made-up context Israel became the villain occupier while the saintly Palestinians were just suffering under the yoke of the cruel Israelis. Thus the link between anti-Israeli attitudes and what was falsely called 'Zionism' was established, and since the Jews of Europe are for the most part supportive of Zionism and Israel, the fury was turned against them too in what amounted to barely disguised antisemitic onslaughts. For many Europeans, it was expedient to divert the anger of their frustrated Muslim populations to anti-Israeli and anti-Jewish channels, in consequence raising Palestinism to the degree of a religious tenet, as reflected in the European Union's blind support for Palestinians despite their proven corruption, and the diversion of those funds to terrorist acts against Israel and to 'educating' their children to the hatred of Israel and Jews.

These trends were particularly salient in France, where, in the election campaign of June 2004, the Europalestine list of candidates, headed by a notorious antisemite – the actor Dieudonne (ironically meaning 'God-given') – made a relatively strong showing in some constituencies and totalled more than 50,000 votes, probably most of them Muslims, judging from their election stickers. Under huge advertisements in the streets of La Courneuve and other heavily Muslim-populated areas of Paris, which announced the link between 'Peace in Europe and Justice in the Middle East', more elaborate statements of faith, hatred, racism and bigotry could not be ignored: 'The martyrdom of the Palestinian people has lasted too long', 'The Palestinian issue has been shamefully marginalized in the corridors of power, in spite of its strong presence in the minds of thousands of citizens', 'Jerusalem to the Arabs!', 'Death to the Jews', 'Allah Akbar!', 'Bush and Sharon got Saddam, but I pray that bin Laden should escape them'.[1] Only when Muslim terrorism transcended the boundaries of Israel, where it was consistently justified and forgiven by the European media, who put the blame on the victims, and struck Western territory, first the Americans and then the Europeans, was some reckoning made, and Israel's position started to find more understanding in European public opinion. In fact, some Euro-Palestinians already began complaining after September 11 in New York, 11 March in Madrid and 7 July in London that 'the media only showed Palestinian [terrorist] retaliation, not Israeli violence', because they suspected that 'journalists were rather pro-Israel. If you watch TV, you will find that all of them are Jewish.' They also accused 'the Jews of splashing mud on us and we do not understand what scares them', or that 'Jews have been deeply dipped in victimhood'.[2]

These extraordinary turns in the fortunes of the Palestinians in the West correlate between Palestinian nationalism and Islam. For as long as Palestinians appeared to be pursuing their armed struggle against Israel in order to gain independence from what many Europeans wrongly dubbed as Israel's 'colonial occupation' of Palestine, no one examined the details or was keen on testing either the application of colonialism on the Israeli–Palestinian case, or the very legitimacy of the Palestinian claim for a state on the ruins of Israel. And only when the Palestinians leaned more and more towards universal Islam, and especially the radical and violent forms thereof on the one hand, as will be shown in some upcoming chapters, while at the same time radical Islam began ravaging the West and declaring a global war against it, did Europe realize the connection between the rise of Palestinian Islam in the form of Hamas, and the direct threat against its own security. That is when Europe understood that its problem with radical Islam was much akin to Israel's problem with the Palestinians, for in both was implicit the threat of the use of violence against the established legitimate governments of Europe and Israel, and that threat was being translated into practice as fundamentalist Islam made headway in the West.

The wrong conception that equalled the situation in the West Bank and Gaza with French colonial rule in Algeria stemmed from a superficial comparison between the occupier and occupied, and the 'colonial condition' in which the invaded people finds itself when the invading nation exploits the natives for the economic benefit of its metropolitan base. Nothing of this sort had occurred in 1967, and therefore the entire comparison has no basis in fact. For one thing, it was not Israel who plunged in to expand its frontier or exploit raw materials, for the West Bank provided neither. Quite the contrary, Israel was attacked by the Jordanian army from the West Bank, and despite its supplications that were passed to Amman through the UNTSO Commander, General Odd Bull, King Hussein, who was trapped in his commitment to fight alongside the 'victorious' armies of Egypt's Nasser, responded by shelling the entire length of Israeli territory and launching a land attack on the UN Headquarters in Jerusalem. Israel had only one option open to it, namely to counter-attack; it did so and within two days of harsh fighting expelled the Jordanians from that territory. Had the Jordanians and the rest of the Arabs agreed to settle, Israel would certainly have withdrawn in return for peace. That is exactly what the Arabs rejected at the time, leaving Israel in charge of those territories until a settlement was reached, because there was no sense in handing over to the enemy the military positions from which it was attacked. To compare that 'rolling', unplanned takeover of a territory in a defensive move to the unprovoked French onslaught on Algeria (or Vietnam for that matter) is missing the point.

Colonized countries were historically situated overseas, and posed no threat to the occupying power, while the highlands of the West Bank are not only contiguous to Israel's territory, but they dominate it and cannot be handed over to an avowed enemy intending, as it had in 1967, to use them as strategic launching pads against the lowlands of the 10-mile narrow waistline of Israel. Unlike the colonizing powers of Europe, who capitalized on the raw materials brought from the colonies and the cheap native labour they could exploit, Israel on the contrary undertook the burden of providing for the Palestinian population, which was poor and underdeveloped, lacking in skills and in resources. How could anyone call that a 'colonial situation'? Be the historical reality as it may have been, the mantra of Israeli 'occupation' caught on pretty early, and under that misleading heading Israel necessarily became the villain 'occupier', thereby lending legitimacy to Palestinian 'resistance' against it. That very theme was embraced not only by PLO nationalists in order to rally their people and world opinion around them, for the sake of their 'war of liberation' that won worldwide currency and sympathy, but also by the emerging Muslim Associations, which came under the one umbrella of Hamas when the first *intifada* was declared (December 1987). Hamas has combined in its ideology ever since the contradictory concepts of national resistance, in order not to lag behind the PLO, which predominated in those days, and the banner of universal Islam, Muslim Brotherhood-style, which would enforce *shari'a* law in its community and thereby make a step towards uniting all Muslims under one caliphate, as of old.[3]

When in 1982 a defeated Arafat and humiliated PLO were exiled from their Lebanese bases, as a result of Israel's incursion to destroy them, some PLO elements began to mellow with regard to negotiations with Israel as the only way to return from their remote Tunisian exile to the Palestinian territories. After the Oslo Accords reached with the Israeli government in September 1993, under which they realized their dream, they established their Palestinian Authority on the land, all the while accusing Israel of continued 'occupation' and forcing it to yield to international pressure to give up more land even as the Palestinians did little to respect their own obligations of collecting illegal arms, putting an end to terrorism, arresting perpetrators of terror in Israel, and trying or extraditing them to Israel. Under the impact of Hamas, which was breathing down their neck and rejecting the Oslo Accords as a 'sell-out' to the Zionists, the PLO leadership, who also managed the Authority, found themselves losing grounds constantly to Hamas, which strengthened permanently in the grassroots by dispensing welfare to the poor, criticizing the corrupt Authority, providing religious solace for the misery of life and gaining the confidence of their masses by engaging in Islamikaze[4] actions. In the process they competed for the mayoralties of cities and towns in the West Bank and Gaza, for student bodies at universities and for professional associations such as lawyers, doctors, architects, engineers, accountants and the like, generally achieving resounding victories.

In short, very close to the establishment of the Authority, Hamas declared itself as an alternative to PLO rule by virtue of its rejection of Oslo, its refusal to participate in the elections which would have legitimized the Authority that derived its existence from those same Oslo Accords, and its continued criticism of the Palestinian government from the outside. The death of the legendary Arafat, who was the symbol that all Palestinian factions adulated, and the rise of the comparatively moderate Abu Mazen, who declared his willingness to strike a compromise with Israel, provided the final impetus for the dramatic rise of Hamas in Palestinian politics. Its leaders, sensing their time had come, consented this time to compete in the elections and won a stunning victory while the veteran PLO, shocked by the results that unseated them from power, grudgingly became the opposition party. As Hamas became the government of the Palestinians, incurring in the process the wrath of the Americans, the Israelis and some Europeans, because of its refusal to deal with Israel, to accept the commitments of the PLO under Oslo or to cease terrorism, it is feared that difficult days lie ahead for the Palestinians and the Middle East in general. While the question of the rapport of force between church and state in the Palestinian entity seems to have been decided for now, it remains to be seen how stable that resolution will be.

NOTES

1. Didier Hassoux, *Liberation*, 15 June 2004.
2. Ibid.
3. See also Meir Litvak, 'The Islamization of Palestinian Identity: The Case of Hamas', *Data and Analysis*, Moshe Dayan Center, Tel Aviv University, August 1996.
4. Islamikaze is a combination of Islam and Kamikaze to characterize the wrongly so-called 'suicide bombers'. See this author's *Islamikaze: Manifestations of Islamic Martyrology* (London: Frank Cass, 2003).

PART I

THE ARAB AND MUSLIM ARENA UNDER
PRESSURE OF CHANGE

CHAPTER ONE

Arab Reckoning in the Aftermath of September 11

INTRODUCTION

In the Arab shame culture, admitting one's mistake is almost tantamount to suicide, for it is almost better to lose one's life than to lose one's honour, and one's honour can be irretrievably stained if one is shown by the finger as having violated the social code and brought shame or dishonour upon himself, his family or his society. Rare, therefore, are the occasions when an Arab leader, cleric or official of any consequence would shoulder the responsibility for any mishap of his own doing, and infrequent are the instances in which an Arab or Muslim intellectual, professional or journalist would dare to criticize his people or leadership for their misdeeds, either for fear of the backlash from those regimes and rulers, or because he or she truly does not sense that they deserve criticism, certainly not in front of foreigners, or in foreign media, which would amount to humiliation and deprecation of the entire Arab-Muslim collective. The occasional exceptions are Arab-Muslim intellectuals who live in the West and feel at ease using the methods of criticism they have learned there to castigate, from a safe distance, their home countries and/or the regimes they run away from.

The Arab-Muslim norm of commenting upon people, events, countries, regimes and rulers consists of self-aggrandizing oneself and deprecating the enemy. Things that go right are, of course, imputed to their great civilization or their prowess, their success in undoing the plots of the enemy and so forth; failure is always attributed to the scheming of the enemies, real or imaginary, or to some *force majeure* beyond one's control, or anything else that allows one to escape self-criticism. Islam and the Arabs are always the generous party, the faithful, the righteous and, conversely, the wronged, the eternal victims, in spite of their impeccable conduct. Others, like the US, are corrupt, tyrannical, aggressive, arrogant and ruthless, while they are gentle, kind, democratic and benevolent. Others are oppressors and merchants of decadence and injustice, while they are the paradigm of justice and the heralds of the future. Their perception of the borders between reality, self-delusion and fantasy are rather blurred, which allow them to impute to others facts that never were, such as massacres, spreading disease, poisoning and the like, while they regularly are the victims of those fabrications.

Each of the fantasies undergoes several stages: first the fabrication of a web of lies that bears no relation to the facts (e.g. the destruction of the Twin Towers by Jews, or the injection by Israelis of Palestinian children with HIV), and which Muslims think that if repeated often enough becomes a reality, in which they begin to believe themselves, even when they cannot prove it to themselves, let alone to others. Then, the stage of denial sets in, when the Muslims realize the outrage and havoc that their delusions have impelled them to foster. At this point, they wish both to detach themselves from the atrocities committed (e.g. the Twin Towers) and also to 'enjoy' their results at the same time. But since facts keep pressing at the door, and Muslim claims of innocence become ludicrous, in the eyes of world opinion, then the stage of projection and laying the blame on others begins. In this Kafkaesque world of the unreal, where there is no cause and effect, only non-Muslims are supposed to sin, to provoke and to lie, and therefore anything projected on them is either true, or could be true even if it is not proven. The enemy is always the murderer and the aggressor, even if he acts in self-defence and self-restraint in order to minimize casualties, for he is de-legitimized to such an extent that he does not even have the right to defend himself. Only Muslims are worthy of what they call self-defence, even when they launch wars of aggression against others.

However, in periods of great national crisis in the Arab and Muslim worlds, voices emerge here and there which seem to want to tell the truth, to take the blame, or part thereof, and to come to some sober conclusions. For example, after the terrible rout of the Arabs in the 1967 War, some politicians among them spoke about their 'glorious defeat' that was due to the war 'of technology and knowledge [Israel's] against backwardness and ignorance [the Arabs]'. Those who speak up and urge their people to abandon hyperbole and self-delusion and accept reality, are often boycotted, criticized and blamed, sometimes even physically attacked, not so much for telling the truth, as for exposing the inherent inabilities of their culture. It requires a great deal of courage, if not audacity, to venture self-criticism of that sort, at the risk of incurring scorn and even accusations of treason, collaboration with the enemy, or simply the corruption and distortion of the noble qualities and intentions of Arabs and Muslims. Maybe, for this reason, few dare to indulge in self-criticism, and those who do would always find fault also with the rival/enemy, in order to make the blow to one's pride easier to absorb.

Therefore, the bouts of self-criticism by Arabs and Muslims about their own society, especially when they come from within and not from expatriates, are a breath of fresh air, and enable us to take a rare look at the mechanisms of self-defence that have characterized Arab society. We will be looking in this essay into some quite surprising manifestations of self-criticism that were occasioned by the aftermath of September 11, when the Muslim world entered into a confrontation of sorts with the West, in an attempt to justify itself in the face of world criticism, and the dismal failure of the Palestinians to gain any achievement from the Aqsa Intifada they had initiated one year earlier in September 2000. Both events are certainly interrelated. We will take a sample of self-criticism, mostly from Arabs who reside in their own countries, and who take a considerable but calculated risk when they criticize as insiders, but also from some expatriates who live in the West, where their criticism of their culture of origin is less risky, but at the same time reflects an outsider's view. The main entries under discussion will be: Arab-Muslim participation in acts of terror, following September 11, women and children's rights, the Arab-Muslim educational system, blasting incumbent leaders and suggesting needed reforms in the regime, and general criticism of the Arab/Islamic world.

ARAB AND MUSLIM TERRORISM

Expectedly, Iran, who opened the way to the Islamikaze phenom-enon,[1] has also been its most virulent advocate, although even there a few defiant dissidents dared to disagree and were dealt with accordingly. Ayatullah Muntazari, for example, who has been under house arrest since 1996, is on record as calling upon the Palestinians to desist from acts of martyrdom, in spite of Supreme Spiritual Leader 'Ali Khamenei's assertion that those acts were the 'pinnacle of Palestinian Resistance, and of audacity, honour and glory to the umma'.[2] A Sudanese author, writing, like some of his peers, from the safety of a London-based Arabic paper, said that the enemy lay within the Arab world itself in the form of 'the mental illness that has affected us since we were defeated by Israel in 1948', and is manifested in the Arab propen-sity to blame others, not themselves, for their setbacks. He declared that 'we, the Arabs, are the lawful parents of Bin Laden, not America'.[3]

In the context of the events of September 11 and their after-math, and the internal debates and soul-searching they provoked throughout the Arab and Islamic world, the prevalent mood remained of blaming the US, the West and Israel for all the malaise that first created and then sprung from that fateful day, but it was also an opportunity for all sorts of oppressed, dissi-dents, liberals, silenced oppositions, exiles, minorities or funda-mentalists to use the general ambiance of criticism and self-criti-cism to air their concerns. An unnamed Egyptian woman (and that is significant in itself) wrote a lengthy dissertation about the position of women in her country, asserting that her female com-patriots were living 'exactly as Afghan women'. She accused the Egyptian press of lauding the liberation of women in Afghanistan after the American attacks there, and of vowing to fight terrorism, while at the same time they disregarded the terror against women in their own country. She was particularly shocked when her son, who grew fanatical under his father's education, was jubilant, as were many Egyptians against their government's best advice, when the destruction of the World Trade Center became known, and at some point she even attempted to commit suicide.[4] This point was also addressed by the Dean of the Faculty of Law at Qatar University, Sheikh al-Ansari, who wrote about his opposition to the kind of Islam that bred terrorists, his commitment to curricular reform in the Arab world, his criticism towards those who called the American counter-attack 'terrorism', and about his plea to eradicate 'all seeds of hatred, repulsion, and fanaticism toward the other, towards women, towards those whose religion is different from ours'.[5]

Similarly, a Tunisian columnist, al-'Afif al-Akhdar, took to task the clerics who issued fatwas to incite others to violence and to legitimize murder. He cited the instance when Tunisian military personnel had refused to participate in a coup against President Bourguiba before obtaining a fatwa permitting them to kill their fellow soldiers and even the President if necessary, and Ghannouchi's deputy himself issued that ruling from his prison cell. The author determines that the connection between the fatwa and terrorism lies in the fact that the religious ruling 'unleashes the terrorist's sadism and instinct for murder. It frees him from all moral restraints and shrivels what remains of his conscience. It also releases him from any sense of guilt.' He says that while the fatwas of the previous decades were secret, like the organizations who issued them, now it has become fashionable for famous sheikhs to make them public and boast about them, and various religious authorities use the media to publicize their competition among themselves permitting the killing of individuals, groups or even nations ... Worse, there were fatwas that were announced after the murder was committed. For example, Ghannouchi himself legitimized the murder of President Sadat twelve years after the deed, thus leaving open the possibility of permitting the murder of other political leaders. Another example, which he criticized, was the Saudi Sheikh al-Hawali, who issued a fatwa that the rulers of the Northern Alliance in Afghanistan were Unbelievers because they supported the Americans against the Taliban government – any support for Unbelievers against Muslims, even if only verbal, constituted blatant heresy and hypocrisy ... The fatwa said that the September 11 disaster was strictly a justified response to the Clinton Administration's missile attack on al-Qa'ida bases in Afghanistan, following the bombing of the American embassies in East Africa in 1998.[6]

This rather strange fatwa meant, as with Hamas attacks against Israel, that only Muslims can target what they regard as legitimate goals, but that when the victims retaliate against them that constitutes a trigger for further Muslim retributions. In other words, the non-Muslim must submit to Muslim attacks, simply absorb and duck them until he got what he deserved at the hand of Islamic justice, whilst any reprisal on his part would be considered a new 'provocation' or 'aggression' deserving of Muslim violent response. This is why the Saudi Sheikh justified the attack on the Twin Towers through their corrupt role as the world 'centre of money laundering', and on the Pentagon, which 'Gore Vidal had himself called 'Hell and a nest of Satans'. Attacks on those targets were thus legitimate by Muslim terms, even more so as retaliation for the American missile attack. That courageous author also condemned those in the Islamic world who mocked the 'weeping and expressing of sorrow and pain over the American victims', arguing that they were all combatants, because they supported their regime ('may Allah not multiply such regimes', said he, the champion of Saudi democracy), and in their case he ruled that it was even permissible to kill the non-combatants among them, the aged, the blind and the *dhimmis*, all Americans without exception. The author remarks that it was such rulings, which were endorsed by other Muslim clerics, such as the eminent Sheikh Qaradhawi, which gave licence to Hamas to eliminate indiscriminately Israeli civilians under the pretext that they were 'combatants'. He wrote that 'fanaticism and hatred for anyone who is different removes the lobe of logic from the brain of the fanatic'.[7]

The lobe of logic fails to function as well when it comes to discussing ways to eradicate hatred from the Muslim writings that generations of Muslims are raised upon. *Al-Jazeera* Television convened a panel of Muslim educators and writers to discuss reform in religious education in the Muslim world. All but one participant, who significantly lives in Washington, denied that there was any need for reform and turned the tables on the Americans by accusing them of all the ills of the Muslim world. Some admitted that though they accepted the need to amend technicalities, such as giving precedence to comprehension of texts over repetition and memorizing, they refuted totally the selective approach of the West to texts they considered as arousing hatred and bigotry. He observed that those who called for jihad against the 'Crusaders' who set off to attack Islam, were inciting the mobs against their governments who voiced their support for America, and deceiving them into demonstrating and acting against the 'enemies of Islam'. The result was that those who acted hastily were destroyed and their families stricken by tragedy, while the imams who incited them pursued their lives of tranquillity and comfort undisturbed without being held accountable for the consequences of their incitement. Sheikh Al-Ansari alone came to the conclusion that declarations of jihad should not be left to any hysterical and irresponsible preacher to utter, but should be confined to the rulers, for otherwise chaos and destruction would ensue, and state interest would be harmed. He consciously stated that since the Saudi Sheikhs had declared that only the rulers had the right to proclaim jihad, he was under the obligation to follow suit and concur. The writer debates those who claim that in the name of freedom of expression, microphones should be afforded to jihad fighters who bring the Arab Nation to the brink of the precipice.[8]

The problem with this voice of reason and moderation is that it challenges the authority of the religious hierarchy, who enjoy, according to his own reckoning based on a poll by *al-Jazeera*, an 83 per cent endorsement of public opinion when they declare that bin Laden is a jihad fighter and not a terrorist. This brings dramatically into focus the illegitimacy of the rulers in place who, for passing interests, not for immutable moral reasons, lend their lip-service support to the West and quell the swelling emotions among their publics in favour of the Muslim jihad fighters. He contends that these terrorists have in mind primarily to oust the existing regimes and install puritanical ones in their stead. But since they have failed, they turn against America, whom they accuse of having produced those corrupt governments, so that they could force it to leave their lands to their fundamentalist mercy. The writer claims that the Muslim soul is naturally disengaged from terrorism, but the fundamentalist incitement falls on receptive ears due to the high profile of fanaticism in Arab societies, which has taken root because of an educational system which has remained impermeable to pluralism. The culture of terrorism, he concludes, can only be fought by education.[9] Like other voices of moderation and self-criticism in the Islamic world, al-Ansari too sparked a very heated debate, first with his articles in his Qatar home papers and then throughout the Arab world, as we shall see below.

Apart from the dreams of world dominion that are blatantly declared by Islamists, and the plans they weave to make them happen through the use of violence, beginning either in Muslim countries or outside of them, many domestic debates between the fundamentalists and their opponents reveal the deepest concerns of those societies about the ramifications that grow out of the bellicose mood of the Islamikaze and their champions. In these debates, attempts are made to convert jihad, the flag ship of the militants, into something more constructive and peaceful, or demands are raised to lend top priority to internal strife, inequities, the status of women and children, education and development, rather than inflame the fire of violence, warfare, killing and destruction. These voices of reason are, for the most part, silenced and not allowed to predominate, but we learn from them, by default, about the ambitions of the Islamists and some of their methods of struggle. Sometimes the writers of reason feel so intimidated that they write anonymously, for fear of being identified and asked to conform. Such a voice, an 'Arab diplomat', wrote an article in the Saudi-owned and London-based *al-Sharq al-Awsat*, where he audaciously suggested to 'replace jihad by development', a temerity that could have cost him his life if it were published in a traditional, or not so traditional, Muslim country. He wrote, *inter alia*:

> Now that the second intifada has ended, at such a terrible price, the Arabs must try, at least once, to grasp the lesson that they have been taught yet again ... And first, we must admit that the ones who pushed the children into the second intifada ... wanted to thwart any initiative that President Arafat sought to promote ... and to make him their and Israel's prisoner ... Demonstrations filled the streets of Arab capitals [in support of the intifada], reminiscent of the giant demonstrations to defend the honour of Comrade Saddam ... Why don't they demonstrate to protest against the deficient

or non-existent basic services in their countries? These countries have no health, education or services, and buckle under the poverty line ... but they are all preoccupied with the Palestinian issue, and no voice rises above the voice of battle there ...

What would happen if every Arab country had, since 1948, turned its attention to building itself from within, without making Palestine its main issue? ... What would happen if every country focused on educating its citizens and on improving their physical and emotional health and cultural level? Wouldn't this have made the battle with Israel a cultural one instead of us sinking into religious and military battles? ... Moreover, I am amazed at the clerics who raise a hue and cry about jihad against Israel ... and compete with each other issuing religious fatwas on martyrdom attacks, but do not encourage the citizens to wage spiritual jihad. Wouldn't this be more useful to the Nation, which since the turn of the century has been subject to *nakba*[10] by its own military, and now marches toward a second *nakba* by its scientists – I refer, of course, to the scientists of religion, and not the scientists of physics, natural science, health or engineering.[11]

Or take, for example, the debates within the Muslim world regarding the very desirability of the Islamikaze phenomenon, which conventional wisdom among them calls *istishhad*, the respectable and much adulated way to die as a martyr, while all those who dare, as in the West, to dub it 'suicide bombing', or plain 'terrorism' or 'murder', are castigated and humiliated into submission to the accepted norms in their society. The Syrian Minister of Information, a euphemism for the supreme commissar for propaganda or 'national guidance' in those regimes, when interrogated during an inter-Arab symposium on the terminology of martyrdom, retorted:

Verily, too many Western terms have been invading our media ... but more dangerous than them is the infiltration of ideas. A few days ago we heard one of them say that acts of martyrdom against the Zionist enemy are acts of violence and terror. Even if the life of the person who said that is dearer to him than his honour and his country ... he must let the shahid [martyr] choose to sacrifice his life for the sake of his country; he must let the martyr fulfil his duty.

WOMEN'S AND CHILDREN'S RIGHTS

An Arab reporter for the Associated Press went to the Gaza Strip, the area where the child Muhammed Dura was killed, at the beginning of the intifada, to gauge the repeated claims about the involvement of children in violence. Her findings are chilling:

> Nearly 20 months of Israeli–Palestinian fighting, and a culture that increasingly glorifies violence has taken a heavy toll on Gaza's children ... Funerals and rallies with gunmen firing in the air are almost daily events. Walls are covered with graffiti glorifying martyrs killed in attacks on Israelis. Their faces stare from tens of thousands of posters, and mosque preachers exhort worshippers to emulate them. 'The climate in Gaza gives the impression that being a martyr wins respect', says Abu Hein together with other experts, while parents, Palestinian media and mosque preachers are not doing enough to shelter their children ...
>
> The economic decline, the fighting and the uncertainty, have filtered down to children in Gaza, with what experts believe to be devastating psychological effect ... Close to 20 per cent of the more than 1,600 Palestinians killed in the West Bank and Gaza since September 2000 were 18 or younger, according to Palestinian health officials. Several thousand minors have been injured ... Most of the death and injury among the children occur when they join protests to throw stones, bottles and sometimes firebombs at Israeli army troops, checkpoints or Jewish settlements. Troops often respond with rubber bullets or tear gas, but they also fire live bullets at times. A March 2002 survey of 2,300 children between the ages of 6 and 13 showed that up to 73 per cent in some parts of Gaza have taken part in violence and that 98 per cent have witnessed events that frightened them ... In some areas, as many as half of those questioned said

that they knew another child who died in the violence, according to the survey by the Center for Social Training and Crisis Management, a Palestinian non-governmental organization ...

With martyrdom now nearly an obsession among youngsters frustrated by the uncertainty and low quality of life, Gazans have been alarmed in recent weeks by a spate of incidents in which teenagers, some as young as 11, tried to infiltrate heavily guarded Jewish settlements or attack Israeli army posts. One such a child was Yousef Zakout, a ninth grader shot dead on 23 April 2002 with two friends aged 14 and 13 by Israeli troops as they tried to slip into the settlement of Netzarim in central Gaza. Zakout left a heart-wrenching will for his family, saying it was his wish to be a martyr, begging his parents' forgiveness and exhorting his six siblings to pray regularly and fast from dawn to sunset twice a week ... His 16-year-old brother, Ahmed, said he too wanted to be a martyr, but he added: 'I will do something that is well planned and effective. I might as well, since these days we can all be sitting here at home and suddenly die from an Israeli shelling' ...

Gazans have traditionally viewed themselves as leaders of the fight against Israeli occupation. Gazan children, some barely out of diapers, have been used by grown-ups to feed this notion. In Gaza's funerals for shahids (martyrs), and in rallies by Palestinian factions such as Arafat's Fatah or the militant Islamic group Hamas, children as young as three or four are outfitted with combat fatigues, masks and toy guns. Such occasions routinely attract hundreds of children, all accustomed by now to the deafening noise made by gunmen firing in the air ... Children are sometimes symbolically wrapped in white sheets to suggest their desire for martyrdom. Muslims wrap their dead in white sheets before burying them, with participants around shouting slogans glorifying martyrdom ... Songs extolling the virtues of martyrdom and praising those already martyred, are played on loudspeakers in large tents erected for the families of children killed by Israeli troops to receive condolences ... Hamas, responsible for scores of suicide bombings in Israel, often pays for the funerals.[12]

The concepts with which the children of Palestine are indoctrinated on their national television, by their own leaders, are supported not only by the harrowing clip of al-Dura that was produced by the Palestinian Authority to elevate the tragically deceased child to a model for others to emulate,[13] but also by the clerics of the Palestinian Authority in general, chief among them being 'Akrama Sabri, the Mufti of the Palestinians. However, in contrast to the clerics who encouraged acts of Islamikaze, obviously in response to the huge wave of popular support for that mode of struggle, there were some mainstream professionals, such as Ashraf al-'Ajrami, a columnist in the Palestinian Authority daily, *Al-Ayyam*, who realized the damage that the outrageous procedure of using children caused to national interest, and counselled to desist from it. He acknowledged the fact that 'the phenomenon of martyrdom was on the increase, especially among minors', but expectedly blamed the 'Israeli occupation' for the 'degradation of life which pushes many to disdain life and seek the shortest way to the hereafter'. He admitted that it was the 'honour and esteem that the Palestinian people give to the martyr that has had a crucial effect on the emergence of this phenomenon'. He also imputed a great importance in this regard to the 'funerals of the martyrs and the celebrations held in their honour, which have always been accompanied by talks of everlasting life and eternal serenity in Paradise'. Therefore, the rationale of these youngsters goes, why wait through the tribulations of life if one can take a shortcut to Paradise by pressing a button, or by purposely coming into close range of Israeli shooting? At the same time, he contends that the enthusiasm among minors to be hailed as heroes and martyrs might encourage their gratuitous exploitation by others. He also concedes that some Gaza children are influenced by mosques and schools, an admission to the ruinous character not only of religious sermons, but also of the Palestinian textbooks,[14] some funded by the European Union, which cultivate the senseless Islamikaze death.[15]

This columnist, who appears to be well-updated on the techniques and motivations of the young Islamikaze, delves into terrifying details and counsels to desist from this practice, not for the moral burden it puts on the Palestinian leadership – that would be too daring a criticism – but for the damage it causes to Palestinian propaganda:

Some are willing to arm them for money – with pistols, hand grenades, and readily available pipe bombs that cost only a few shekels. These brainwashed children are imbued with motivation to approach the nearest settlement where they are shot dead by the soldiers of the occupation ...

The children's martyrdom promotes the hostile propaganda of the enemies, particularly in reinforcing their claims that the Palestinians send their children to the front line. These are false claims aimed at justifying the indiscriminate shooting at all the Palestinians ... The phenomenon also causes the children to rebel against their parents, insofar as the children threaten their parents that they would martyr themselves if the parents did not accede to their demands or did not turn a blind eye on their inappropriate behavior ... Moreover, some of the children have used pipe bombs during arguments amongst themselves ...

Collective efforts should be made to contain this phenomenon ... All activities having an ill-effect on the children's emotional stability, pulling them in directions outside the normal matters of children, must be monitored ... The security apparatuses should apprehend the arms traffickers and collaborators, who are acting among the youths to make money or to exterminate this generation together with its nationalist enthusiasm and its will to fight ... It is also important to stop the mosques from engaging in exaggerated political activity and providing grounds for anyone who wants to abuse the minds of youth and minors ... The Palestinian media also have a role in refraining from broadcasting pictures affecting the emotional state of children, and from exaggerating in reporting tragic news that arouses the children's feelings of frustration and despair.[16]

Another rare courageous Arab voice against the self-immolation of children was raised by a female Arab journalist, Huda al-Husseini, who was incensed at the systematic sacrifice of children in a war they did not initiate and perhaps ill-comprehended:

Some Palestinian leaders ... consciously issue orders with the purpose of ending the childhood [of their youth], even if this means their last breath. I want to know why we, the Arabs, insist on dying rather than living for our homeland. If these children have nothing to lose, and they think the training is a game, are we supposed to continue pushing them with hypocrisy and stupid enthusiasm to actually lose their lives? Have we exhausted all means and used every argument, have we exhausted our brains, and have nothing left but to gamble with the lives of children and push them to confront Israel? Or maybe the Palestinian leaders – those who are in the PA or those who get ready to fill a role in it – put their trust in the humanity of Israel? If this is what they do, they are wrong ... What kind of independence is based on the blood of children while the leaders are safe and so are their children and grandchildren? ... Are only the miserable destined to die in the spring of their lives? Those children who are killed may not, in their short lives, have enjoyed a fresh piece of bread, sleeping in a warm bed, the happiness of putting on a new piece of cloth, or carrying books with no torn pages to school ...

The time for Arafat and those around him has reached its dusk ... First of all, these children deserve to live, before we push them to find death. But, what are we doing to them? We abuse their innocence, we supply them with tons of stones, while we sit in our offices and commend their death. Then we accept an invitation for a working lunch or dinner and talk about those children who died holding stones, those that died, probably hungry.[17]

However, as one must have noticed above, those who dissent in the Arab world from the conventional wisdom which supports Muslim terrorism do not usually do so out of empathy for the non-Muslim victims, but out of concern for what terrorism does to Muslims themselves, notably the children among them. In other words, except for rare expressions of general humanistic remorse, Arab and Muslim writers are primarily concerned with their own societies. Similarly, when an Egyptian woman dared to criticize her gender's status in her country, she was rather sedate as regards general issues or policies in the Arab-Muslim world, perhaps preoccupied as she was with her personal lamentable situation. In the

Egyptian weekly *Akhbar al-Yaum*, a lengthy letter was published from an unnamed Egyptian woman, who described what it was like to be married to a Muslim fundamentalist. The editor decided to publish it, though it was extraordinarily lengthy, after he was prodded to do so by colleagues who had 'heard similar or worse stories'. She wrote with rage, that while the Egyptian press was lauding the liberation of Afghan women from the Taliban government, it refrained from reporting on the situation of women in Egypt, which was no less depressing. Excerpts from the story of her relations with her husband are edifying:

> his [pre-marital] tolerance, which had attracted me during our engagement, turned overnight into rigidity, domination and tyranny ... A week after the wedding he asked me to sit down with him to hear his instructions:
>
> First [he said], you must terminate all your contact with your workplace. Do not resign, just do not show up, and they will fire you, according to the law without giving you your rights, and you do not need them;
>
> Second, ... make up will not improve your appearance, so you must immediately rid yourself of all those sins [make-up] ...
>
> Third, ... men hungry for women have become widespread in Egyptian society, and you are prohibited from arousing their lust. Therefore, you have to wear garments that conceal you from their adulterous eyes ...
>
> Fourth, to expose your face and hair is a grievous sin ... you are fortunate that I can save you from the torments of Hell ... when you married a believer like me ... You must rip up your clothing, silk garments and lingerie ... You will wear the only garment a Muslim woman needs to wear, which will cover you from head to toe, and will have only one opening to allow you to see and avoid bumping into things ...
>
> I now have many garments, all covering every centimetre of my body, and in only two colours: black for outdoors, white for the house ... In all my 25 years of marriage I knew perhaps only one week of happiness. I am the mother of six, since my husband thinks that the only reason for marriage is to increase the birth rate of the Nation of Muhammad. Were

I not already 55, he would not have settled for only six children ...

My husband also forbade laughter in the apartment soon
after the honeymoon, since laughter was from Satan, who
aims at corrupting believing Muslims ... Imagine a house full
of children who are forbidden to laugh, play or even smile ...
A blind sheikh came to the house and drilled my children to
memorize the Qur'an, hour after hour ... Then he demanded that I cover the hair of my daughters when they reached
the age of 4, and dress them like me at 7. I could not remove
my head to toe cover even in the house, lest the girls learn
the bad example from me and removed it when they were
outdoors, far from his watchful eyes ...

Our house has no radio or television, because they are forbidden by Islam, as they distract children from their purpose
in life ... Only recorded tapes of preachers reciting the
Qur'an and commentaries were allowed, and we were made
to gather and listen to them day in, day out ... When my
daughter asked her father why he did not bring home the
cassettes of the great preachers of al-Azhar [appointed by
the establishment], my husband said that they are agents of
the unbelieving government and speak its words, and therefore there was no place for their cassettes in the house ...

He thought that education was appropriate for boys, but
pointless for girls ... and after they attended an elementary
religious school, he decided they should stay at home. They
are ignorant of the government curriculum and hardly know
how to write and read ... though they know the Qur'an and
the Hadith by heart.[18]

And on and on, a whole litany of suffering, which brought this
unfortunate woman to the brink of committing suicide on some 20
occasions, and to a real attempt from which she was rescued,
according to her own reckoning. She was particularly hurt by her
son who became a harsh copy of her husband, and who on
September 11 came home jubilant about the horror in the US,
assuring his crying and desperate mother that he saw and knew
hundreds of other people who reacted like him. She could not
comprehend how his mind was taken over by violence, enmity and

hatred, when he callously declared that that war would 'consume all those who are not Muslim, or do not implement what Muslims expect of them'. She lamented the 'spread of the virus of inter-religious violence in Egypt, which destroys the minds of young people', not necessarily from the deprived and disaffected social strata. That happened, she said, because many homes, like hers, were opened to fanatic preachers to brainwash the young girls and boys, something that would assuredly reflect on the next genera-tion of Muslim terrorism, and ended with a plea to the world to realize that Egyptian women lived like their Afghani counterparts, while movements of human rights were looking on inactively.[19]

ARAB-MUSLIM INTELLECTUALS AND THE EDUCATIONAL SYSTEM

Majdi Khalil, a former Egyptian now residing in the US, took part in a debate with fellow-Arabs over *al-Jazeera* Television network. He lashed out at the takeover by political Islam of the education-al systems of the Islamic world, comparing the 3,000 madrasas in Pakistan in 1978 with the 39,000 today. He said that although Israel pursued political violence today, there was not a single case where a Jew blew himself up in New York or London, and at any rate there are fewer Jews altogether in the world today (some 17 million) than there are terrorists among the billion-strong Muslim population. He asserted that a wall of concrete surrounded the Islamic world which prevented democracy, globalization, devel-opment and modernity from getting in, and emphasized that the pretexts advanced by Muslims for this state of affairs were so scanty and shallow that no serious forum could accept them. He said that all those who pretend to speak in terms of science or medicine, i.e. medicine according to the Prophet of Islam, cannot seriously expect to be heard at any gathering in London or New York. He added:

> The Muslim Brothers are the source of all trouble in Egypt and the world, in combination with Saudi Arabia and Pakistani Islam of the Mawdudi brand. That trio – the Muslim Brothers, the Wahhabis and Mawdudi – are the source of all disasters that have befallen the Muslim world. In Egypt, since the times of the King and then Sadat, a great

deal was invested in Muslim education. Faculties of education were erected and deans were appointed, all among the
Brothers' membership. Two million graduates are churned
out every year from religious schools, who studied religion
for 20 years ... What can they do for society? Do we need
two million sheikhs a year? They teach topics that belong to
the seventh century. Pakistan churns out four million of
them annually, and in Saudi Arabia 70 per cent of the graduates of higher education are likewise. We do not need all
these quantities, and I am opposed to the contents of their
schooling too, which talk against the homeland[20] and accuse
people of heresy ...

It is true that the West acted violently during the
Crusades, but now it no longer practises religious violence ...
Religious violence today is only practised by Islam. Political
Islam advocates holding texts in one hand and a gun in the
other. The education they talk about is no education at all;
it is a hate club ... It is education against everything, against
modernity, against science. When modernity was Islamized,
a distorted system was created, like a Mongoloid child
suffering from Down's Syndrome. We do not oppose
religious education per se, but the religious education that
breeds hatred, encourages people to fight others and their
thoughts, advocates fanaticism, racism and isolationism and
borders on metaphysics, accuses intelligent people of heresy,
and opposes modern science ...

The basic textbook in our faculties of education, 'The
Fundaments of Education', says, for example that Christianity
emanates from Judaism, but that Judaism is not a faith ... In
page 15 of that book, they say that Jesus had never existed,
and that Christianity was full of pagan ideas that were drawn
from the trinity of gods in ancient Egypt. Not only are others
accused of heresy, but these books are full of repulsion from
nationalism, and they contain nothing but Islam at the
expense of Egyptian, Arab and human identity ... If this
system of education which calls upon its followers to kill others, and is not much different from the Terrorism Manuals
that were found in the Afghani caves, don't the others have
the right to interfere and clamour for its reform? And I am

not talking only about education, but also about free communication and democracy. It is the absence of this trinity which created the atmosphere of terrorism, therefore if there are reforms, they must apply to all three.[21]

Sheikh Al-Ansari, who was introduced in the previous section and is credited as a 'prominent liberal voice in the Muslim religious establishment', was interviewed for *al-Raya* daily in Qatar, following his daring remarks in *al-Hayat* mentioned above. He proclaimed his commitment to curricular reforms in the Arab and Islamic worlds with a view to 'removing all seeds of hatred, repulsion, and fanaticism towards others, towards women, towards holders of other faiths or those professing different schools of law within Islam'. This audacious statement, which goes a long way to admit the deficiencies in the existing curricula, certainly cannot be made without reference to other great reformers in Islamic history, who had been greatly appreciated and respected, and whose new reinterpretation was needed to make them relevant once again for the current crisis that he courageously acknowledged. He invoked the great figures of Sheikh Muhammed al-Ghazali and Sheikh Muhammed 'Abduh, who had striven, in his words, to 'eliminate the elements of divisiveness both within the umma and between it and the rest of the nations'. He argued that since tolerance reigned supreme in Islam it was necessary to reinstall that notion in school curricula. He enumerated several examples:

- In Islam, he said, studies focused on those 'who will be saved', i.e. Muslims, to the exclusion of all the others, whose inheritance was Hell. He explained that students who are educated in that vein grow to believe they hold the exclusive Truth while all the others will remain deceivers and ignoramuses.
- Similarly, he claimed, when students are educated on the notion that foreign relations are determined by the differentiation between Dar al-Harb and Dar al-Islam (see 'Arab and Muslim Terrorism' above), and jihad is prescribed as the way of intercourse between them, then aggression becomes possible in the name of jihad. He even asserts that while 'some ideas exist in several religious law books, allowing Muslims to attack

non-Muslims', those ideas are wrong. He says that since the Qur'an allows man the right of choice, then anyone can be a Believer or Unbeliever, therefore the rationale of waging jihad by Muslims against non-Muslims is removed.

- He comes out virulently against the 'type of Islam which breeds terrorists', since that in itself is 'a crime against true Islam and the Muslims themselves'. He condemned the schools of thought which produced extremist groups that 'cannot deal with modern reality', and blamed the preachers in mosques who portray the war in Afghanistan as a Crusader battle between Islam and Christianity. He ridiculed those preachers of hate, asserting that if Allah had listened to them and destroyed the Christians, they themselves would not 'have a microphone to preach with, or the air-conditioner or the car they so enjoy'.

- He dubs as 'unfair' the naming of the American counter-attack in Afghanistan as 'terrorism', because doing so would be confusing terrorism with self-defence, or response with aggression. He says that Arab history is replete with examples where acts of terrorism of the scale done in America had warranted total annihilation of the perpetrators.[22] He commends America for trying other avenues before they moved decisively against the Taliban.

- He asserts that even if there is considerable collateral damage during the punitive attacks against the terrorists, and many innocent civilians are killed, the blame lies squarely at the door of the terrorists who had kindled the reprisals against them. What was done in Afghanistan was named by the author as a 'liberation of our Muslim brothers by the Americans, though unfortunately not by Muslim hands'.

- Al-Ansari maintains that the attraction of the Arab world to bin Laden is only the latest link in the long chain of 'liberating heroes, grounded in Arab mentality', beginning with the legendary 'Antara, and then Saladin, 'abd-al-Nasser and Saddam Hussein. For the populace who adored those heroes, it did not matter if they were liars, adventurers, tyrants or terrorists, because 'Arab mentality ascribes to them a sanctity that covers their sins'.

- Al-Ansari links this state of mind of the Arabs with their frustration emanating from their 'political, social and ideological repression, backwardness and inability to change', and the incitement to hate the 'colonialist West' and 'American hegemony'. He particularly accuses *al-Jazeera* for carrying bin Laden and his aides' propaganda and incitement, and making them stars, thus lending their screens to murderers to spread their propaganda ...

- The author also attacks 'hollow' Arab intellectuals who echo the incited masses, by sacrificing the truth and scientific analysis in favour of appeasement of tempers, and by 'hypocritically' linking September 11 to the Palestinian issue, which had never been invoked in al-Qa'ida literature before.[23]

A Kuwaiti columnist, Ahmed al-Baghdadi, engaged on a campaign of painful self-flagellation that echoed, in some respects, the concerns of his Qatari co-religionist, but it also opened new vistas of self-criticism not heard or allowed often in Arab lands. The article, which made its debut in a Kuwaiti daily, *al-Anba'*, was later picked up by other Arab media, notably the Egyptian magazine *Akhbar al-Yaum*.[24] It should be noted, however, that Baghdadi had already been embroiled with his religious authorities, who had sentenced him to one month's imprisonment for blasphemy. His angle was quite innovative, inasmuch as by condemning Israel and the West he actually implied criticism of his country, his countrymen, his co-religionists and his culture. He accused Prime Minister Sharon, for example, of terrorism, but at the same time insisted that the 'Zionist entity' never exercised terrorism against its own intellectuals and never put its writers in prisons, and that its prime minister was duly and democratically elected, while the Arab and Islamic world could not boast of any leader who likewise attained legitimate power. He also said that not only did Arabs and Muslims commit a horrendous act of killing innocent civilians on September 11, by a group of 'martyrs', but that prior to that Arab rulers had practised terrorism towards their own citizenry, something without parallel in either Israel or the West.

Baghdadi's list of condemnations of Arab regimes is long: they let Muslim fatwas come to pass, which sanctify the killing of people for their beliefs, something that had not occurred in Europe since the Middle Ages (he even sarcastically suggested that Arabs should be awarded the Nobel Prize for their novel 'invention'); they sue intellectuals in courts for their views and indict them for blasphemy, and in some cases force a couple to separate because one of them was sentenced for heresy, something that amounted to terrorism in his eyes; their intelligence services have executed hundreds of intellectuals and dissidents, a form of terrorism that the Zionists have never adopted; people disappear at the hands of secret apparatuses, a form of terror never practised in the West or in Israel, but where Arab and Islamic regimes, notably Iraq, excel; Arab Muslims even introduced that hell into Afghanistan and brought about its demise and destruction; Arab Muslims, like Hizbullah and the Palestinians, have invented plane hi-jacking and sown terror into the hearts of innocent passengers. In short, he posited the Arabs and Muslims as the masters of terrorism, which began in their domestic policies against their own citizenries, and ended in international terrorism. For that reason, he justified the West, who had been humiliating Arabs and Muslims and rejecting them from its midst. He determined that while stating that it is a religion of tolerance – and Saddam Hussein begins his speeches with a blessing of peace – Islam does not tolerate other's opinions and even undercuts its own intellectuals, at a time when the 'heretic' West and Israel do not practise that kind of terror.[25]

Reactions, some of them violent, were not slow in coming. In order to appreciate his lonely courage, one must take a look at what happened next. The day after al-Ansari's interview, *al-Raya* kept its distance from its 'deviant' interviewee, stating that the 'published material reflected the views of Dr Ansari, not the paper's', but also courageously assuming responsibility and refusing to disown the published interview, arguing that Dr Ansari 'can defend his own views'. What was more disheartening were the virulent attacks by readers of all walks who heaped personal abuse on the writer, one of them claiming that his words were published 'in preparation of the attack against Iraq'. Many readers and radio listeners were outraged by what they regarded as blasphemy on the part of the writer and demanded to ban further publication of those views. Others accused al-Ansari of Americanizing Islam to the extent that he encouraged people to perform the pilgrimage to New York rather than to Mecca.[26]

But the worse was to come. An op-ed in *al-Raya*, by 'abd al-Halim Qindil, complained that America, not content with invading other nations and instigating other governments to wage war on its behalf, had also determined to 'educate other nations' over the heads of their governments. Not content with Sunnite and Shi'ite Islam, the US had resolved 'to install a new school of Islam of the Bush brand, depleted of spirit, honour, and will of jihad. It wants to turn the Arab and Islamic countries into a shameful emulation of the tank-secularism of the Turks', all the while covering her designs under slogans of tolerance, love and democracy.[27] Another writer, Muhammed al-Maliki, made the point that even should the current curricula be turned into non-curricula, 'Islam will remain rooted in our midst for ever, and we shall continue to teach our children that all evil emanates from the West, that Zionists cannot be trusted because they entertain no good intentions toward humanity. We shall continue to cultivate the morality and values that will protect them against openness and permissiveness, and we shall continue to nurture them with honour, force, pride, freedom, struggle, resistance to occupiers and jihad for the sake of Allah'. The writer vowed that should the curricula be altered, Arabs and Muslims would not submit to the 'pervert will of the West' and would continue to remind their children that the change had been forced on them, thus keeping the old curricula in the minds of generations ...[28]

Other writers, such as 'Aisha 'Abidan, a columnist in the same al-Raya, also attacked al-Ansari for inviting the Americans to tamper with Arab and Muslim school curricula, after they had already taken possession, through globalization, of all the political, social and moral aspects of life. She contended that al-Ansari did not reflect the views of the Muslim majority, and his views therefore deserved to be refuted by both preachers in the mosques and intellectuals in order to avert a new American hegemony. For America's aim was to tear the Muslim world apart and generate its ideological and cultural disintegration; its behaviour in Afghanistan amounted to terrorism, and therefore it should not be allowed to take control of the school curricula or of Muslim civilization.[29] Similarly, but even more vitriolically, Dr Ansari's predecessor as the Dean of Islamic Law at Qatar University, Dr Ali Muhammadi, came out against American subversion of the

Islamic umma in 'order to destroy it and re-shape it by foreigners and at their tune', and against those who 'elect to live like slaves in American farms, at a time when their Islam assures them of their freedom'. He distinguished between two sorts of Americans: those who follow only greed and material profit and are out in Africa and Asia trying to enforce their material and economic yardsticks of human behaviour; and those who live in their own country where they promote murder, rape and robbery against their own countrymen. They cause misery to others by their pollution of the earth, their accumulation of weapons of mass destruction, and their tampering with the human genome. Therefore, he concluded, it would be self-defeating to let the likes of Rushdie alter Muslim curricula which have remained as the last dam against globalization.[30]

Many other columnists, public figures, members of the Muslim establishment and intellectuals joined the fray, with a minority, like Dr Ahmed Bishara from Kuwait, decrying the Islamic takeover of education systems in the Gulf countries, which had resulted in 'Arab and Muslim terrorism carried out in the name of Islam, of which the Arabs themselves are now victims'; but the overwhelming majority of them condemned Ansari out of a genuine outrage. For example, Dr Tabtaba'i, Chair of the Legislative Committee of the Kuwaiti Parliament, lashed out at Ansari for aiming to 'drag us to Americanizing our identity and abolishing our Muslim identity'. He reaffirmed that 'Allah was the Guardian of the Islamic Faith, thanks to the Mujahideen who have been spreading it to all parts ...'. He expressed regret that Ansari, who 'accused Islam of terrorism, was an academic in charge of educating the young in Qatar and the Gulf'.[31] The Egyptian columnist Hassan ak-Harawi also condemned those who had gone astray by 'supporting Machiavellism and turning us into Indians at the hands of Americans, so that we accept aid and weapons, and in return we alter our curricula, and our Qur'an and Sunna, to please America who wants to create a new mixture of Islam and Christianity ... We are expected to be tolerant, turn the other cheek and then all other parts of our body'. He insisted that if tolerance is predicated on the respect of the other, then Islam too must be allowed to act with tolerance as it understands it, even if this involves the use of force. He explained that there was no

logic for a 1,400-year-old faith to give way to one hardly four centuries old, which was constructed 'on the ruins of the Indians,
debauchery and tyranny, and is now looking for new Indians'.[32]

Another Egyptian, the fundamentalist Sheikh Qaradhawi, who
had initially founded the Islamic Law Faculty in Qatar, and some
of whose fatwas have been discussed above, naturally joined Dr
Ansari's detractors, and refuted America's desire to

> strike off jihad, doing good and avoiding evil, removing sin
> by force when persuasion fails, struggle against oppression
> and resisting tyrants ... they do not want us to use the word
> Unbelievers even when these are aggressors ... We can fight
> easily against colonialism and occupation, but the invasion
> of our minds via ideological and cultural war is much more
> dangerous ... They want to enslave us, drive us by rods and
> pull our ears as if we were cattle.

This kind of discourse has been prevailing in the Gulf States, supposedly the most open, modern, moderate and in desperate need
of American protection, since the explosion of hatred against
America and the West surfaced after September 11. The few daring voices of dissidence that expressed themselves were almost
universally drowned in protest, condemnation and intimidation.
There are probably many more moderates who dare not surface
for now, but their silence is known to emit many voices.

REFORMS OF THE REGIME

Dissidents in the Arab and Muslim world, who demand reforms by
their home regimes, act for the most part abroad, for what they say
and write in Western countries can hardly be tolerated at home.
Dissidents are both of the fundamentalist kind, which aims at
toppling the tyrannical regimes of the secularists and substituting
for them the rule of Islam; and of the liberal sort, which professes
liberalization and democratization in their countries. The Arab
regimes are depicted as corrupt, subservient to the West and
enjoying no popular support, hence the reluctance of the rulers to
submit their rule to elections. As such, they are certainly subject
to toppling through violence. Understandably, most critics and

calumniators of the domestic scene in Islamic countries do it either from the comfort and safety of their Western exile, where they can exploit the openness of their host countries to attack the regimes they have escaped, or, more rarely, from within when circumstances allow. It is noteworthy that there are critiques not only on the right, by fundamentalist Muslims, but also on the left, by courageous and conscientious liberals who want to implement Western-style reforms so as to stop the Islamists and pull their societies out of the obscurantism that has been reigning there. The reformers' comments are usually countered by others, from within and without, mainly by fundamentalists who are outraged by the attempts at, or even the mere talk about, the much-needed reforms. Some of those controversies, which tie in domestic with external issues, will be illustrated in this section.

The most notorious critics and sworn adversaries of the existing regimes in Muslim countries are probably al-Qa'ida and its branches, which have sought asylum either in rogue countries such as Iran, Afghanistan and the Sudan, or in the heart of the West itself. From the safety of their exiles, they not only attack those regimes violently, but also mount formidable terrorist networks, often manned by fanatic Islamikaze, to subvert, fight and destroy those regimes. The rationale was eloquently and horrendously worded both in bin Laden's now famous fatwas and declarations, and also in the Training Manual of that organization, which was seized and published after September 11:

> After the fall of our orthodox caliphate on 3 March, 1924,[33] and after expelling the colonialists, our Islamic nation was afflicted with apostate rulers who took over in the Muslim nation. These rulers turned out to be more infidel and criminal than the colonialists themselves. Muslims have endured all kinds of harm, oppression and torture at their hands.
>
> These apostate rulers threw thousands of the Islamic Movement youth in gloomy jails and detention centers that were equipped with the most modern torture devices and experts in torture and oppression. Those youth have refused to move in the rulers' orbit ... but they opposed the idea of rebelling against the rulers. But the rulers did not stop there; they started to fragment the essence of the

Islamic nation by trying to eradicate its Muslim identity. Thus, they started to spread godless and atheistic views among the youth. We found some that claimed that social- ism was from Islam, democracy was the Shura (religious council), and the Prophet, blessed be He, propagandized communism …

These young men realized that an Islamic government would never be established except by the bomb and rifle. Islam does not coincide or make a truce with unbelief, but rather confronts it … The confrontation that Islam calls for with these godless and apostate regimes, does not know Socratic debates … but it knows the dialogue of bullets, the ideals of assassination, bombing and destruction, and the diplomacy of the cannon and machine-gun.[34]

Together with bin Laden and his associates, the radical expatriate Sheikhs Bakri and al-Masri, whom we have known in detail in Britain, are probably the most outspoken against their former governments in the Islamic world. Abu-Hamza al-Masri, for example, admits that his life prior to his re-birth as a devout Islamist was tantamount to jahiliyya,[35] that is, the era of 'igno- rance' which had prevailed in pre-Islamic times, before humanity benefited from the Prophet's divine message. The borrowed term of jahiliyya from the pre-Prophetic era has been prevalent among Muslim fundamentalist leaders, foremost of them Sayyid Qutb, the spiritual mentor of the Muslim Brothers in Egypt, executed by the Nasserite regime in Egypt in 1966. The use of this vocabulary has far-reaching implications for radical Muslims, because it implies a mode of action following the blueprint of the Prophet himself: first, since he could not bear the jahili environment of his native Mecca, he migrated (the famous hijra that took place in AD 622 and signalled the beginning of the Muslim Calendar), to create a new Muslim milieu; that, of course, justifies the 'migra- tion' of today's radicals to the West, once their native lands under their godless rulers have made Muslim existence untenable. Secondly, exactly as the Prophet used his base in Medina to con- quer his native Mecca and then the world, so would they. They conceive of the generosity and leeway they receive in the West as an-Allah ordained opportunity to launch their onslaught for the re-conquest of their lands of Islam from the present corrupt and illegitimate governments.

At the other end of the ideological gamut, Arab liberal reformers take their leaders to task for their failures. Arab writers, like Subhi Fuad, the editor of *al-Masri*, an Arabic journal appearing in Australia, blamed the Egyptian leaders, first Nasser with his pan-Arab dreams and then Sadat, who introduced Islam into politics, for Egypt's backwardness, and suggested that had a separate Egyptian identity been cultivated, his country would today be developed and advanced.[36] A Sudanese author, writing like some of his peers in the safety of a London-based Arabic paper, said that the enemy lay within the Arab world itself in the form of 'the mental illness that has affected us since we were defeated by Israel in 1948', and is manifested in the Arab propensity to blame others, not themselves, for their setbacks, and he declared that 'we, the Arabs, are the lawful parents of bin Laden, not America'.[37]

In a letter addressed to President Yasser Arafat that was made public, Nabil 'Amr, one of the senior members of the Palestinian leadership, scathingly listed the failures of the Authority and of Arafat since the Oslo process began in 1993. He wanted the course corrected, because he was concerned about the first attempt of the Palestinians to rule themselves, but his incisive criticism nevertheless stood out in an autocratic regime such as Arafat's:

> I do not know if this letter will be published or if it will be shelved for political considerations. What I know is that addressing Yasir Arafat directly has its pros and cons. The pros are that the letter will be sent to the correct address even if it contains sharp criticism and disturbing revelations. The cons are the way some inexperienced individuals will interpret the letter; they will interpret it either as traditional and naive hypocrisy or as a ferocious war that smacks of disloyalty. Weighing up the pros and cons of the letter, I believe the balance is tilted in favor of the pros. This is because I am certain that the President, who is known for his fondness of following up everything written, might spare us intervention by the busybody.

Mr President: What makes you present in a favorable light the continuing alienation within the establishment – be it Fatah or the PLO, the Legislative Council or the Government? In the time of the revolution, this alienation was unjustifiable; in the time of the PA and the road to the state it is forbidden.

Mr President: You accepted the 'Gaza-Jericho First' idea not because it would result in the liberation of two dear towns. You accepted it because it would be a practical translation of the principle of a 'state on probation', a state that would start with a tiny geographic entity and a tinier sovereignty framework. With time and when these harsh conditions are fulfilled, it would become a state with a wider area and a wider sovereignty. When you accepted this principle, you were aware that there were Arabs, Palestinians, and Israelis who did not want this probationary period to succeed. All these had strong justifications to reject and serious tools to foil and sabotage the project. In our internal conflict and in our negotiating struggle with Israel, we abandoned one of our most important weapons – that of building establishments worthy of receiving support from the world and capable of winning the trust of the Palestinians and pulling the rug from under the feet of the Israelis. What did we do to the Legislative Council? What did we do to the judiciary? What did we do to the Finance Ministry? What did we do to the administration? What did we achieve on this level? I speak in the plural 'we' because I believe the responsibility for failure is a collective one, although you shoulder the greater part of the responsibility in view of your post, jurisdiction, and power.

What did we do to the establishments of the PLO, which had a strong and broad international legitimacy? What did we do to Fatah and to its conferences, regions, committees, and offices? If we did something essential, I am certain it was not in the direction of developing and activating these establishments but in the direction of dissolving their role, canceling their capability, and annulling their personality and tradition. If the most important research center in the world tried to know the reasons for all this self-inflicted punishment, it would find only one reason: our inability to understand our project and serve it in a way that wards off the dangers and provides the chances of safety. Some voice the opinion that what happened were logical manifestations of a revolution that had suddenly become an authority. Although this opinion is valid, it is not enough to explain our behavior. We started the solution experiment knowing full well our commitments and obligations. We were not combat units that climbed mountains and crossed jungles; we were the proprietors of frameworks and establishments. Didn't we boast that we had more embassies than Israel had? Didn't we boast that our democracy and pluralism were better than the democracy and pluralism that existed in stable states and societies?

Therefore, there is something as important as the sudden shift from the culture and mentality of the revolution to the new situation. It is simply the challenge of swimming in the sea of the Palestinian masses. In the past, dealing with this sea took place from distant shores. In the past, the leadership that was exiled to everywhere except the homeland only knew about the Palestinian people that they are an inexhaustible storehouse of blood and loyalty. The shortcomings of the relationship between a leadership in exile and its people cannot be understood except when the real merger with the people occurs. Before the merger, the leader and the people understood each other through pictures for which we chose their colors according to the needs of each side. The leader needed to depict the people as unanimously supportive of the leadership. The people saw in the exiled leadership an ingenious gathering of noble values and unique heroic personalities. However, when the reunion took place, simple things began to matter. The leadership is a group of individuals some of whom are brilliant and have a proven track record in struggle and some of whom are black sheep whose behavior does not tally with the idealistic picture formed about them through the phases of the long struggle. As for the people, their main traits are steadfastness and firmness. However, this people also contains ordinary individuals with their demands, whims, and interests.

Mr President: When the reunion took place, we did not

operate well this major historic process. We did not enact firm laws to regulate the relationship between the authority and the people who would form this authority and grant it legitimacy and credibility.

Mr President: We treated our project with the mentality of sharing booty, not with the mentality of participating in shouldering grave burdens. Not a single committee was formed to study the qualifications of those who were assigned big and small posts. In forming our governments we did not pay attention to professional and behavioral considerations. We returned to the tribe as the main consideration. We backed down on political considerations that used to have some presence in the formulas and establishments of the PLO. We were very lenient in the beginning so much so that we justified the behavior of some ministers who made their ministries close to their homes. We turned a blind eye to the allocation of one ministry to an individual who hailed from Hebron, another ministry to an individual who hailed from Nablus, and a third ministry to an individual who hailed from Jerusalem. We did nothing when a high-level official carried his job and took it to Amman. We did nothing when a veteran struggler demanded that he be appointed a minister as a condition for returning to the homeland on the road to which – according to him – he nearly got martyred.

Mr President: I do not want to remind you of the story of the lists. We all colluded so that these lists would become the basis for polarization in our new situation in such a way that all our people became directors. The result was that every government post had lost its credibility and halo. We did all this, unaware that all the friends before the enemies were recording all our moves and steps and watching the rhythm of the state that would be born in the twenty-first century in the most dangerous spot in the world (the Middle East). They also monitored the billions of dollars that they had committed to give to the difficult project. How naive were we when we did not expect that lean years would come during which we would pay the price for all this.

Mr President: We relied on a naive assumption that influenced our mind and behavior, namely, that the world needed our signature to any solution and that we could do what we wanted. Who would dare to harass us while we held the key to international and regional stability? However, our strong foes found an effective medicine to this magic key, a medicine that was very simple: they took this key from us. Let us be frank with each other: There is something other than conspiracy that has made the whole world either stand against us or incapable of helping us. Because we have a just cause does not mean we are entitled to do what we want. Does the justness of our cause justify all this chaos in our house? You complain about this chaos more than others do, although you are accused of encouraging it as a tactical step to confound the enemy.

Mr President: We will remain in a state of constant retreat as long as we have the extraordinary ability to consider what happened to us in terms of attrition, destruction, and defeat a great achievement by a leadership that finds nothing to boast about except promising the Palestinians all the catastrophes of the world. All this so that history would record that it was a firm and stubborn leadership! Didn't we jump for joy over the failure of Camp David? Didn't we throw mud at the picture of President Clinton who dared to submit a proposal for a state with some modifications? Didn't we do this? Were we sincere with ourselves? No, we were not. This is because after two years of bloodshed we accept what we rejected, perhaps because we know that it is impossible to achieve. How many times did we accept, reject, and then accept? Our timing in saying yes or no was never good. How many times were we asked to do something that we could do but we did not do it? When this something became impossible, we begged the world to re-propose it to us. Between our rejection and acceptance the world either distanced itself from us or set new conditions that we could not even think of.

Mr President: Now, what shall we do? Now means that the Israeli tanks firmly control the West Bank and encircle the Gaza Strip. Now means that the chances of opening the political file have dwindled and been replaced by contacts to obtain facilities, such as the movement of ministers in ambulances. Now means a big retreat from the point when we

stood on the threshold of a state during Bill Clinton and
Camp David to the point of Gaza first in which Bethlehem is
rewarded by lifting the curfew on it. Now means that every
Palestinian militia in the homeland behaves without checks
and controls in the name of the legitimacy of the resistance
and the inevitability of steadfastness until doomsday. Now,
after all this, what shall we do? Certainly a delegation visiting Washington is not a solution when there is an absolute
Israeli–US alliance, when the United States prepares for war
on Saddam, and when Rumsfeld speaks about the West Bank
and Gaza Strip in a language that Sharon does not dare to
speak. Certainly, phone calls by Solana, visits by Moratinos,
and attempts by the EU to open dialogue with the fighters to
resort to reason will not work. What works is frankness and
admission that a grave failure has occurred. Admitting failure, even if it is grave, does not mean the end of the world
or the burial of an issue that has all the prerequisites for survival. It means courage in dotting the Is and crossing the Ts
and preparation to avoid the causes of failure and replace
them with the requisites for success.

Mr President: What prevents us from holding a serious
domestic dialogue with Hamas, Islamic Jihad, and all
factions and asking them frankly for a period of calm for
redressing the Palestinian wounds and attempting to create
a climate that would help us renovate our cracking home
and eroded alliances? Doesn't the 'giant fighter' (the
Palestinian people) deserve some time to rest and take a
breather even if Sharon harasses us? Is it not wise to besiege
Sharon with calm, perhaps we will win the third party that
we have lost because of our miscalculated steps?

After this dialogue for which there are no strong justifications for its non-success, what prevents us from implementing
the Legislative Council's document on internal reform? This
document is the best comprehensive plan for a real reform
that will pave the way for a real state of which we have
always dreamed even in the darkest circumstances. What
prevents us from opening an urgent workshop for reforming
the Palestinian judiciary after the issuance of the law on its
independence – this law was violated on the next day? What

prevents us from acting immediately to stop the chaos
spreading in the administrative department where the army
of employees has reached 130,000 persons, three quarters of
whom do not know what their work is?

Mr President: Sharon's tanks cannot prevent the
rearrangement of our house because you still issue decisions,
possess legitimacy, and can issue more decisions without a
comprehensive plan – with my apologies to those who
coined the stupid phrase the '100-day plan'.

Mr President: We have not done yet what we must do.
Perhaps we have become accustomed to finding justifications
for our failure. How easy it is for Sharon's tanks to carry all our
sins over their sins! Mr President: We have committed a serious mistake against our people, authority, and the dream of
the establishment of our state. However, we can be forgiven if
we admit our mistake and get to work immediately. What this
people deserve is for us to work a lot with them and for
them—not to place their destiny at the mercy of a coincidence
blown by new international winds or mortgage them until
doomsday without opening a window of hope for them.[38]

ARABS AND MUSLIMS UNDER SCRUTINY

Nothing exemplifies the internal intellectual strife that tore the
Muslim world apart in the aftermath of September 11 than the
conspiracy theories that were rife then and thereafter. Indeed, in
addition to the usual fabricated stories about the use of depleted
uranium by the Americans against the Kosovars, or the 'massacres' that are or were allegedly committed against Muslims, or
the accusations of poisoning wells, lands and innocent people
that are hurled regularly against Israel, September 11 afforded
novel opportunities for imagination to work overtime and make
up all manner of stories without foundation. The comments of
two Saudi columnists on the fantasy-ridden stories of an Islamist
Egyptian journalist, Fahmi Huweidi, go a long way to opening a
window on the conspiracy theories which haunt much of the
Muslim world. While Huweidi presented his stories in Saudi papers,
notably in *al-Watan daily*,[39] the Saudi columnists responded in
Egyptian papers. To Huweidi's allegation that it was 'probable' that

extremist American militias carried the September 11 attack, Hamad al-'Isa retorted that it was unthinkable that the Egyptian writer did not as much as mention that the fatwa calling for the murder of American civilians had been issued in 1996 by an 'Afghani' Arab, presumably bin Laden himself. To Huweidi's claim that the Arabs could not have concocted that attack due to its complex and sophisticated planning and execution, al-'Isa answered that it was Arabs who had tried to blow the World Trade Center up in 1993, that Arabs knew how to fly airplanes and how to mount Islamikaze operations in southern Lebanon and in Palestine. He also insisted that it was the Arabs who invented the hijacking and blowing-up of civilian airplanes in the 1970s, and they gave that up only when they realized that the method had failed dismally.[40]

Countering Huweidi's exultation over that barbaric attack, 'Isa said that the terrorists' success was due to the good and peaceful American people's civilized treatment of anyone who went to America legally, and was allowed to tour freely everywhere, including the White House and the FBI Buildings, even if he wore Muslim fundamentalist attire. He drew attention to the fact that Arab and Muslim preachers were free to curse the US on its own home soil without being harmed. He also denounced Huweidi's call for an international investigative committee to find out what happened on September 11, on the grounds that due to America's superb judicial system, it was well able to investigate itself and to protect the rights of the accused. He also ridiculed Hizbullah Television, which had claimed that the '4,000 Israelis who worked at the World Trade Center and were absent on the day of the attack' had 'demonstrated that it was Mossad who carried out that crime'.[41] Another Saudi columnist, al-Nkidan, also published a scathing critique of Sheikh Huweidi, whom he otherwise venerated as an 'enlightened' cleric, and other Muslim conspiracy theorists, accusing them of marketing absurdities and nonsense that were no better than those of the 'Kandahar cave-dwellers'. He also lambasted 'modern Arab thought which was collapsing under the weight of delusions, since it lacked the rationality or critical spirit required for Arab and Islamic societies today and in the future'.[42] He thoughtfully concludes:

Most of the Arab and Muslim commentators have not eliminated the possibility of conspiracy in one way or another.
Naturally, the conspirator is always Israel; alternatively
the finger is pointed at the Jews. If it seems inconceivable
logically and in the light of events that this catastrophe was
perpetrated by the Zionist movement or that Jewry had a
hand in it, we tend to stress the Jewish influence on decision-
making and public opinion, or even their control over the
American business and financial community. These claims
appear somewhat convincing, but there remains an important point to notice, and that is that American society is democratic and open and there is no way of hiding the truth from
it to please anyone, even if it concerns Israel itself ...

Throughout history, there has not been one single case of
proof of the veracity of the assumptions underpinning this
conspiracy theory. But Arab thought has remained enamoured
of it ... The truth is that we are not capable of formulation and
interpretation of events, and therefore we recycle this idiotic
culture, the same improbable and stupid theory ... Despite
the changes in the Arab world, and in the world around us,
the Arab citizen still does not have a complete character that
could enable him to independently impose on the Arab
rhetoric his own position regarding events ... In conclusion,
do any of us remember the Protocols of the Elders of Zion?
They too spoke of a Jewish conspiracy against the world,
even though no one in his right mind in the world today can
view them as the truth.[43]

Important in raising the American people's awareness of the new
threats and challenges facing it are certain voices among the Arabs
in general, Arab-Americans in particular, who reject the anti-
American consensus and choose to side with their country. Chief
among them has been Fouad Ajami who, from his prestigious academic chair at Johns Hopkins, adds the clout of his knowledge and
the authority of his experience as a former Lebanese, to his instinc-
tive and rare loyalty to the country that not only gave him shelter
but also catapulted him to international prominence. Some of his
scathing remarks about Arab politics, beyond his learned and per-
ceptive books about the world of delusion of the Arab rulers, have

been cited worldwide. But less famous Arab-Americans also feel the need to call to task their fellow Arabs and Muslims, not only in the American press in order to alleviate the sometimes unjust suspicions raised about them, but, more importantly and significantly, in the Arabic press abroad. The London-based *al-Hayat* published a selection of Letters to the Editor, one of them from Zuheir Abdallah in the US, where he essentially castigated the Arabs, and especially their media, for following a delusive and destructive course. He detected three phases, which were actually watersheds in the development of that press over the past 60 years:

1. The broadcasts of Yunis al-Bahri from the Arabic station in Berlin under the Nazis, where he instigated the Arabs to act against the West and Britain, and lauded Hitler, Nazi Germany and the Axis Powers. Abdallah commented that though the Arabs were the lowest in the ladder of Nazi racism, the Arabs used to cluster around radio receivers and to swallow avidly those incitements; then
2. Ahmed Sa'id from Cairo's 'Voice of the Arabs', who gathered Arab masses around his curses of Arab moderate leaders and the West. He imputed to that demagogy the fact that moderate Arab regimes in Iraq and Libya succumbed, to be replaced by 'tyrants and fascist parties that the Arab world has been still suffering under their burden'; after the 1967 defeat, the influence of the 'Voice of the Arabs' receded when the masses realized that they were pushed to a war they were ill-prepared for; and
3. The present phase of *al-Jazeera Television*, whose reporter in Kabul became the spokesman for the Taliban. He has been in the custom of reporting the civilian casualties in order to raise sympathy for them, but concealing the military defeats of the Taliban and overlooking the massacres they perpetrated. They also fail to report the joy of the inhabitants in the areas liberated from the Taliban, but nevertheless have attracted to themselves the third generation of Arabs. However, with the fall of the Taliban came an end to *al-Jazeera*, exactly as the demise of the Nazis and then of the Arabs in 1967 brought to an end the media heroes that accompanied them.

Abdallah concluded, nevertheless, that the new generation of

Arabs had learned nothing from the experiences of their predecessors. For with the onset of Ramadan, other Arab stations began to air television series imbued with hatred, such as the Crusaders of one millennium ago, who are revived as if they happened today. But, while the media have encouraged the mending of fences between warring nations, like France and Germany or Japan and Russia, in the civilized world, the Arab media continue to educate for incitement and hatred, lick the wounds of the past, and so encourage young people to commit suicide and to kill people they know nothing about, just because they are members of other nations and religions.[44] This self-criticism by an Arab who has tasted the delights of Western culture is naturally music to the ears of Westerners, and therefore as credible and 'Faithful' as the Biblical 'wounds of a friend'.[45] It also encourages Westerners in their belief that there is something wrong with the Arabs, if some of their kin admit it. Even more so when such words come from an Arab national, like the Kuwaiti Ahmed al-Baghdadi, who audaciously and innovatively lashed out at the Arabic press which focuses on Israeli deeds but overlooks what is happening in the Arab world itself. This self-flagellation came from someone who had been condemned to one month's imprisonment in Kuwait in October 1999 for 'insulting Islam' by claiming that the Prophet had failed to convert non-Muslims to Islam.[46] He 'conceded' to his readership, that Prime Minister Sharon had 'committed acts of murder and terror against the Palestinians', but, and this is his point, he stressed that no Israeli official had ever terrorized his own society, because the 'Zionist entity does not terrorize its intellectuals and writers and does not throw them into prisons ... We have to be honest towards our enemies, as our Qur'an prescribes, and recognize that the governments of the Israeli entity are elected democratically, while no elected prime minister is to be found in the entire Arab and Muslim world.'[47]

Kuweiti columnist Baghdadi's analysis is nothing short of revolutionary with regard to the Arab world. But he also falsely claimed that Arabs and Muslims did not usually terrorize others, until September 11, when a 'group of shahids killed 7,000 innocent people; but they did terrorize their own people'. Even as he was disregarding the sustained campaign of Muslim terrorism against Israel and Jews abroad in the past two decades, he could not help enumerating the sins of his own people and culture:

1. The Arab world alone permitted the publication of fatwas which indicted and condemned people to death, while no such verdict has been issued by any Christian cleric since the Middle Ages. He sarcastically attributed the Nobel Prize to the Muslims for their 'invention that permitted the survival of such verdicts which retributed against people of dissenting opinions'.
2. The prosecution of Arab intellectuals in courts of law, their indictments for heresy, and in consequence the verdicts that destroyed families when a spouse was ordered to abandon his or her 'heretic' partner. This exists only in the Islamic world. Is this not terrorism?
3. The intelligence apparatuses have cut short the lives of hundreds of politicians, intellectuals and clerics. The Zionist entity has never acted likewise against its citizens, he contended. Is this not terrorism?
4. The phenomenon whereby any security apparatus in Arab and Muslim countries can arrest people or cause them to disappear does not exist in the West or in Israel. Isn't that terror?
5. Iraq alone is a never-ending story of terror against her people and neighbours.
6. The Afghans had led a quiet and healthy life, albeit their internecine wars, until the Arabs and Muslims got there and introduced them to the circle of terror and hell for which they pay the price today.
7. Who hijacked a Kuwaiti airplane and killed the Kuwaitis aboard? Wasn't it the pious Hizbullah?
8. The Palestinian Arabs were the first to invent hijackings of planes and terrorizing peaceful passengers. Is this also not terrorism?
9. The Arabs and Muslims have no competitors: they are the masters of terrorism against their own citizens, their terrorism often extends to other innocent people in the world, with the support of some of their clerics.

He concluded that the Muslims were now paying the price for terrorism by being humiliated in the entire civilized world. They are rejected everywhere: in restaurants, airplanes and buses, and one cannot blame the West for that, because all the governments and people of the Muslim and Arab world are 'lying with regard to terror'. He claimed that while they are proclaiming Islam as the 'religion of peace and fraternity', al-Azhar university students launch demonstrations against 'Banquet for Sea Weeds'.[48] He said that the

> ignorance of our nation provokes laughter in the world. The Muslim and Arab worlds are the only ones where prisons are full of intellectuals whose only sin was that they wrote ... For the past 500 years, no writer or intellectual was murdered in the heretic West, while the indictment and death warrants issued by clerics in the Arab and Islamic worlds are cheap. And since the people and governments observe their silence, it means that they agree to those ways ... Now is the day of reckoning. Nothing goes without retribution, and the account is longer than the beards of all the Taliban put together. The West's message to the Arab and Islamic worlds is clear: either you improve your ways, or else.[49]

A Muslim-American, Dr Muqtedar Khan, of Adrian College, Michigan, of Indian descent, took the Muslim world in its entirety to task when he addressed an open letter to his fellow Muslim-Americans, after duly paying the lip-service of Israel-bashing. It turns out then, that teachings of reason and humanity do not necessarily emerge from great scholars at major universities as Harvard, but can emanate from decent human beings in more remote colleges such as Adrian:

> What happened on September 11 will forever remain a horrible scar on the history of Islam and humanity, for no matter how we condemn this act ... the fact remains that the perpetrators of this crime against humanity have indicated that their actions are sanctioned by Islamic values ... Muslims have been practicing hypocrisy on a grand scale. They protest against the discriminatory practices of Israel but are silent against the discriminatory practices in Muslim states. While acknowledging the ill-treatment of the Palestinians by Israel, I must remind you that Israel treats its 1 million Arab citizens with greater respect and dignity than most Arab nations treat their own citizens ... Today, Palestinian refugees can settle and become citizens of the

US, but in spite of all the tall rhetoric of the Arab world and Qur'anic injunctions [Sura 24:22], no Muslim country except Jordan extends this support to them ...

Have we ever demanded international intervention or retribution against Saddam for gassing Kurds, against Pakistan for slaughtering Bengalis, against Saudis for abusing the Shi'is, against Syria for the massacre at Hama? We condemn Israel not because we care for the Palestinians, we don't. We condemn Israel because we hate 'them'. Muslims love to live in the US, but also love to hate it. Many openly claim that the US is a terrorist state, yet their presence here is testimony that they would rather live here than anywhere else ... As an Indian Muslim, I know for sure that nowhere on earth, including India, will I get the same sense of dignity and respect that I have received in the US. It is time that we acknowledge that the freedoms we enjoy in America are more desirable to us than superficial solidarity with the Muslim world. If you disagree, then prove it – by migrating to whichever Muslim country you identify with ...

The culture of hate and killing is tearing away at the moral fabric of Muslim society. In the pursuit of the inferior Jihad [of violence and war], we have sacrificed the superior Jihad [of spiritual striving]. It is time we faced these hypocritical practices and struggled to transcend them. It is time that American Muslim leaders fought to purify their own lot ... While encouraging Islam to struggle against injustice ... Allah also imposes strict rules of engagement ... he also encourages Muslims to forgive Jews and Christians if they have committed injustices against us ... Islam has been hijacked by hate and calls for murder and mayhem ... Bin Laden has become a phenomenon – a cancer eating away at our moral foundations. Yes, the US has played a role in the creation of Bin Laden, but it is we who have allowed him to grow and gain such a foothold. It is our duty to police our world. It is our responsibility to prevent our people from abusing Islam. We should have made sure that September 11 had never happened ...

Islam is not about defeating Jews, or conquering Jerusalem, or competing with the American Jewish lobby for power over American foreign policy. It is about mercy, values, sacrifice and duty. Above all, it is the pursuit of moral perfection ... The worst exhibition of Islam happened on our turf. We must take responsibility to undo the evil it has manifested. This is our mandate, our burden but also our responsibility ... I hope that we will now rededicate our lives and our institutions to the search for harmony, peace and tolerance. Let us be prepared to suffer injustice rather than commit injustices ... If we wish to convince the world of the truth of our message, we cannot even be equal to others in virtue, we must excel, and we must be more forgiving, more sacrificing.[50]

HOPEFUL SUMMARY?

This almost unprecedented outpour of self-criticism in the Arab and Muslim world, some destructive and aimed at removing regimes in place in order to replace them with something that might even be worse; others constructive and directed to achieving reforms in the existing regimes; and still others simply meaning to remove old stereotypical thinking and replace it with a new measure of rationality and realism, has not ended even one year after September 11, which had occasioned it. Quite the contrary, self-criticism seems to have picked up some momentum, as more and wider circles join the fray, thinkers and intellectuals come out of the closet, and the realization grows that self-criticism does not bring the skies down nor cause chaos. The best sign of his hopeful development is that not only the same critics persist in hammering their messages into their public, in spite of the humiliation and intimidation that they had to incur, but that their ranks are being swollen as more and more dare to utter out loud their dissatisfaction with the current state of affairs. Admittedly, the shrieks of the fundamentalists, who threaten to topple the regimes in their countries, have also intensified in volume, but while their threats, violence and vocabulary are known and repetitive, the new critics who advocate reform, peaceful means and renouncing violence, constitute the new breath of fresh air that Arab and Muslim societies are beginning to get accustomed to.

It is true that, with some important exceptions, most of the calls of the peaceful reformists and the liberal critics of their own regimes seem to have emanated, thus far, not from humanist persuasion but from utilitarian considerations of gaining favour with the West, but in the past even those considerations had been drowned in the rhetoric of self-righteousness. Nobody had prevented 'Abd-al-Hamid al-Bakkush, the former Prime Minister of Libya, for example, from uttering the self-deprecating, almost sycophantic, self-criticism that he has been spreading these days from London about the 'inherent and built-in cultural, political and economic deficiencies of the Arabs',[51] when he was in office and had the power also to change things. Nor was Nabil 'Amr, the former cabinet member of the Palestinian Authority, muzzled when he was in office from criticizing the corruption, autocracy, miscalculations and mistakes of Arafat during the peace process with Israel. Neither of them had risen, in real time, to tell their people and the world about the mishaps under Qaddafi or the scuttling of the Oslo process by Arafat, respectively, until they found themselves outside the establishment, and bent, one suspects, on taking personal vengeance on their previously adulated leaders. One may suspect the same tendency when one scrutinizes the current efforts deployed by Arab countries, notably Saudi Arabia and Egypt, to mend fences with the US.[52]

One should not disregard either, the tone of settling accounts between Arab countries and regimes, and between them and others, when suddenly, in an ostensible bout of remorse and self-flagellation of the Arabs and Muslims as a whole, one detects subterranean streams which point to the need of the author to flagellate others, not the self. For example, since the Palestinians lost favour with Kuwait in the Second Gulf War (1990–91) due to their support for Saddam, Kuwaitis would look for every opportunity to tarnish Arafat's image. Therefore, when a Kuwaiti paper suddenly 'discovers' that Arafat deposited in his personal bank account millions from the foreign aid he begs for, in order to cover the expenses of his wife and daughter's extravagant life in Paris,[53] it cannot be suspected of morality or care for the rule of law, as long as it does not dare to expose and condemn the many-fold larger corruption and waste of the Kuwaiti (and Saudi for that matter) princes. The same can be said of the condemnation of institutionalized corruption in the Arab world, by Arab expatriates in Europe.[54] Conversely, there is no doubt that there are

Arabs who try to battle against prevailing stereotypes, for the sake of straightening the record, like 'Ala' al-'Arabi, who lambasted the Arab and Muslim media which claim, based on certain passages of the Qur'an and its commentaries,[55] that the Jews are 'descendants of pigs and monkeys', and termed them pure anti-semites.[56] Another example: when the Hebrew University Cafeteria was blown up in early August 2002, a number of Palestinian personalities came out severely against the wanton killing of students, Israeli and foreigners,[57] though their condemnation emanated, at least in part, from the consideration of the bad image and disservice that those acts did to the Palestinian cause.[58]

One cannot help admiring people like Sheikh al-Ansari of Qatar and Tunisian liberal columnist al-'Afif al-Akhdar, who were repeatedly cited above, for their courage and consistence in self-criticism in spite of the hostile voices which condemned them for 'protecting' the West and sometimes Israel, in defiance of the near-unanimous torrents of bigotry around them. For example, al-Akhdar did not hesitate to touch upon the Islamikaze bombings which have been the hottest and most 'untouchable' topic in Arab politics in recent months. Al-Akhdar's essay in July 2002, in *al-Hayat* (London – it is doubtful that it could be published anywhere in the Arab world), is probably the most daring act of defiance of Arab and Muslim public opinion on this issue. Under the title 'The Missed Opportunity and the Intifada of Suicide', he wrote, inter alia:

> My generation had opened its eyes to the loss of Palestine, and it is about to close them to the loss of the opportunity to retrieve any of it ... Until the year 2000, the solution was at hand, but the Palestinian leadership refused to extend their hand to it. That amounted to missing the last rare opportunity to retrieve the land, with enough honour to cause the wound to heal, which has been bleeding since we were first defeated by Napoleon in 1798 and then by Ben Gurion in 1948 ...
>
> Clinton presented the Palestinians with proposals on a golden platter, but they answered with intifada and suicide bombing ... and so, in one stroke, we lost both the land and our reputation ...

Before the suicide attacks against Israeli civilians we had the image of freedom fighters, but after the most important Palestinian organizations, including Fatah, became involved with those attacks, followed by the majority of Arab intellectuals, the Arab street and 80 per cent of Palestinians, the new image stuck to us of those who take lightly human life, their own and others' ... It is thus likely that the Arab–Israeli conflict will be resolved by coercion and humiliation against the Arabs, reflecting the present balance of power ...

To our repeated defeats in the past two centuries, we responded by becoming less and less courageous to ask the painful questions, and we sunk into the culture of producing excuses and laying the blame on others, condemning the traps into which the West and Israel had pushed us ... The neurosis of defeat is what caused the leaders, especially the Palestinians among them, to punish themselves with more defeats, even where success was guaranteed. This is due to many factors:

1. We suffer from a frozen thinking which prevents us from evaluating the local and international balance of power;
2. Political backwardness that bars the way to changes in leadership when they are due, and gives precedence to private relationships over skill and knowledge;
3. We have become obsessed by the mania of armed struggle, until it became a goal unto itself. We have thus missed all opportunities since 1937 to this day, while advancing pretexts that right, time, geography and demography are on our side;
4. Our inability to define what our national interest is ...
5. Our banning any freedom of debate and moderate discourse, emanating from a cool and rational analysis of the situation. Instead, we are carried by the radical rhetoric of our culture and the emotional significance of words, where logic, moderation, compromise are lacking ...

We cannot retrieve our rights as long as for us words are equivalent to substance. Therefore most Palestinians with a spirit of criticism have remained outside the present leadership.[59]

All this is not to say that all is lost. It is very likely that in the long run, maybe a very long run, the length or the time of which cannot be foretold, more and more Arabs who come into contact with the West or study there, and return to their countries after years of mixing with Western culture and norms of conduct, some of them will come to realize the vanity of their past dreams and aspirations, and through a painful process of soul-searching awaken to new opportunities. Only then will they learn to shoulder responsibility, to blame themselves for their failures, to respect their own and others' lives, to open their societies to debate and criticism, to embark on the road of participatory democracy, and to embrace human and civil rights as part of their programme. These norms cannot be enforced from the outside; they must grow organically from within. A hopeful sign in that direction came up in the heated debate that followed the publication of the Arab Fund for Economic and Social Development, which caused a storm throughout the Arab world. That report pointed out the fatalism and the helplessness of the Arabs when it comes to development, resulting in the Arabs marking the lowest rate of development in the world, with the exception of Central Africa, in spite of their immense resources. That report, compiled by Arab experts and technicians, concluded that while worldwide populations need ten years to double their income, in the Arab world 140 years are required.

A liberal Arab columnist of Iraqi origin, Khaled Kashtini, commenting on the report, identified in it three major factors inhibiting development in the Arab world: the stifling of civil and human rights; the limitations on women, who constitute one half of the workforce; and the restricted flow of knowledge. He said that those were only symptoms of a deeper malaise in Arab society: the stifling Arab heritage, political totalitarianism and the obsession with the Palestinian issue. He said the Arab heritage engendered limitations because of past glories that the Arabs try in vain to revive, due to its restrictions on women's development, and to the focus on the Arabic language and grammar, instead of directing students to the sciences. He says that Africans could adopt democracy more easily than the Arabs, because they had no heritage which negated democracy. He emphasizes that the Palestinian issue was ill-tackled, due to Arab ignorance, errors of judgement, misunderstanding and opportunism (personal and national), until it grew to such an extent that it inhibited Arab development. He suggests that:

> The liberation of Palestine has become a slogan under which all the enemies of democracy, the nouveau riche and the merchants of nationalism and pan-Arabism found cover ... They shut off anyone who demanded reform, liberty for the people, women participation, or just simple things like getting a passport, or a building permit, for all those wishes were made subservient to the liberation of Palestine first ...
>
> This bitter conflict with our able enemy has forced upon us kinds of jihad which generated acts of sabotage, plane hijackings, suicide and all manner of violence ... Together with the military coups which succeeded each other, they produced instability in the area, caused us huge expenditures, and led us to use methods of terror and torture that were taken straight from hell, and to stifle the independence of the judiciary.[60]

The author also claims that Western support for Israel had sent the Arabs into the arms of the communists, hence the failure of the political and economic systems that they copied from the communist bloc. That alliance was convenient for Arabs, he submits, because of Arab hatred towards the West and because of their authoritarian political culture. Corruption, squeeze and embezzlement did the rest, as the Arab citizen became dependent on the bureaucracy to survive.[61] It is this sort of criticism, unthinkable a decade ago, and obviously the product of Arab and Muslim rulers' inability to prevent the fresh air of global news to seep through their walls of secrecy and oppression via the Internet, which gives reason to hope that the trend will continue, no matter how long it takes.

NOTES

1. Islamikaze is the term coined by this author, combining Islam and Kamikaze. See R. Israeli, 'Islamikaze and their Significance', *Journal of Terrorism and Political Violence* (February 1997).
2. *IRNA* (Iranian News Agency), 1 May 2002.
3. *Al-Hayat* (London), 19 January 2002. Memri 334, 23 January 2002.

4. *Akhbaral-Yaum* (Egypt), 29 December 2001. See Memri 329 and 330, 11 January 2002.
5. *Al-Raya* (Qatar), 6 January 2002; see also *al-Sharq al Awsat* (London), 28 September 2001 and 25 October 2001. All in Memri 337, 29 January 2002.
6. *Al-Hayat* (London), 13 January 2002.
7. Ibid.
8. Ibid.
9. Ibid.
10. Literally 'catastrophe', but the term is used for the Arab defeat by Israel in the 1948 War, and has come to symbolize all the Arab defeats since.
11. *Al-Sharq al Awsat* (London), 8 May 2002.
12. *Washington Post*, 14 May 2002.
13. See Daphne Burdman's article 'Education, Indoctrination and Incitement: Palestinian Children on their way to Martyrdom', in *Journal of Terrorism and Political Violence,* 15, 1 (Spring 2003), pp.96–123.
14. For details on Palestinian textbooks, see R. Israeli, 'Education, State Building and the Peace Process: Educating Palestinian Children in the Post-Oslo Era', *Journal of Terrorism and Political Violence*, 12, 1 (Spring 2000), pp. 79–84.
15. *Al-Ayyam* (Palestinian Authority), 3 May 2002.
16. Ibid.
17. *Al-Sharq al Awsat* (London), 27 October 2000. Ibid.
18. *Akhbar al-Yaum* (Egypt), 29 December 2001.
19. Ibid.
20. Fundamentalist Muslims shun the modern nation-state in favour of re-establishing the caliphate which ought to encompass all Muslims.
21. *Al-Jazeera* Television (Qatar), 17 December 2001.
22. Probably reference is made to President Assad's reaction to acts of terrorism by the Muslim Brothers in Syria, in which he flattened large sections of the city of Hama (their stronghold) and eliminated over 20,000 of them by conservative estimates (1982).
23. See *al-Raya* (Qatar), 6 January 2002; and also al-Ansari's articles in London-based *al-Sharq al Awsat*, 28 September and 25 October 2001. All in Memri 337, 28 January 2002.
24. 3 November 2001.
25. *Akhbar al-Yaum* (Kuwait), 3 November 2001.
26. *Al-Raya*, 7 January 2002. Memri, No.26 (Hebrew).
27. *Al-Raya*, 8 January 2002. Ibid.
28. Ibid., 12 January 2002.
29. *Al-Raya*, 12 January 2002.
30. *Al-Quds al-'Arabi* (London), 10 January 2002.
31. Ibid.
32. Ibid.
33. That was the official end of the Ottoman Empire, the last for now, when it was defeated during the First World War and modern Turkey emerged, which substituted under Ataturk for the deceased Empire, together with other independent nations which declared their independence. It has become a basic element of faith among practically all Muslim fundamentalist movements to call for the re-establishment of the universal Muslim caliphate as the panacea for the ills of Muslim countries.
34. J. Post (ed.), *The Qaeda Training Manual: Military Studies in the Jihad Against the Tyrants* (London: Frank Cass, 2002), published as a special issue of *Terrorism and Political Violence*, 14, 1 (Spring 2002), p.17.
35. *Al-Ayyam* (Yemen), 8 August 1999. See Memri 72, 16 October 2001.
36. *Al-Quds al-'Arabi* (London), 23 January 2002.
37. *Al-Quds al-'Arabi* (London), 7 October 2001.
38. IMRA (Independent Media Review and Analysis), 2 September 2002.
39. *Al-Watan* (Saudi Arabia), 18 and 25 September 2001. See Memri 294, 31 October 2001.
40. *Al-Qahira* (Egypt), 23 October 2001. Memri, ibid.
41. Ibid.
42. *Al-Sharq al Awsat*, 25 October 2001. Ibid.
43. Ibid.
44. *Al-Hayat* (London), 21 December 2001. Memri 37 (Hebrew), undated.

45. Proverbs: 27:6.
46. After the death of the Prophet (AD 632), most of the tribes of Arabia that had converted to Islam as a personal oath of allegiance to him reneged upon learning of his passing away. It became incumbent upon his successor, the first Caliph Abu Bakr, to fight the bloody and cruel 'Ridda Wars' (The Wars of Apostasy), when the tribes were subjugated one after the other at a terrible human price.
47. *Akhbar al-Yaum* (Egypt), 3 November 2001.
48. That book, by the Syrian writer Khaydar Khaydar, was published in 2000 in Cairo, eighteen years after it was completed. It led to the demonstration by al-Azhar students, who were incited by the Muslim Movement in Egypt. See Memri 37 (Hebrew), undated.
49. *Akhbar al-Yaum* (Egypt), 3 November 2001.
50. From an article published in the *New York Post*, 19 October 2001. See http://nypost.com/seven/10192001/postopinion/opedcolumnists/34049.htm.
51. See *al-Hayat* (London), 31 July 2002.
52. See Dr Abdallah al-Jasir, Saudi Deputy Minister for Information, in *al-Sharq al Awsat* (London), 13 November 2001; Saudi Prince Kahled al-Faisal, in al-Sharq al-Awsat, 14 January 2002; and *al-Hayat* (London) 6 June and 8 August 2002. All cited by Memri.
53. *Al-Watan* (Kuwait), 7 June 2002. See also the interview of Mu'awiya al-Masri, member of the Palestinian Legislative Council to the Jordanian paper, *al-Sabil*, 3 July 2002.
54. See, for example, the Sudanese writer Dr 'Abd-al-Wahhab al-Effendi, who lives in London, in *al-Quds al-'Arabi* (London) 6 August 2002. Cited by Memri.
55. Surat al Mai'da, verse 60, and Surat al-a'raf, verse 166. Major classical commentators, like Tabari, Qurtubi and Ibn Kathir, who are often referred to in that and other contexts in the contemporary media, had come to different interpretations of those passages.
56. *Al-Qahira Weekly* (Egypt), 7 May 2002.
57. See the statement by Hana Nasser, President of Bir Zeit University; and by Rashid abu-Shubak, Head of Preventive Security in Gaza.
58. This point was particularly stressed in the statement made public by fifty-five members of the Palestinian leadership on 19 June 2002. Text in *al-Quds* (Palestinian Authority), 19 June 2002; elaborations in interviews given to *al-Sinara* (Israel), 21 June 2002. A wide-ranging debate within the Palestinians, for and against the Islamikaze bombings against Israeli civilians, took place during the months of April–June 2002. See, for example, *al-Hayat al-Jadida* (Palestinian Authority), 9 June 2002; *al-Quds* (Palestinian Authority), 29 May 2002; al-Ayyam (Palestinian Authority), 4 and 20 June 2002; and *al-Sharq al Awsat* (London), 2 May 2002.
59. *Al-Hayat*, 21 July 2002. The same writer, al-Akhdar, also published a very scathing critique of Hamas and took it to task for poisoning young Palestinians with nonsensical indoctrination about the impending liquidation of Israel. *Al-Hayat*, 14 July 2002.
60. *Al-Sharq al Awsat* (London), 15, 16 and 17 July 2002. All cited by Memri.
61. Ibid.

CHAPTER TWO

Islamic Fundamentalism in the Public Square

THE PUBLIC SQUARE AS A BATTLEFIELD

Reputedly, the philosophic rationale for separation of church and state lay in the argument that religion was a matter for individual concern, therefore no state institution could be invoked to enforce it. All this is conceptually and practically accepted and applied in the modern world – Western style. Thus, the public square can be kept more or less neutral, give or take several manifestations of 'indecent' mores and norms of conduct, generically known as 'the new morality', which have come to be tolerated by the general public as a price for maintaining this universally supported separation.

In traditional and conservative societies, the Muslim world included, there is little tolerance for the new morality, and its expressions in public are usually countered by outrage on the part of clerics, often by violence, and in consequence by religiously inspired legislation to curtail those liberties. Among Muslim fundamentalist groups, the outrage with the public square goes much further: not only do they reject Western values lock, stock and barrel, which they fault for the general degradation of mores, but they accuse the West of having schemed to undermine Muslim societies from within by corrupting their youth with its new morality that is visible in the public square. Therefore, they battle the visibility of the West with their own mores, and if they cannot uproot it with rhetoric and competition for the souls of their constituencies, they have no qualms about resorting to violence in the public square in order to get the attention of the public both domestically and externally.

Capitalizing on the general disapproval of many of the Western norms by the conservative public, these movements extend their criticism of the public square to include the entire political systems in their own countries, which they regard as subservient to the decadent West – hence, the public-squarization of the political-religious debate which encompasses all spheres of life. Since in Islam religion is part of life, and life is part of the religion, the latter by necessity is dragged into the public square. But it is not only the fundamentalists who set the agenda in the public square; the authorities who defend themselves against the fundamentalist onslaught also do, as well as established Islam which serves the governments in place, on the one hand, and regards itself as menaced by the fundamentalists, on the other. The debate is not conducted in words only, although the *da'wa* (call, or propaganda) is an essential tool of the fundamentalists in appealing for public support. They also commit acts of sabotage, kill government officials, foreign tourists and other designated enemies, and terrorize common people into submission; but they also build an infrastructure of social welfare, provide leadership and solace to their people, profess social and political revolution, and teach that Islam is the panacea for all ills of their society.

While the activities of the fundamentalists, both inoffensive and violent, unfold in and from the public square, the government's reactions cannot help but occur publicly too. Governments also use propaganda to denigrate and condemn the fundamentalists, finding support in the *'ulama* (learned men) of established Islam. They use the public media at their disposal to launch vendettas against the fundamentalists and to claim that the latter do not represent 'true' Islam.

The authorities also conduct massive arrests, engage in shootouts in the streets of their cities, mount mass demonstrations, run show trials, and otherwise attempt to curtail the high profile of the fundamentalists, all within the purview of the public. This compels the common people to take sides in the debate, and often to take part in fundamentalist activities or in demonstrating against them. All this is done in the open, in the very centre of the public square. However, while the governments wish to cleanse the public square from the impact of the fundamentalists, the latter strive to cleanse it of 'Westoxication', which they see as caused directly by or via the regimes in place, deemed to be collaborators of the hated West.

VOCABULARY AND SYMBOLS

Underlying the Islamic discourse in the public square are a vocabulary and an entire system of symbols which have been imposed by the fundamentalists and which have become universalized to an extent that even their opponents, such as the governments in place who battle against them, are compelled to make use of them. Very often, the incumbent regimes, who are in constant quest for legitimacy, must resort to those vocabulary and symbols in order to pose to their constituencies as no less Islamic than their opponents, who precisely delegitimize them and offer themselves as an alternative in Islamic terms. These terms encompass such concepts as *jahiliyya* and *hijra*, *shahid* and *fida'i*, government by shura as democracy, the *zakat* as the paradigm of the welfare state, jihad – both spiritual and actual, Jerusalem and Hudaybiyya as powerful symbols of redemption, 'Umar ibn al-Khattab and Salah a-Din as worthy predecessors of the fundamentalist struggle, Israel and the West as the source of all evil, the old and new Crusaders as the paradigm of the enemy of Islam, and revivalist Islam as the panacea for all ills.

Jahiliyya and hijra, which refer to the times of the Prophet, were extensively used by Sayyid Qutb, the great Islamic luminary who was executed by Nasser in 1966 for allegedly plotting to overthrow the revolutionary regime in Egypt. His fundamentalist followers in the Islamic world have since extensively resorted to those concepts to define themselves and the world about them. In these terms, jahiliyya is not only the era of darkness and ignorance which had reigned prior to the coming of the Prophet of Islam, and the epithet for the culture and way of life which had surrounded humanity before Muhammad's prophetic message to the world, but also the deserved attribute to characterize any society today which does not follow the path of Islam. Not only is the West plunged in its ignorance, but even Muslim societies which are ruled by non-Islamic tyrants of all sorts, are themselves suffocating in a jahili atmosphere which only a revived Islam can remedy.

The Prophet of Islam, who could not sustain a meaningful life in the jahili sinful city of his native Mecca, found the remedy in hijra (i.e. migration into a sane Muslim environment where Islam could be brought to bear and a worthy life carried to full bloom). His migration to Medina in 622 CE marked not only his personal salvation, but also the rescuing of Islam from crisis and persecution and the beginning of a new era for humankind which was inaugurated right then – year 1 of the Islamic calendar. This major and far-sighted demarche of the Prophet, the most perfect of all humans, has necessarily become, like his other deeds and utterances, the model for all others to follow. Muslim fundamentalists review contemporary world history in these terms; they diagnose jahili societies as being unliveable and prescribe hijra from them as a way out. Following the Prophet again, who had used his Islamic base to battle against the Unbelievers in their jahili lands, they also vow to pursue their enemies into submission. They may choose a spiritual hijra, namely remaining in their places among the jahili society, but creating their own enclaves of study, education, social welfare or even neighbourhoods (i.e. the Muslim Brothers in Egypt and elsewhere), or they may actually migrate from their milieu and create their own (i.e. the Takfir wal-Hijra faction in Egypt).

A self-definition of the fundamentalists as the hijra people, so to speak, also entails a definition of the others – the people of kufr (unbelievers) or of jahiliyya, or the New Crusaders, from whose environment one must migrate and/or against whom one must struggle. Muslim fundamentalists have clearly identified their enemy: the regimes in the Islamic world which practice non-Islamic law; the West which has been undermining Islam from within and corrupting it with its norms of behaviour in the public square, with a view to tottering it and replacing it; and Israel-Zionism-the Jews, who are intrinsically the enemies of Allah and humanity, in addition to their being an arm of the West in the heart of the Islamic world. All these enemies must be depicted in evil terms so as to make them free prey for Muslims to attack and destroy. A rhetorical delegitimation of their enemy is a prerequisite towards making the use of violence permissible, even desirable, against him. Hence, the systematic and virulent attacks of these movements against what they perceive as their enemies, both domestic and external, even if at times they borrow a Western vocabulary, lending to it their own connotations and interpretations.

The underlying justification to launch war against such evil enemies,[1] domestic and external, is distilled in the quintessential notion of jihad. Etymologically, this word was meant to signify an intellectual striving, and by extension also a physical striving, for a cause. In Islamic law, however, jihad has principally one meaning: military action to expand the outer borders of Dar-al Islam (Pax Islamica) or to protect them from encroaching Unbelievers. This idea is founded on the notion that Islam is not simply one of the revealed religions, but the prevailing and most updated faith which has come to substitute for, and to supersede, the other monotheistic faiths. It is then incumbent upon Islam to extend its rule all over the world by peaceful means if possible, by force if necessary. Jihad is usually viewed as a collective duty (fard kifaya) binding the Muslim community (the umma), as a whole. Namely, when the Muslim authorities pursue jihad, every Muslim individual is viewed as having discharged this duty. However, since Muslim countries have desisted in practice from this idea, mainly due to pragmatic considerations, Muslim fundamentalists have come to take this duty as a personal one (fard 'ayn), and so have consecrated any struggle of theirs against non-believers or against Muslim regimes not to their liking, as a pursuit of that holy duty. This is what the Hamas group has to say in this regard:

> When our enemies usurp our Islamic lands, jihad becomes a duty binding on all Muslims. In order to face the usurpation of Palestine by the Jews, we have no escape from raising the banner of jihad. This would require the propagation of Islamic consciousness among the masses on all local, all-Arab and Islamic levels. We must spread the spirit of jihad among the Islamic umma, clash with the enemies and join the ranks of jihad fighters.[2]

According to this view, and along the lines charted by Sayyid Qutb[3] and others before them, Hamas views the war against Israel and the Jews as a religious war,[4] and therefore Muslims ought to swell their ranks and fight it to the finish, whatever the price. As one of their leaflets says, 'our struggle with the Jews is a struggle[5] between Truth and emptiness, between Islam and Judaism'.[6] So it goes for the struggle against others which are targeted as the enemies of Islam. For example, during the Gulf War (1991) one jihad recruit, instructed to set up and detonate a car bomb on a busy street in one of the countries fighting against Iraq, told a *Times* correspondent that the fate he awaited in the afterworld was far superior to the rotten life he had at present. But he added that his life was not all that miserable, for he was readying himself to die for his cause. He said that all lives were moving towards Heaven or Hell, and he chose Heaven.[7]

In spite of the wide variety of interpretations given to jihad in modern times, some of which are soft and subtle, it is evident that the Muslim radicals, including Islamic Jihad, Hamas, Hizbullah, and certainly international Muslim fighters such as those who were battle-hardened in Afghanistan (the "Afghanis") or in Bosnia, are uncompromisingly committed to the violent brand thereof. They refer to many Qur'anic passages which assure the martyr, that is, the dead in the course of jihad, all manner of rewards in the next world.[8] This is the reason why jihad has become the rallying slogan of many of these radical groups of Muslims, as in 'Allah is the goal, the Prophet the model, the Qur'an the Constitution, jihad the path, and death for the cause of Allah the most sublime creed'.[9] Death in the course of jihad becomes, then, an expected and even desirable outcome, especially when jihad is taken as the explanatory motif of history. Indeed, radical Islamic movements regard the present generation's struggle in the path of Allah as only one link in the chain of continuous jihad, inasmuch as the precedent fighters/martyrs had opened the path and the living in each generation must follow in their footsteps. In fact, the symbol of the Muslim Brothers is constituted by a Qur'an book hemmed in by two swords, their explication being that force, i.e. jihad by the sword, defends justice as encapsulated in the Holy Book.

Hence, the powerful appeal for jihad, and for death in jihad if necessary, is reinforced by the Islamic legal prescription that all are liable to jihad except for the blind, the handicapped and the old, who cannot expend the requisite effort in the battlefield. In the macho-prone youth of the Islamic world, going to jihad is proof that one is not afflicted by those inabilities, Allah Forbid! One of the heads of the Muslim Brothers in Egypt called upon the jihad fighters to brandish the banner of jihad until all Islamic lands are liberated and the Islamic Caliphate is reinstated. Similarly, Hamas leaders have repeatedly emphasized the importance of jihad by according to it the validity of a Sixth Pillar of the Faith. In a fatwa circulated in the West Bank under Israeli rule, spiritual leaders of the Palestinians have determined that jihad is a personal duty binding on each and every individual 'until the usurper has been removed from the land by force of the sword'. They rejected peace with Israel, if only because that would amount to cessation of the jihad and the obstruction of the road of jihad before the coming generations.

The fundamentalists have also forced on the public square discourse about the Arab–Israeli conflict in Islamic terms. In fact, supposedly secular leaders in the Arab world are dragged into that discourse in a match of one-upmanship in order to demonstrate that they master its vicissitudes no less than their opponents. And so, they discuss wars against Israel in terms of jihad and the casualties in those wars in terms of shuhada' (martyrs). Yasser Arafat, for example, has reputedly taken on an Islamic nom de guerre (Abu 'Ammar) and the brigades of the PLO have been named after renowned battles in Islamic history (Hittin, Yarmuk, Ein Jalut) or after Islamic Holy Places (al-Aqsa). Similarly, the war communiqués issued by the PLO have always begun with the Basmalah, as do Arafat's statements – written and oral. Arafat, as did the late Anwar Sadat, frequently uses Qur'anic citations as a way to win the hearts of his audience.

Nothing illustrates the public-squarization of the Islamic political discourse among the Palestinians better than Arafat's fiery speeches, in which Muslim vocabulary and symbols abound. Not only has he drawn a parallel between himself and 'Umar ibn-al-Khattab in the context of retrieving Jerusalem for the Muslims, but he also used Jerusalem as a mobilizing factor to arouse Palestinians, and other Muslims worldwide, for the battle of jihad to liberate the holy places there. He also often compared his signing of the Oslo Accords with Israel to the Hudaybiyya Treaty made by the Prophet with the people of Quraysh in Mecca and later revoked when that was found expedient. This linguistic usage in the public square, which the late President Sadat also did in his time, goes a long way to tell the public that the war objectives, as well as the peace objectives, are founded on, emanate from, and are geared to Islamic bases and goals.

IDEOLOGICAL UNDERPINNINGS OF THE ISLAMIC DISCOURSE

The Islamic discourse which has been imposed on the public square by the fundamentalists rests on firm ideological commitments and beliefs which are spelled out in a persistent and repetitive manner throughout the Islamic world. As an example, we could examine the platform of Hamas which was published in the beginning of 1988 and encompasses all the vocabulary and symbols discussed above. Essentially, this platform is the public response of Hamas to the PLO Charter, meaning that the debate in the public square should not consist of a PLO monologue, but should be challenged by an equally attractive platform which would appeal to the same constituency. By tossing the question of two competing ideologies into the public square, Hamas intended not only to signal the end of monolithic rule, PLO-style. The attendant questions of authoritarian regime, or other systems of government, which set the public agenda, determine national priorities, define national needs, and decide upon national objectives, goals, and aspirations also came to the fore and raised the thorny question of legitimacy of government.

No regime in almost any Islamic country can claim a credible legitimacy as it is understood in the West. No one has truly elected the regimes in place: they have either inherited absolute monarchical power, or have taken it over by force and perpetuate their hold on it with military coercion. Almost none of these rulers is backed by a permanent and predictable popular base, and this is where the Islamists can stake their strongest grievance against these governments. To acquire some legitimacy, these autocrats take on Islamic titles: the Curator of the Twin Holy Sites (Mecca and Medina) for the Saudi King; the Heir of the Prophet and the Guardian of al-Aqsa Mosque for the Jordanian monarch, another Descendant of the Prophet and the Chairman of the Jerusalem Committee of the Islamic Conference Organization for King Hassan of Morocco, etc. Even godless Saddam Hussein announced during the Gulf War that he was adding the Islamic war cry 'Allah Akbar!' to his national flag, in order to make his war against the Americans, the 'New Crusaders', a novel version of the War of the Believers against the invading Unbelievers.

Lack of legitimacy means that someone is waiting in the aisles and posing as an alternative to the incumbent faltering power. The best organized and the most zealously poised to take over are usually Muslim radicals who claim their own legitimacy in Islam and its teachings. When they are in opposition to autocratic rulers, one hears them speak for democracy, free elections, human rights, freedom of speech, and the like. They are, therefore, often perceived as moderate, reasonable, operating within the system, as long as they do not use violence to attack or overthrow the regimes in place (the Muslim Brothers in Egypt and Jordan, the Islamic Movement in Israel, Islamic Movements in the West). But when they do, they are ruthlessly suppressed by the rulers, usually with the silent support of the West which clearly leans towards autocratic regimes loyal to it (Turkey, Egypt, Algeria, Jordan, Morocco, Saudi Arabia, the Palestinian Authority, etc.), rather than to Islamic regimes inimical to it (Iran, Sudan, Afghanistan).

In the past decades, the power of the international media, which passes over local restrictions and makes the idea of the global village applicable to authoritarian Islamic countries as well, has evidently eroded the almost absolutist nature of the regimes there. The sight of the collapse of tyrannical rulers in Eastern Europe, which was shown in real time all over the world, also triggered a dramatic rise in belief in the power of the people and in the ability of the common man, if determined and resourceful, to force down the tyrant. It is as if a third player has come into the public square to broker power between the authorities and their Islamic opposition. It is true that following the fall of such tyrants in Islamic countries as the shah of Iran (1979) and the Rabani clique in Kabul (1996), they were not succeeded by democratic regimes, but it seems that the fall of Suharto in Jakarta (1998) has been generated by a democratic current of yet uncertain orientation as long as it is not taken over by Muslim fundamentalists.

In order to gauge the depth of the ideological commitment of the Islamists to the debate in the public square, let us examine, for example, the political platform of Hamas already cited above. The following points of debate, both in the domestic and external arenas, illustrate the very tangible alternative, on all levels of politics – diplomacy, economy, society, culture, and even art – that radical Islam purports to pose to its rivals presently in power:

1. Exactly as the Palestinian Authority has its basic constitutional document – the 33-article PLO charter, Hamas posits its parallel – the 36-article charter of the Islamic Resistance Movement. The difference between them immediately puts the latter at a superior level of legitimacy and credibility over the former. For while the PLO document has been debated and adopted by the Palestinian National Council, as a secular manmade platform, the Hamas document was adopted by no one in particular. Every one of its articles is backed by a citation either from the Holy Qur'an or the Sunna of the Prophet, thereby creating an impression of timelessness and divine validity. The consequence is clear: while the PLO constitution is amendable, as its Article 33 provides and as it was in 1968, the Hamas document appears as immutable as its sources of inspiration themselves. Legitimacy is preferably due, then, to the eternal and the divine, not to the fleeting and ephemeral.

2. Together with addressing specifically the Palestinian plight, the Hamas Charter juggles with Palestinian nationalism in order to merge it into a universal Islamic nationalism under the aegis of the Caliphate. Here, rather than forego the Palestinian cause specifically, with the attendant danger of losing its constituency, Hamas opted for tackling the Palestinian issue as part of the malaise of the world of Islam which can be remedied by the return of Islamic rule. Therefore, unlike the PLO Charter which claims loyalty to Arab nationalism, Hamas proclaims itself a wing of the universal Muslim Brotherhood, whose aim is to restore Islam to its original splendour. Once again, as against the disappointing ruling national governments in the Islamic states, Hamas proposes to resort to the much more hopeful and promising overarching umbrella of the future united Islamic Caliphate.

3. Unlike the PLO and other secular trends in society, which

have taken to a blind and uncritical imitation of Western ways, Hamas proposes to mobilize society – human resources, economic resources, culture and art, in the service of purifying itself from 'Westoxication'. To attain that goal, not only the regimes have to be replaced by more legitimate ones, but all the systems of education, the media, youth and women, must be reorganized and assigned their roles in society. For example, women ought to be considered as dutiful 'factories' to produce Muslim jihad fighters who will grow to carry out the will of Allah. Another example – since plastic arts and sports are of a jahili nature, they should be eliminated and replaced by other forms of art – photography, films, and poster drawing for the sake of explaining and propagating Islam. This would entail, naturally, cleaning up the public square from all corrupting accretions brought about by the West and Israel. This is totalitarianism at its highest point.

4. Hamas urges the shelving of all internal difficulties among the Palestinians in order to devote all attention and resources to external battles against the enemies of Islam. Here again, they appeal to the authorities-that-be to desist from persecuting them in order to please the West or Israel, and to respond instead to the public desire to see the Islamists act without limitations or restrictions. The only chance for Hamas and its kind to survive is to let the public square be open to them to make their case and plead for their cause. Yet their banishment from the public square, whether under pressure from the West or threats of Israel, can only serve them in the long run by alienating the masses of Believers from the authorities.

5. On the matter of the non-Muslims who live in Islamic societies, Hamas proposes other solutions than the flowery promises of equality under the current governments. The Islamists proceed from the assumption that only under Islam can the members of other religions prosper, as long as they accept and submit to its superiority and hegemony. The rationale is clear: when Islam rules, fraternity, harmony, peace and love reign; when Islam does not rule, it is hatred, friction, discontent and bloodshed which prevail.

6. As regards members of other faiths who do not submit to Islam, their lot will be jihad until submission. The Hamas

Charter takes a particular interest in the Jews who live outside the perimeters of Islamic rule: they are, by definition, the enemies of Allah and humanity; they have concocted all the wars, the revolutions and the evils of the world; they prepare and scheme to corrupt all societies of the world via such organizations as the UN, B'nai B'rith, the Free Masons, and the Rotary and Lions clubs, in order to overtake them from within. The Charter cites liberally from the Protocols of the Elders of Zion as a document of history, and confirms the wretchedness and final disposability of the Jews according to Islamic sources which call upon the Believers to eliminate them. Unlike the PLO, which has avoided sounding antisemitic, and has been willing to negotiate with the Jews and come to a political settlement with them, Hamas remains totally committed to fighting the Jews and expunging them from the land.

7. The political consequence of the above is that since the Jews are evil by nature, their Zionist movement as well as their Israeli state can only be evil like them and must be fought to the finish. Therefore, all forms of negotiations with Israel are thoroughly condemned. From their viewpoint, since the land of Palestine (including the territory of Israel) is a *waqf* (holy endowment) given to the Muslims by Allah for all generations to come, it is not given to any Muslim to negotiate it away. And as difficulties in the application of the Oslo agreements abound, Hamas is in a position to adopt a 'we told you so' stance, which may become very popular among the Palestinian public and erode the moral authority of the Arafat and his successors regime in the public square.

8. Finally, the Islamic militants also offer in their discourse their own interpretation of history. Humanity has been polarized, in their view, between Believers and Unbelievers, the latter sometimes are represented by the Tatars or the Crusaders. This polarity is made of good guys, that is Muslims, the holders of the divine truth, and of bad guys, namely, the enemies of Allah such as the West and Israel. Muslim heroes, such as 'Umar and Saladin, are the liberators of the Holy Places and the dispensers of humaneness and equity to the world, while their enemies, the Crusaders, the Tatars, and the Nazi-like Jews, are

the oppressors who are bound to fail in the final analysis.

FROM WORDS TO ACTION

On 18 November 1997, the terrible massacre of foreign tourists in Luxor, Egypt, brought once again to public consciousness the fact that Muslim radicals not only have an agenda which they try to propagate in their public square, but that they are prepared to use violence to enforce it, and not only in the public square of Egypt but of the entire world. They signalled to the world that they were no longer willing to accept their own oppression at home and their obliteration from their public square, while the world was watching indifferently under the pretext of non-interference in Egyptian internal affairs. By using violence against innocent tourists who had no part in the internal debate in Egypt, they forced both Egypt and the countries of the victims to take note of the situation in the country where their voice had been silenced. In other words, they transferred the debate from an artificially muted scene to a much more open arena which the Egyptian authorities could not ignore.

Similarly, the 'Islamikaze' activities worldwide, and specifically those launched by Hamas and Hizbullah against Israeli targets, are primarily intended to bring to the public square, both local Palestinian and local Lebanese respectively, as well as the world scene, the concerns of those Islamic radicals which would have otherwise been ignored. The difference is that while the *Gama'at*[10] in Egypt aim at punishing the Egyptian government by hitting it where it hurts most (tourism revenue and international image), the other two movements battle the enemy on its soil, on the soil that they perceive as occupied by Israel, not their own governments with which they wish to debate on the domestic front for now. But these violent activities, which we term 'terrorism' in our parlance, are neither the only nor the main domain of normative action on the part of the Muslim fundamentalists. No less effective to impose their agenda on the public square are their constructive, long-term, socio-political and religio-economic activities which, in the long run, bring them the most dividends.

Basically, the fundamentalists, without stating it, constitute a sort of anti-state in order to rival the governments in place and to fill in some of their yawning deficiencies, especially in the economic and spiritual domains. They capitalize on the assumption that even if they are today banned from participating in the political process (as in Egypt and Algeria), they can build up a vast base of popular support which will certainly stand to their credit when the day comes. The Algerian scenario certainly confirms this assumption: for years the FIS[11] was allowed to act only religiously and socially under the aegis of FLN[12] monolithic rule, but when the Islamists were finally recognized as part of the political game leading up to the first free elections in 1991, they swept the electorate before they were quelled by the military with Western acquiescence. To some extent, this is what happened with the Welfare Party in Turkey, which gained a majority of the votes in 1995, and constituted a government before it was removed from power under military pressure.

This quietist attitude of building a base and waiting for the opportunity, which has been adopted by Muslim Brothers and their like out of recognition that confrontation with the regime might bring about their elimination, stands in sharp contrast with the militant and violent stance taken by such groups as the Gama'at in Egypt which regard terrorism as the only way to make themselves heard in the public square. They are far smaller than the Brothers, and their scarce resources, insubstantial penetration into all strata of society, and the restricted pattern of their diffusion in all parts of the country do not permit them a firm grip on a wide popular base. The Brothers and their clones, on the contrary, do possess all those attributes and can therefore take advantage of their ubiquitousness to air their concerns and grievances in the public square, not only through rhetoric but also through action in the open. Their domains of activity abound:

1. They publish a wide array of magazines, posters, books, leaflets, and also audio and video tapes which are diffused either free of charge or at very low and affordable prices. These publications address themselves not only to exhortations to return to the faith or to scholarly dissertations about the merits of Islam and its historical heroes, but mainly to the daily agenda of the common people: where to find help and

solace, how to solve particular economic, education or health problems, how to conduct oneself in daily life, etc. For lack of guidance and care on the part of the hardened official state bureaucracy, the common man feels neglected and left to his own devices, and this is where the Muslim movement steps in to fill the gap. This is also where the public square echoes the inefficacy and carelessness of the authorities with the warmth and accessibility of the Islamists.

2. Not only the common people, but also growing sections of the middle class, such as intellectuals and bourgeois, are aghast with the always unfulfilled promises of the rulers, with the increasing and spreading poverty, with corruption at all levels of government, even with the Islamic establishment which is sycophantically subservient to the rulers, and the rulers' own exclusive hold on power in spite of the lip-service they pay to participatory democracy. They look around and see the Islamists as the only viable alternative. The latter do not seem corrupt; they project an image of purity and devotion to a cause; they care for the people; and striving without remuneration, they give without taking and are there when needed. They provide guidance and direction; they give hope; and they seem to know what to do in situations of helplessness. Above all, their leaders are of them and for them; they live modestly and are accessible at any time; and they seem to be the repository of wisdom, serenity, savoir-faire, and resourcefulness. Naturally the very presence of these people in the public square, and the long trail of good deeds that follows them and often turns into an aura of charisma, more than offsets the omnipresence of the rulers' cult which often invades all the media and the public space.

3. Muslim fundamentalist leaders are masters of public relations: they address national and international media, and by getting a worldwide hearing they assure their place in the public square. Not only do they make headlines following acts of terror, but also as a result of daring statements, either critical of their authorities or of the West, threats they voice against their enemies, and particular exploits that they boast of, such as hijackings, sabotage (actual or imagined), taking of hostages, extortion of money, and release of their prison-

ers, etc. Every one of these occasions assures them a high profile in the public square, both nationally and internationally,
and on the same occasion they can also voice their general
grievances and profess their ideology. Two specifically
Islamic means to attain high visibility in public are the Friday
sermon (khutba) and the occasional legal verdict (fatwa) in
response to a problem. This means that all current matters of
the day, in all spheres of life, have an energetic, immediate,
and authoritative response which is tossed into the public
square together with the prevailing views.

4. Fundamentalists have turned mosques into their bastions, not
    only because of their inherent symbolism as a place of wor-
    ship, but also because of their intrinsic immunity from intru-
    sion. Any authorities in a Muslim country would think hard
    before they turn a mosque or its yard into a flashpoint, much
    less into a battlefield. Therefore, not only do we witness a fre-
    netic pace of mosque construction in areas of fundamentalist
    activity, but we also notice that the functions of the mosques
    have greatly expanded. Typically, a new multi-story mosque
    building would include a floor for social services (welfare,
    clinic, service offices), a floor for education (Qur'anic school,
    day school, but also computers, girls' education, etc.), a floor
    for sports activities, and the main hall, usually more sumptu-
    ous than the others, for prayer and meetings. This expanded
    sanctuary, where the anti-state can function and provide its
    alternative services with impunity, has become in itself a sort
    of public square where things are said and done as a matter
    of course, which usually go unchallenged by either the
    authorities or other opponents from among the general pub-
    lic.

5. To finance all this array of activities, the fundamentalists
    have reverted to levying the zakat, the alms that had become
    one of the Pillars of Islam since the time of the Prophet and
    had constituted the public treasury which had financed the
    'welfare state' of early Islam. At the time, it was a regressive
    tax, imposed on all Believers, which amounted to some 8 per
    cent of income. But today, with the modern states' tax sys-
    tems, and as the zakat is no longer levied by the state and is
    left to individual generosity as a sort of charity, the Islamists

have stepped in and filled that vacuum. For them, this is the legal way to finance the people's needs, and each person is taxed according to his capacity: the businessman gives money, the building contractor – building materials, the destitute – manual labour, the professionals – time to serve the public with their skills, and scholars – teaching and spiritual guidance. And so, the zakat has made a comeback via the back door, virtually as a tax, since people in a Muslim community are under public pressure to conform in order to validate, as it were, their membership in the congregation of Believers. Again, the public square is rendered active not only for the sake of congratulating the generous and condemning the miser, but also for the sake of creating an alternative public treasury to finance the Islamic community and to show the efficacy and honesty of the spending.

6.   The zakat is spent on welfare for the needy and on education, etc., which sometimes escape the public eye. But the Islamists also go for vast expenditure on public works which helps to enhance their popularity and visibility in the public square – such as the centrality of mosque building in fundamentalist activities. They also organize camps for youth to spend the summer in neglected and underdeveloped areas in order to conduct public works such as road repair, build mosques and public facilities, or bring solace to the poor, the old, and the handicapped. Two goals are thus attained: welfare work with high visibility in the public square and the corresponding credit the Islamists get in the public eye, and also keeping the youth off the streets during the summers of indolence and misdeed and channelling their vigour and enthusiasm into creative and positive activity, much to the delight of their parents. To gauge the tremendous achievements of the Islamists in the public square, all one has to do is visit the places under their jurisdiction and to realize their efforts in beautifying the environment, fighting crime, cleaning up local government, and making a good reputation for themselves. They prove that the problem of local neglect is not only due to lack of funds, but mainly to corruption, carelessness, and the inability to raise taxes or to efficiently spend the available money. The fundamentalists, aided by the zakat levies, prove able to

provide for all that.

7. The Islamists have also turned the Muslim holy places, some of which had been neglected and allowed to disintegrate, into a mobilizing factor for their cause. As part of the zakat payments and the summer camps, or independently of them, they are able to rally donations and volunteers to clear and clean Muslim cemeteries, rebuild and restore old mosques, and insist that waqf properties be dedicated to their stated purposes, namely, religious and welfare. By so doing, and especially by involving women and youth in these endeavours, they can publicly claim that they command a wide following of volunteers and dedicated experts, in contrast with the authorities who can only enforce their law on a reluctant citizenry, thereby accumulating more bitterness and anger against them.

8. The fundamentalists have also imposed on the public square their mores and moral standards. All one has to do is watch the change in dressing habits in the Islamic world in recent years: more women than ever wear the *zai shar'i* or religious dress, a sexless, neutral garb, with or without a head cover and sometimes even with a veil and long sleeves, which impart to the woman in the street a look of a mobile tent, exuding neutrality, asexuality, unavailability and hands off, in order to escape the scrutiny and voracious stares of men who are deprived of any sexual contact unless in a marital context. Also, co-ed classes at school are eliminated as soon as the children reach puberty. Men and women are separated on buses and in stations, and married women are generally relegated to house work. The new mores also include the abolishment of coffee houses and of alcoholic consumption, and encourage the frequenting of mosques as well as the growing of beards by men in order to emulate the hallmark of the Muslim Brothers.

9. One of the largest spheres of Islamist activity in the public square is participation in professional and social associations other than the Islamic Association. This is especially vital in countries where they are not allowed to run for elections as part of the political system (i.e. in Egypt and Algeria), or only as individuals and not parties, as in Jordan. Thus they cam-

paign and win high positions in the teachers, lawyers, doctors, and accountants associations, or in the vanguard of student bodies on university campuses or in such charitable bodies as the Islamic Red Crescent and philanthropic organizations of all sorts which oftentimes act as a cover to illicit
fundraising and the like. When they win elections in such
bodies, they capitalize on them not only to gain influence in
those organizations per se, but also to enhance their popularity as a whole and to make believe that they are up and coming as the alternative way of the future.

10. Finally, there is the question of technology and its thorny relation to the West. Fundamentalists do not mince their words
when they accuse the West of corruption and tag it as the
enemy of Islam. How, then, can they justify, in the public
square, their usage of Western vocabulary and worse, Western
technology, which has become so vital to their propaganda
and to the very diffusion of their cause? For the vocabulary,
they found a solution by appropriating it to themselves and
claiming Islamic antecedents to every one of the modern
accretions to Western thought: for democracy there is rule by
shura, for socialism and the welfare state there is zakat, for
sovereignty of the people they posit the sovereignty of the
Almighty, and for parliaments as legislative bodies they present the shari'a as the supreme and unsurpassed act of divine
legislation. For them, tolerance, generosity, human rights, and
liberal rule were practiced by Islam long before the West discovered them. Technology also has its justification even if the
West is more advanced today. There was a time in the Middle
Ages when Islamic science ruled the world; today there is a
temporary reversal of the situation. Technology in itself is
merely a tool, and its judicious use in an Islamic way turns it
into a useful means. For example, television, tapes, radio, and
posters can be used to spread the Qur'an, the exploits of
Muslim heroes, and to raise Muslim awareness in general,
instead of the films, music, culture, insidious propaganda, and
pornography of the decadent West.

CONSEQUENCES AND LESSONS

Muslim fundamentalists have introduced a revolution of sorts in the public square inasmuch as matters never discussed publicly before have now been imposed and have become part and parcel of the public discourse in Islamic countries, in spite of government oppression. This new discourse, in which Muslim oppositions and governments equally participate, is precipitated by four streams which converge into one powerful rapid that sweeps everything in its course:

- First and foremost, the countries where Islamic fundamentalism has taken over the government (to date, Iran, Sudan, and Afghanistan) have also been the first to toss the new discourse into the Islamic public square. The success of the Islamic revolution there, and more so the explicit efforts made by those Islamic governments to sponsor other revolutionary Islamic movements elsewhere, have forced all Muslims to be either on the offensive or on the defensive in this regard. It is no longer possible to clamp down on this discourse, much less to ignore it.
- The fundamentalists in practically every Islamic country, from Morocco to Indonesia, and from Tajikistan to Black Africa, reinforced by the success of the Islamic Revolution in the above countries, and aided financially, morally, politically, and sometimes militarily by them, have the means and, more and more, the audacity to speak up and act to advance their cause as we have seen above. Moreover, even in non-Islamic countries, in Africa, America, Europe, Asia, and the Middle East, the Muslim fundamentalists, who constitute more or less insignificant local minorities, gather momentum from other Islamic movements around them and participate in the discourse. Significantly, it is the latter who act with the most daring and conduct their activities the most publicly, since they can take advantage of the liberal regimes under which they operate to propagate their Islamic message. Chief among these are Great Britain, which is ironically accused by the Egyptians of sheltering Islamic terrorists; the United States, where fund-raising for radical Muslim movements (termed terrorists in Western parlance) goes unhindered; and Israel, where Muslim radicals sit

in the Israeli Knesset or as mayors of a number of Arab towns, something they cannot do in most Arab countries.

- The Islamic establishment in the Muslim countries, which is customarily subservient to the governments in place, and has at its disposal the governmental apparatus and state media, counters the fundamentalists' propaganda with its own, trying to prove to the populace that it is representing true Islam and appealing to the crowds to skirt the dangerous ways of the far more popular and down-to-earth fundamentalist leaders and preachers. So, paradoxically, while attempting to protect themselves and the regime, they slide down the slope towards the radicals by borrowing their vocabulary and addressing their agenda, much to their own disadvantage.

There are significant numbers of converts to Islam in practically all non-Muslim countries where Muslim minorities reside, or among non-Muslim minorities in Islamic countries. These new adepts of Islam, just like other converts to other faiths, tend to become more Muslim than those born Muslim, either a natural outcome of their newly found illumination and enthusiasm, or in order to show their co-religionists that they are no less Muslim. Many converts on all continents remain anonymous and do not attract much attention, such as the Black Muslims in North America, in South Africa, or among the Copts in Egypt. But when a celebrity, such as Cat Stevens (renamed Yussuf Islam), Cassius Clay (now Muhammad Ali), or Professor Hamid Algar, the eminent American Islamologist, embraced Islam, that became a cause for celebration for the radicals because it signified that those enlightened minds had vindicated the superiority of Islam and would bring with them countless others. These celebrities, who usually become very fervent Muslims, also contribute materially, spiritually, and morally to their new faith by speaking for it and proclaiming it as the root cause of their fame.

Unlike all the others who may harness themselves to the radical Islamic cause as a tactical device, or out of a temporary gain or personal satisfaction, the fundamentalists are strategically committed to bringing their convictions to the world. They possess not only a socio-political program which they intend to carry out to the letter, but being men of action, they have already launched, in their more or less modest way, the social revolution in the public square as a precursor to the total application of their plans. They seriously provide an alternative to the governments in place by hailing their triple slogan: 'Islam is the solution', 'Islam is the Truth', and 'Islam is the alternative', which, in a situation of despair and lack of legitimacy, becomes a viable option.

In order to remain in the public square in the face of oppression by the existing regimes, the fundamentalists may show flexibility and readiness to accept the rules of the game. Indeed, most fundamentalist groups have shunned violence internally and are prepared to resort to the ballot if they were allowed to do so, in order to show their mettle in public. However, the authorities have learned from the Algerian scenario and are wary of letting the game of democracy run its course lest the fundamentalists exploit it to get power and then there is no telling what they might do with it. If we listen to their insistence on the shari'a state they envisage, and the rule by shura that they profess, then maybe free elections, which would get them to the helm, would also be the last. In the meantime, their moderate and 'reasonable' discourse allows them to gain political asylum for their persecuted leaders in the West, where they freely publish their propaganda and collect funds without restrictions.

Political bargaining in contemporary Islamic societies is nearly impossible due to the totality of the Islamic claim. In theory, then, the rulers can choose between total democratization, to which they pay lip-service but by which they may be swept from power as in Algeria, or they may practice total oppression, banning, exile, persecution, elimination, and exclusion of the Islamists. A small degree of liberty is not possible in the long run, because once it is accorded, more will be demanded, and with growing insistence and urgency, often backed by violence, in the name of the same liberty that the rulers had recognized and partly accorded. The murder of President Sadat by Muslim radicals whom he had helped surface from clandestineness, and more so the removal of the reformers from the political scene in the Soviet bloc – those who had initiated partial liberty – are enough evidence of the futility of the halfway measure syndrome which consumes its initiators.

The Islamic groups, having embedded in their worldview the

legitimacy of jihad to battle their illegitimate rulers and the West that sustains them, cannot simply be shut off by oppression. They are accumulating popularity and strength in the public square, paradoxically under the protective wings of the West which accords them shelter. Instead of taking sides between fundamentalists who want democratic means to gain power, and their oppressors who, under the guise of democratization in fact quell any attempt to challenge their rule, the West should perhaps encourage the democratic process and non-violent debate in the public square, whatever its outcome. If the current autocrats should win, then they might achieve legitimacy and will perhaps become less autocratic and more responsive to the public debate. If the fundamentalists should win, as they have in a number of places, then perhaps the constraints of government will moderate them in the long run and make them less impervious to dialogue with the West. Legitimate governments which promote transparency, namely, debate in the public square, will, in turn, reduce violence and promote democratization.

NOTES

This was first published in *Jewish Political Studies Review*, II, 3–4 (Fall 1999), pp. 141–62.

1. See, for example, Ahmed Rifa'i, *al-Nabi al-Musallah* (The Armed Prophet) (London, 1991), pp.107–8, 120–48, where the onslaught of Shukri Mustafa, the head of a Muslim radical group in Egypt, against the Egyptian authorities, is described in detail.
2. Article 15 of the Hamas Charter.
3. Sayyid Qutb was the great luminary of Muslim fundamentalists in Egypt and elsewhere in the Islamic world. He was executed by Nasser in 1966, but his martyrdom has only enhanced his stature.
4. The entire Hamas Charter is interspersed with the vow for jihad. Almost every Article repeats the Hamas commitment in that regard.
5. The term used in the text is jihad, which can be a spiritual as well as a military struggle.
6. Article 16 of the Hamas Charter.
7. See Boaz Ganor, 'The Islamic Jihad: The Imperative of Holy War', in *Survey of Arab Affairs*, Jerusalem Centre for Public Affairs, 15 February 1993, pp.1–2.
8. One of these rewards is free sex with 70 virgins who regain their virginity after intercourse, thereby giving the martyr supreme pleasure.
9. Article 8 of the Hamas Charter.
10. Gama'at, literally 'groups', refer to the radical Muslim groups in Egypt who shun the quietist attitude of the Brothers and try to achieve their goals through militant means.
11. Front Islamic du Salut (Islamic Front for Salvation) is the name of the Algerian fundamentalists who strove to gain power by democratic means and won the elections of 1991, which were later scuttled by the military junta.
12. Front de Liberation Nationale, the nationalist party of Algeria which led the independence war against the French in the 1960s and ruled the country until the 1991 elections.

CHAPTER THREE

From Bosnia to Kosovo:
The Re-Islamization of the Balkans

THE PROBLEM

On 12 February 1997, on the occasion of the 'Id al-Fitr Festival, the Uighur rebels in Chinese Central Asia published, on their Internet site, an appeal to all Muslims to heed the unfolding events in Bosnia. 'What kind of festival is this', they asked, 'when 250,000 Muslims are being murdered, tortured and raped in Bosnia?' They sent their heartfelt thanks to the 'Iranian people who are sending help in spite of the West's embargo', and accused the West of 'stopping the Muslims when they were about to win, while at the same time aiding the Serbian Fascists'. Evidently, the Uighurs in China's Northwest had their own axe to grind when they used the universal festival which linked all Muslims together to draw attention to their own plight in Xinjiang, where their own land was being 'robbed' by the 'fascists' of China. However, as they thanked the Iranians for their assistance to the Bosnians, they might also have been referring to the backing the Islamic countries in the Middle East were providing the Uighurs and other Islamic groups in China,[1] something that was recognized by and caused alarm in the midst of the China leadership.[2]

In April 1998, the State Department published its annual report on global terrorism. Among other things, it referred to the unidentified terrorists who acted against the international presence in Bosnia, and especially to the Mujahidin who had served in the Bosnian army during the civil war, but were now engaged in warrant killings. According to that report, the Bosnian government began arresting some of those loose terrorists, and by November 1997, it had incarcerated twenty of them, who were identified as Arabs or Bosnian Muslims.[3] In the same year of 1998 there were reports that Iranian intelligence agents were mounting extensive operations and had even infiltrated the American program to train the Bosnian army. According to those reports, more than 200 Iranian agents were identified as 'having insinuated themselves into Bosnian Muslim political and social circles ... to gather information and to thwart western interests in Bosnia'. Those agents, it was believed, could be helpful in planning terrorist attacks against NATO forces or targets.[4] Taken together, these reports do identify the 'unidentified terrorists' mentioned above. Moreover, these reports link together into an Islamic International centred around Iran indicating that most of the major terrorist activities are carried out by Islamists: from the Israeli Embassy in Buenos Aires (1992); the international gathering of Islamic terrorist organizations in Teheran (1997); the Hizbullah stepped-up activities against Israel in the late 1990s; the arrest in Israel of Stefan Smirak, a would-be 'suicide-bomber' for Hizbullah (November, 1997); the attacks against American interests in the Gulf, East Africa and on American soil (throughout the 1990s),[5] to say nothing of the Muslim separatists in China, and the Islamic resurgence in Bosnia and Kosovo.

People today speak of the clashes between Serbs and Muslims in Bosnia, and Serbs and Albanians in Kosovo, in terms of ethno-national conflicts, with the more numerous Serbs figuring as the oppressors and their rivals as the underdogs and the oppressed. Prima facie, the very usage of the terms 'Serbs' (and 'Croats' for that matter) against Muslims, equates the latter (essentially members of a faith and civilization) to the former who clearly belong to religio-ethnic groups. This points to the fact that not only did Yugoslavian statism and universalistic communism fail to obliterate ethnic and kinship identities (real or imagined), but that communal interest overrides the state umbrella, economic interest or even sheer common sense. But this also raises the question of whether Islam, a universal religion predominant in more than fifty countries around the world, is, or can be perceived as a nationalism that is particularistic by definition.

THE HISTORICAL UNDERPINNINGS

After the Arab conquests had exhausted the immense primeval energies released by Islam since its inception in the seventh century and up until the ninth century, the Turks of Central Asia who arrived on the scene in the eleventh century gave a new impetus to Islamic expansion, this time into the heart of Europe. As Bat Ye'or put it:

> The Islamization of the Turks within the Muslim Empire integrated new and unlimited forces. Uncouth and hardy, they had, since the 9th Century, supplied contingents of slaves exclusively reserved for the Abbasid Caliph's guard and for military service. Thus, quite naturally, the ideology and tactics of jihad inflamed the warlike tendencies of their tribes, already roaming the Asiatic borders of the Greek and Armenian lands. They joined its ranks with the enthusiasm of neophytes, and their ravages facilitated the Islamization and Turkification of Armenia, the Greek territories of Anatolia, and the Balkans. Yet, it is also true that their depredations could not be controlled by the Muslim state and often harmed its economic interests.[6]

The Ottoman state, which reached Vienna at the pinnacle of its existence, was multi-ethnic and multi-religious, and under its Muslim-majority dominance, Christians, Jews and others lived side-by-side for many centuries. However, this coexistence was not born out of a modern concept of tolerance of the other on the basis of acceptance of differences and equality to all, but on a sense of superiority, which tolerated the others in spite of their inferiority. Thus, even though Turks, or Muslims, may have constituted the minority population in some areas of the Empire, they reigned supreme by virtue of their Muslim master status, while the various Christian groups (and Jews for that matter), were relegated to the status of 'protected people' (the *dhimmi*).[7] Christians and others who had integrated into the Ottoman system by embracing Islam, speaking Turkish and going into the Imperial service, soon became part and parcel of the Ottoman culture even when they kept their attachment to their ethnic origin and to their mother tongue. The case in point were the Bosnians, many of whom felt privileged to go into the *devsirme* system by enrolling their boys in the prestigious Janissary corps, and in the course of time were Islamized though they preserved their Slavic roots and language.[8]

The Balkans were conquered by the Ottomans from the middle of the fifteenth century on. Serbia fell in 1459, and four years later Bosnia, with Herzegovina succumbing to the conquerors in 1483. Caught between the economic interest of milking the tax-paying *dhimmis*, which necessitated maintaining the conquered population in place instead of expelling or converting it by force, and the military and security needs which required that the Muslim population be numerous enough to ensure the loyalty to the Empire, the Ottomans tended to implement the latter choice in the Balkans. They adopted a policy of deporting the native populations and settling their own people, or other conquered people, in their stead, thus ensuring that no local minority should envisage any insurgency among a Muslim population. In Bosnia, the process of Islamization was reinforced by the turncoats who flocked to Islam and became the worst oppressors of their former co-religionists; so much so, that the Bosnians were notorious for their role in the Ottoman administration, military and especially the Janissaries.[9]

As late as 1875, long after the introduction of the *tanzimat* reforms which were supposed to redress the situation of the non-Muslims throughout the Empire, the British Ambassador in Istanbul reported that the Ottoman authorities in Bosnia recognized the impossibility of administering justice in equality between the Muslims and the Christians, inasmuch as the ruling Muslim courts accepted no written or oral evidence from Christians. One 1876 report from Bosna-Serai (Sarajevo) by the British Consul in town, tells the whole story:

> About a month ago, an Austrian subject named Jean Udilak, was attacked and robbed between Sarajevo and Visoka by nine Bashi-Bazouks. The act was witnessed by a respectable Mussulman of this time named Nouri Aga Varinika, and he was called as a witness when the affair was brought before the Sarajevo Tribunal. His testimony was in favor of the Austrian, and the next day he was sent for by the Vice-President and one of the members of the Court and threatened with imprisonment for daring to testify against his coreligionists.[10]

As Hans Majer tells us above, Muslims, Christians (and Jews for that matter), could keep to themselves in their own communities, with their lifestyles, rituals and festivals running without hindrance, except in case of intermarriage. For here the only allowed combination was Muslim men taking in Christian (or Jewish) wives, which consecrated their joint offspring as full-right Muslims. The result was that while non-Muslim culture merged into the predominant Islam, there was also an outside input into the Muslim culture with material culture (food, dress, habits, language, etc.) growing to become common to all. All this was acceptable to the Ottoman authorities who were reluctant to interfere, but as soon as the *dhimmis* became wealthy and were conspicuous in their dress and demeanour, it was considered a provocation to the Muslim population and dealt with accordingly. Christians who wanted to improve their lot in Bosnia and Albania could always do so through conversion to Islam or seek the protection of their Muslim family members.[11]

Towards the end of the Ottoman rule, as economic problems arose and the state was no longer able to enforce law and order in the face of the nationalist awakening in the various provinces of the Empire, local rule grew more despotic in an attempt to hold on to the territories that were slipping out of the Porte's grip. The notions of equality coming from liberal Europe, which made the maintenance of legal and religious inequities untenable, conjugated into national terms, and spelled out independence from the Ottoman yoke since the idea of a ruling Empire held together by Islam was no longer operative. It was ironically the Ottoman attempts at modernity, opening up the system, addressing individuals instead of traditional communities, which brought its downfall and opened the new vistas of nationalism and independence in the Balkans as elsewhere, a situation not unlike Eastern Europe after the Gorbachev Perestroika in the late 1980s and early 1990s. But in view of the Greek and Bulgarian plans for a Balkan Federation under their aegis, to take over from the Ottomans,[12] and the tax repression imposed by the Bosnian Muslims, the Serbs rose up in arms (1875), and many of them ran into hiding, leaving behind children, the old and women, something reminiscent of the horrors of the Bosnian War and then the Kosovo War more than one century later. Preydor and Banja Luka were the most harmed by the insurgents when Serb churches and homes were burned.[13]

According to reports from the time of the rebellion, the Bosnian Muslims, descendants of converted Slavs who had become the landowners and acceded to the status of aristocracy by virtue of their conversion, now practiced their faith fanatically and ruthlessly towards their Orthodox compatriots who would rather die in battle than submit to the tax exactions. What made things worse, again as in the recent events in Bosnia, was that the Catholics allied to the Muslims against the Orthodox Serbs. An eyewitness of the time reports:

> United under oppression, it was natural that the Serbs should respond by rebellion. But in the entire northern part of Bosnia and Turkish Croatia ... the antagonism between the two [Catholic and Orthodox] denominations is vast enough for us to have eye-witnessed Catholics marching on the heels of the Turks against Greek insurgents ... By an inexplicable aberration, the priests of the two denominations entertain hatred [towards each other] and we could say without exaggerating that, if given the choice, the Catholics would rather be dominated by the Turks than by the Orthodox Serbs.[14]

The reporter concluded that the Muslims of Bosnia maintained their loyalty to the Ottomans, and therefore there was no chance of a fusion between the populations, in view of the fact that those Serbs whose ancestors had embraced Islam as a political expediency, were now too imbued with it and too captured by the teachings of their Holy Book to relent from their intense hatred which had germinated in their bodies and taken them over completely.[15] But this was to be only a foretaste of things to come, as henceforth the politics of Bosnia would be dominated by the alliance of two of its major religious groups, and later ethno-national communities, against the third. After the Berlin Congress and the occupation of Bosnia by the Austro-Hungarian Empire, the Serbs allied with the Muslims against the occupiers, who were supported by the Catholics in the province. The Hungarian governor of the province tried valiantly but unsuccessfully to create a new

Bosnian identity merging together its three principal communities.[16] But the annexation of Bosnia by the occupiers in 1908, created a new alliance: the Serbs, who wished their merger with Serbia, were pitted against the Croat–Muslim coalition who would rather reconcile to their occupation than allow the Serbs to implement their dream. As a result, repression of the Serbs in Bosnia, coupled with the expulsion of Serbs from Kosovo, brought the bitterness of the occupied Serbs against their oppressors to a record level. Sukrija Kurtovic, a Bosnian Muslim, sought the differentiation between ethno-nationality and religion, and pleaded for the unity of the Bosnians with the Serbs in one single national group by reason of their common Serbian roots, arguing that Islam was a common religion of the Bosnians and the Turks, but that in itself did not make them share any national common ground.[17] The idea of Yugoslavism, a larger entity where all the ethnic and religious groups could find their common identity, came to the fore after the Balkan wars and precipitated World War I following the Sarajevo murder of the heir to the Austro-Hungarian throne in 1914. That war reinforced the Croat–Muslim alliance in Bosnia, which swore to expel the Serbs from Bosnia altogether and acted upon its vow by perpetrating large-scale massacres of the Serbs, and demonstrated the vanity of an all Yugoslavian identity.[18]

A Yugoslavian state was created in 1918 nevertheless, which once again attempted to fuse its components in the ethnic and linguistic domains and leave, as befits a modern European state, the question of religion to the realm of each individual. However, while the Serbs and the Croats of Bosnia could look up to Belgrade and Zagreb respectively, the Muslims were left to vacillate between their Muslim, Ottoman, local and Slavic roots. At first they allied with the stronger Serbs and turned their eyes on Belgrade where they ensured for themselves some privileges, but wary of the competition between the Croats who championed their nationalism and the Serbs who regarded themselves as the guardians of Yugoslavian unity, they focused more and more on their local and religious identity in the form of a Muslim Party (JMO), while the Serbs and the Croats continued to claim that the Muslims of Bosnia were of their respective origins.[19]

During World War II the renewed Croat–Muslim alliance had

tragic consequences inasmuch as under the shelter of its collaboration with the fascists and the Nazis, it brought about the murder, forced conversion or expulsion of a million Serbs. After 1945,
Yugoslavia was reconstituted, this time on its Soviet model, with
its various components recognized on ethnic or linguistic
grounds, and since 1971 on religious grounds for the Muslims of
Bosnia. Since then, what was ethnic and religious sentiment for
the Bosnians turned into a national identity, in spite of the paradox under which communism offered them nationalism based on
faith.[20] This immediately reinforced their coalition with the Croats
in order to scuttle Serbian hegemony in the federated communist
Yugoslavian state, especially in view of the demographic presence
of Serbs in all the federal republics, particularly in Bosnia and
Croatia. So, once again, instead of using the idea of Yugoslavia to
merge the populations of Bosnia-Herzegovina, the idea of faith
(Islam and then Orthodox and Catholic Christianity) became a
vehicle for reinforcing the hatreds and suspicions, which only
waited for the end of the Tito rule and the Communist regime to
burst out in violence and war. After the disintegration of
Yugoslavia in the early 1990s, the Croats and Serbs of Bosnia
expressed their wish to join their respective national republics,
while the Muslims naturally regarded such a dismantling of what
they viewed as their national state as detrimental to their national existence. None of the rival national groups possessed a demographic majority to claim legitimacy to rule all the rest, and the
road was wide opened to war.

THE IDEOLOGICAL UNDERPINNINGS

In 1970, well before the collapse of the Yugoslavian order
imposed by Tito and the outburst of communal nationalism
which instigated the process of its disintegration, a political manifesto was written by an unknown Muslim in Bosnia, Alija
Izetbegovic (born in 1925), but not immediately released to
the public. It was, however, duplicated and made available to
individual Muslims who circulated it among their co-religionists
apparently to serve as a guide for a Muslim order to replace the
Godless communist system in Bosnia. That pamphlet is known as
the *Islamska Deklaracija* (Islamic Declaration). In 1983, after

Tito's death but while the communist state was still held together, a trial took place in Sarajevo where the author and some like-minded individuals were prosecuted for subverting the constitutional order and for acting from the standpoint of Islamic fundamentalism and Muslim nationalism. Significantly, after the fall of communist power, the accused were publicly rehabilitated, and the Declaration was then officially published in Sarajevo (1990). Izetbegovic, at the head of his Democratic Action Party (SDA) won the majority of the Muslim votes in the first free elections in Bosnia-Herzegovina (November 1990), but his pamphlet was obscured and not heard of again. Judging from the wide appeal of his later book, *Islam Between East and West*, which was published in English in the USA (1984), in Turkish in Istanbul (1987), and in Serbian in Belgrade (1988), and from the developments in the Bosnian war in the mid-1990s, one might be well advised to take a look at it.

The declaration, which in many respects sounds and looks like the platforms of Muslim fundamentalists elsewhere (e.g. the Hamas Charter),[21] assumes that its appeal will be heeded by Muslims around the world, not only by its immediate constituency. It accuses the West of wishing to 'keep Muslim nations spiritually weak and materially and politically dependent' and calls upon the Believers to cast aside inertia and passivity in order to embark on the road of action.[22] And like Muslim radicals such as Sayyid Qutb of Egypt, who urged his followers to reject the world of ignorance around them and transform it according to the model of the Prophet of Islam, the Declaration of Izetbegovic also calls upon the millions to join the efforts of Muslim individuals who fought against the *jahiliyya* (the state of ignorance and godlessness which had preceded the advent of the Prophet),[23] and dedicates the text to the memory of 'our brothers who have laid their lives for Islam',[24] namely the *shuhada'* (martyrs) of all times and places who had fallen in the cause of Islam.

The manifesto, again like other Muslim radicals, not only addresses itself to the restoration of Islam in private life, in the family and society, but also expressly shuns local nationalism of any sort and substitutes for it the creation of a universal Islamic polity (the traditional *umma*), 'from Morocco to Indonesia'.[25] The author awakens his people to the reality where 'a few thousand true Islamic fighters forced England to withdraw from the Suez Canal in the early 1950s, while the nationalist armies of the Arabs were losing their battles against Israel', and where 'Turkey, an Islamic country, ruled the world', yet when it tried to emulate Europe it dropped to the level of a third-world country. In other words, it is not nationalism that makes the force of Muslim nations, but their abidance by Islam in its universal version. Therefore, it does not befit Muslims to fight or die for any other cause but Islam, and it behoves Muslims to die with the name and glory of Allah in their hearts, or totally desert the battlefield.[26] Translated into the Bosnian scene, Muslims ought not take part in, or stand for, any form of government, which is not Islamic, and any cause, which is not connected to Islam. To the Bosnians, whom Izetbegovic addressed, there were only two options left: either to subscribe to Muslim revival and its political require-ments, or be doomed to stagnation and oblivion.[27]

The manifesto then goes into a long dissertation explaining the reasons and history of the 'backwardness of the Muslim nations' (pp. 5–11). Basically, it refutes modernists who regard the notion of the Islamic *din* as only religion in the European sense, and insists on viewing it and living by it as an entire religious, cultur-al and political way of life, which unifies 'religion and science, ethics and politics, ideals and interests'.[28] In the typically funda-mentalist fashion, it attacks established conservative Islam and its 'hodjas and sheikhs, who organized themselves as a caste unto itself and arrogated to itself a monopoly over the interpretation of Islam, and placed itself in the position of mediator between the Qur'an and the people'.[29] It also mocks the modernists for emulat-ing the West and worshipping its material life, ultimately produc-ing corruption and decadence instead of spiritual uplifting. In this context, the author belittles the role of Mustafa Kemal in modern Turkey because he wrongly thought that by ordering the fez out, the heads, which wore it, would also be transformed.[30] That was the reason, in the author's mind why Turkey and Japan, which began from the same starting point at the turn of the century grew in totally different directions: Japan, who knew how to inte-grate her own culture with modernity, but kept her traditional writing system, became a great power, while Turkey, who abol-ished her Arabic script which 'ranks among the most perfect and the most widely used alphabets' to introduce the Latin script, remained a third-world country.[31]

This total rejection of Kemalist Turkey's model of course stands in contradiction to Western hopes to 'sell' that very precedent of modernity, Europeanization and moderation to the emerging Muslim entities in Central Asia and the Balkans. As against the perceived failure of Turkey and other Muslim countries due to 'the weakening of the influence of Islam in the practical life of the people', the author posits that 'all successes, both political and moral, are the reflection of our acceptance of Islam and its application in life'.[32] Therefore, while all defeats, from Uhud at the time of the Prophet to the Sinai War between Israel and Egypt, were due to 'apostasy from Islam', any 'rise of the Islamic peoples, every period of dignity, started with the affirmation of the Qur'an'. The author complains that in the real world the Qur'an is being recited instead of practiced, mosques are 'monumental but empty', the form took over from substance, as the Holy Book turned 'into a mere sound without intelligible sense and content'.[33] This reality was caused, laments the author in line with other Muslim fundamentalists, by the Western-inspired school system in all Muslim countries.[34]

Secularism and nationalism, the products of that foreign educational trend, took over the minds and hearts of the new generation of Muslims. The masses, who do not submit to these fleeting concepts which are foreign to Islam, chose indifference; but if they are rightly guided they can rise to action provided they are spurred by 'an idea that corresponds to their profound feelings, and that can only be the Islamic idea', instilled by a new intelligentsia that 'thinks and feels Islam' and would ultimately 'fly the flag of the Islamic order and together with the Muslim masses initiate action for its realization'.[35] This new Islamic order should unite 'religion and law, upbringing and force, ideals and interests, the spiritual community and the state, free will and coercion', for 'Islamic society without Islamic rule is incomplete and impotent; Islamic rule without Islamic society is either utopia or violence'.[36] This in effect means, in the vein of other Muslim fundamentalist platforms, that the Muslim state ought to enforce ('coerce') the Islamic order, short of which violence would erupt by necessity. For, according to this scheme, and contrary to the European concept of a liberal society where the individual is prized, a Muslim 'does not exist as an individual entity', and he must create his Islamic milieu in order to survive, by way of changing the world around him if he does not want to be changed by others.[37]

The manifesto holds that there is no point to legislate laws, as is Western wont, because they end up corrupting society. It is infinitely better to educate people and teach them to obey the decree of Allah, for this will put an end to corruption and lawlessness[38] which is the reason for the 'incompatibility of Islam with non-Islamic systems'. Therefore, 'there can be no peace nor coexistence between the Islamic faith and non-Islamic social and political institutions'.[39] This means in effect that Muslims should not submit to a non-Islamic rule and that they should strive to create an Islamic order where none exists, due to the assumption that 'Islam clearly rules out any right or possibility of action of any foreign ideology [supposedly including democracy, pluralism, tolerance, freedom, equality etc.] on its turf'. As a result, 'there is no room for the lay principle, and the state should be an expression of the moral concepts of [the Islamic] religion and supportive of them'.[40] In light of these principles, which shun mysticism and stagnation and assume the right of innovation to make things adaptable to every time and place, the pamphlet defines and traces a long series of rules and regulations which ought to guide the individual Muslim (pp. 25–40) in practically all spheres of his societal life. The core of this orientation is that:

> Islamic society may not be based upon social or economic interest only, or on any other external, technical factor of association as a community of believers; it is based on a religious and emotional aspect of affiliation. This element is most clearly visible and enshrined in the *jemaat* as the basic unit in Islamic society.[41]

This would mean in the Bosnian context that only a religiously-based society, on the model of religious associations (*jemaat*) is viable, and no provision is made for non-Muslims or for a multi-religious or multi-cultural society in its midst. (See the question of minorities below.)

The question of life in such a Muslim community is left

unclear. On the one hand, the manifesto assures the 'equality of all men'[42] and discards divisions and groupings according to race or class. But, if man's value is determined according to one's 'integrity, and spiritual and ethical value',[43] and these noble qualities are grounded in Islamic creed and value-system, then only if one is a good Muslim can he be considered worthy. This is all the more so when the concept of the *ummet*, the universal congregation of all Muslims is taken as the 'supranationality of the Muslim community', and Islam and Pan-Islamism define its boundaries: 'Islam determines its internal and Pan-Islamism its external relations', because, 'Islam is its ideology and Pan-Islamism its politics'.[44] By Islam, the author means certain limitations on private property in order to ensure a fair distribution of wealth based on Qur'anic precepts. The restoration of *zekat* (paying of alms, one of the Five Pillars of the Faith) to the status of a public obligation as of old, and the enforcement of the Qur'anic prohibition of collecting interest, are seen as the instrument to achieve social justice.[45]

Izetbegovic, in intending to establish the 'Republican Principle', namely that power should not be inherited, defeats his purpose by positing at the same time the Qur'anic 'recognition of the absolute authority of Allah, which means the absolute non-recognition of any other omnipotent authority', for 'any submission to a creature which implies unsubmission to the Creator is not permissible'.[46] This, of course, would have a direct ramification on the entire question of sovereignty, democracy, authority and power. In this scheme, the idea of the inviolability of the individual is totally rejected, as it is made clear that in statements of equality of all men notwithstanding, and 'irrespective of man's merits' he must submit to the Islamic order where there is a 'synthesis of absolute authority (in terms of the programme) and of absolute democracy (relative to the individual)'.[47] It takes a lot of intellectual acrobatics to extricate the meaning of this 'absolute democracy' that is strapped to the 'absolute authority' of the Divine Qur'anic message under which the Believer is expected to operate. For, while the author subscribes to the idea that all men, including the Prophet, are fallible and worshipping them is a 'kind of idolatry', he assigns 'all glory and praise to Allah alone, because Allah alone can judge the merits of men'.[48] This, of course, would render any process of election between men impossible, and anyone who reaches a position of authority can only gain legitimacy if he submits to the 'absolute authority' of the Qur'anic teachings.

Part of this brand of democracy is insinuated to us when the author suggests that in his envisaged Islamic order the mass media 'should be controlled by people of unquestionable Islamic moral intellectual authority. Perverts and degenerates should not be allowed to lay their hands on these media ... and use them to transmit the senselessness and emptiness of their own lives to others. What can we expect if people receive one message from the mosque and a totally opposite one from the TV relay?'[49] The author does not spell out the criteria to judge the 'emptiness and senselessness' of journalists under his regime, nor does he explain how he, or anyone else, can judge any person when all judgment is left to Allah. But he dares, under the heading of 'Freedom of Conscience',[50] to suggest all those limitations on the media, which would certainly make them anything but free, the protestations of the author notwithstanding.[51]

While the statement that 'there can be no Islamic order without independence and freedom' may still sound plausible, in view of the Islamic regimes of Iran, Afghanistan and Saudi Arabia, it is vice-versa, namely that 'there can be no independence and freedom without Islam',[52] which seems a bit presumptuous by any stretch of the imagination. For that would mean that the freest and most democratic nations of the world are in fact deprived of freedom and independence as long as they do not see the light of Islam. Unless, of course, he means that the idea applies only to Muslim peoples. In that case, the author argues, only if the Muslims assert Islamic thought in every day life, can they achieve spiritual and political liberation. Moreover, he claims that the legitimacy of the ruler in any Islamic nation will always depend on the extent of the ruler's commitment to Islam, short of which he turns for support to foreigners who maintain him in power.[53] Conversely, if he acts according to Islamic requirements, he thereby achieves true democracy by consensus which is inherent in Islam and which alone makes violence redundant.[54] But the road to this utopian state of affairs is not obtained in 'peace and tranquillity, but in unrest and challenge'.[55] That means, that like other Muslim fundamentalist movements which promise their constituencies sweat and blood, and that earn credibility and appeal in so doing, the Islamic Declaration under discussion treads the same road to contrast with the empty promises of rulers in the Islamic world who make sweeping pledges of peace and prosperity but are unable to deliver.

Now comes the problematic issue of the relations between the Muslim host culture and minority guest cultures under the Islamic order. The manifesto provides religious freedom and 'protection' to the minorities, 'provided they are loyal', something that smacks of the traditional Muslim attitude to the *dhimmi* (protected people) under its aegis. The interesting aspect of all this is that when the situation is reversed, namely Muslim minorities dwelling in non-Muslim lands, their loyalty is made conditional on their religious freedom, not the other way around. Moreover, even under such conditions, the Muslims are committed to carry out all their obligations to the host community 'with the exception of those that are detrimental to the Muslims'.[56] The question remains unanswered as to who is to determine what is detrimental to Islam, and when and where. Assuming that the status of Muslim minorities would depend on 'the strength and reputation of the Islamic world community', it would mean two things:

1. There was a possibility, in Izetbegovic's thinking, that the Muslims of Bosnia would remain a minority; indeed, their rate is about 40 per cent of the total population (and growing, due to a higher birth-rate) and if the Catholic Croats and Orthodox Serbs of Bosnia should gang up against them (something quite unlikely), this manifesto still provides them with a chance for survival.
2. In either case, the Bosnian Muslims are counting on the intervention of the world Muslim community, something that was to be corroborated during the Bosnia and then the Kosovo wars.

Again, like Hamas and other branches of the Muslim Brotherhood, this manifesto proclaims the primacy of education and preaching, in order to conquer the hearts of the people before power, a prerequisite of the Islamic order, is conquered. 'We must be preachers first and then soldiers',[57] is the motto of the manifesto. Force to take over power will be applied 'as soon as Islam is morally and numerically strong enough, not only to overthrow the non-Islamic rule, but to develop the new Islamic rule', because 'to act prematurely is equally dangerous as to be late in taking the required action'.[58] The author is confident that this can be done, because 'history is not only a story of constant changes, but also of the continual realization of the impossible and the unexpected'.[59] The model for the new Islamic order, which the manifesto puts on the pedestal, is Pakistan, the Muslim state that, in spite of its many deficiencies, remains the 'great hope' of Izetbegovic.[60] But his great goal is the unity of the Muslim people, and in the meantime every Muslim country should be concerned about all the rest: Egypt ought to care for the Muslims of Ethiopia and Kashmir,[61] and by inference, the Muslims of Bosnia and the Balkans should be the business of all the rest of the Islamic world. The fact that feelings of affinity for oppressed Muslim brothers everywhere are not translated into action is the fault of the Western educated Muslims who substitute nationalism for Pan-Islam.[62]

Under the heading 'Christianity and Judaism', the manifesto determines the future relationships of the envisaged new Islamic order with those two faiths, which the author considers 'the two foremost religions' and the 'major systems and doctrines outside the sphere of Islam'.[63] Nonetheless, the author distinguishes between Jesus and the Church. The former, he says, in line with Qur'anic teachings, is part of divine revelation while the latter, as embodied in the Inquisition, is abhorrent to his heart. At the same time, however, as is the normative Islamic wont, he accuses Christianity of 'distorting certain aspects' of the divine message while accusing the Church of intolerance.[64] Similarly, he differentiates between Jews and their national movement – Zionism, idealizing the times when they lived under Islam, but he totally rejects their plea for independence and nationhood.[65] So, as long as the Jews are submissive and stateless in their *dhimmi* status within the Islamic state he envisages, all is well, but to dare to declare independence and stand up to the Islamic world, that is unforgivable. He claims that Jerusalem is not only a Palestinian city but first of all a Muslim one, and therefore he warns the Jews, who 'have created themselves' the conflict with the Arab regimes (not the Arab or the Muslim people), that a prolonged war will be waged against them by Muslims until they release 'every inch of captured land'. He threatens that 'any trade-offs or compromises which might call into question these elementary rights of our brothers in Palestine will be treason which can destroy even the very system of moral values underpinning our world'.[66]

In sum, this passionate message of Izetbegovic, based on the Qur'an and the revival of Islam, addresses the universal congregation of all Muslims, and strives to establish an Islamic world order based on Qur'anic precepts. The idea of nationalism, any nationalism, is totally rejected in favour of the Islamic Republic, which alone can respond to the challenges of the modern world and restore to Islam its glory and preponderance. Like the platform of Hamas and other fundamentalists, the text of the Qur'an, rather than the commentaries of the Muslim establishment, provides the rationale for the cultural, social and political revolution that the author proposes to undertake. Indeed, the profuse citations from the Holy Book that we find interspersed throughout the text of the Declaration, bear witness to Qur'anic hegemony in the thought and plans of the author. Moreover, by positing the listed principles as deriving from the Holy Scripture, namely the eternal and immutable Word of Allah, the document creates the impression of a divinely guided program, which is not given to debate or consideration. The vow insinuated in this declaration, that Islam would reconquer its people peacefully if possible, by force if necessary, might throw some light (or rather obscurity) on some of the events that took place in Bosnia in the 1990s, including Iranian and other Mujahidin which participated in the battles, and seem to be accelerating in Kosovo at the turn of the millennium.

While in Serbia in 1998 and 1999, when I met academics, politicians from the opposition, and journalists who did not hold much sympathy for their government, but were at the same time concerned about the revival of Islam in the Balkans, I was given more details about Izetbegovic and his Islamic activities. It is said that immediately after the Second World War, in Spring 1946, as

a member of the 'Young Muslims', he, together with Omer
Behmen (later Vice President to SDA Party), and Dr Shachirbay
(father of Muhamed Shachirbay, the Bosnian Ambassador to the
UN), started an illegal magazine, *The Mujahid*, in which the following song was published:

> The earth throb, the mountains quake
> Our war cry resounds through the land
> Heads held high, men old and young,
> In a holy jihad our salvation lies
>
> *Chorus*: The time has come, onward brethren
> Onward brethren, onward heroes
> To the Jihad, to the Jihad let us go.
>
> Proudly the green banner flies,
> Close ranks beneath it in steel-like file,
> Let the brotherhood of Islam bind us,
> Let us scorn death and go to the battle
>
> *Chorus*: The time has come, onward brethren ...
>
> With our war-cry 'Allah Akbar'
> Rot the old and corrupt world
> For the joy and salvation of mankind
> Boldly, heroes, let us go into battle!
>
> *Chorus*: The time has come, onward brethren ...

These themes are strikingly similar to those propagated in cassettes by the Hamas organization[67] to glorify the death for the
cause of Islam in the course of jihad. They also strikingly form the
same thinking which produced the Islamic Declaration analysed
above. It is not surprising therefore that as early as 1992, at the
genesis of the Bosnian War, the Islamic community newspaper in
Sarajevo, *Prepared*, published the following poem:

> Go into battle with a clear mind and with full confidence
> In Allah. If you survive, you will be a *ghazi* [a Muslim fighter].

If you die, you will be a *shahid* [martyr]. Otherwise,
You will not be one or the other, and most surely you will be humiliated.
Go into battle, if possible with *abdest* [ritual ablution] and, obligatorily,
With Allah's name in your heart and on your lips.
On no account must you go unbathed, because any such individual can be the cause of disaster both to himself and to others.
During the attack on the enemy, or in combat with him, shout the *tekbir*.
[Allahu Akbar– Allah is the Greatest].
If possible, carry the Qur'an with you.
After all, this the Muslim must know that he is fighting on the side of justice and is following the path of Allah.
Allah promises assistance to such men. The man on whose side Allah is, no one can defeat. This and next world are his.[68]

In yet another song popular among the Muslim fighters, one could hear:

Wake up soldiers, it is dawn, it is time for prayers.
We are the army of the jihad; there is no God but Allah.
This is the remedy for every pain; there is no God but Allah.
In the Bosnia River Valley, an army corps is being formed.
We are brothers like steel, every Chetnik fears us,
And every Ustasha; there is no God but Allah.
We are the army of the jihad; there is no God but Allah.[69]

THE CONCEPT OF GREATER ALBANIA

During the turmoil, which swept the Balkans on the eve of the Berlin Congress (1878), the Albanians, as an ethnic group, came up with the concept of including within their fledgling national entity all the Albanians of the Balkans, beyond the geographic boundaries of Albania itself. Being Muslims, the Albanians, like the Islamized Bosnians, enjoyed a privileged status in the Ottoman Empire. In 1878 the Albanian League was established in Prizren, which presented the Greater Albania plan. While the

Albanians constituted the majority in the core areas of Albania proper, their proportion in Kosovo did not exceed 44 per cent.[70] Like in the case of Bosnia where ethnicity was religion-bound, there could not exist an Orthodox Croat, nor a Catholic Serb, nor a Bosnian who was not Muslim.[71] So in Albania, Islamized Serbs, Greeks and Bulgarians became ipso-facto Albanians. In 1912 an attempt was made under Austro-Hungarian auspices to implement the idea, followed by another such attempt under the Italian fascists in 1941. The third attempt, initiated at the end of the 1990s as a result of the collapse of the Soviet Union and Yugoslavia, translated into tearing Kosovo, by now predominantly Albanian-Muslim, from Serbian sovereignty, following up on the Bosnian experience which had subtracted that province from Serbian-Yugoslavian hegemony.

The precedent of Bosnia, which had allowed in 1971, ironically under the communist rule, the recognition of Bosnia's nationalism as Muslim, would now propel the ethnic Albanians to revive their Islamic heritage and claim their Muslim identity which ipso-facto would justify their separation from the Serbs. At first, the awakening of the Albanians was undertaken along the ethno-national track. Prior to 1971, the break between Maoist Albania and Yugoslavia had occasioned the Albanian revolt in Kosovo (1968), but after the normalization of their relationships in 1971, the Albanians turned to cultural propaganda by peaceful, if subversive, means. Interestingly enough, like the Palestinians who are competing with Israel over their ancestral land by conveniently claiming that they are the descendants of the ancient Cana'anites who had preceded the Israelites on the land, the Albanians now advanced the claim that they inherited the ancient heritage of the Illyrians who were the original inhabitants of Kosovo.[72] This resulted in the Albanian rebellion of 1981, in which they demanded the status of a republic (no longer an autonomous region within Serbia, like Voivodina in the north), still within the six-republic Yugoslavian Federation. After the fall of Communism in Albania, the new regime recognized in 1991 the self-declared Republic of Kosovo, and its head, Ibrahim Rugova, opened an office in Tirana.[73]

The disintegration of Yugoslavia by necessity revived the old dreams of a Greater Albania, which now eyed not only Kosovo, but also parts of Macedonia, Greece, Serbia and Montenegro where an Albanian population had settled over the years. The rising of Muslim consciousness in the Balkans, after the Bosnian precedent, and the spreading of the Izetbegovic doctrine, now acts as a catalyst to draw together, under the combined banners of Greater Albania and Islam, all the Albanian populations of that region. In 1992 Albania joined the Conference of Islamic Countries, and it has been working to attract support of other Islamic countries to the Greater Albania plan, actually presenting itself as 'the shield of Islam' in the Balkans.[74] It has been noted that while the Albanian demographic explosion in Kosovo, which has allowed them to predominate and demand secession, has not taken place in Albania itself,[75] perhaps an indication, as in Palestine and Bosnia, that the 'battle of the womb' heralded by nationalists and Muslim fundamentalists, is not merely a natural growth but may be also politically motivated.

CONCLUSIONS

While in Serbian national terms, the loss of Kosovo to the Albanians is equivalent in their eyes to Israel losing Jerusalem,[76] in international terms, the importance of this issue lay in the emerging pattern of the re-Islamization of the Balkans. True, the immediate concern of the Serbs is to what extent can a minority which achieves a local majority within their sovereign territory, demand the right of secession, especially when that demand is backed up by irredentist claims of a neighbouring country. If that should be the case, then entire areas of the US populated by Mexican-Americans, or parts of Israel where the local Arab population has achieved the majority, or the Kurdish populations of Turkey, Iraq, Iran, and Syria, or Arab enclaves in France, could raise the question of their autonomy and ask for their right to secede. For that matter, the Croats and Serbs of Bosnia could also revert to their initial demand at the outset of the Bosnian crisis to merge with their respective national entities. The larger concern, however, is to what extent the settling patterns of the Albanians can disrupt the physical continuity between the Christian countries of the Balkans: Greece, Macedonia, Serbia, Bulgaria, and Romania; or, more importantly, whether a new continuity of Islamic settlement, from Bosnia through Kosovo and now southern Serbia, can link up with the

Muslims of Bulgaria to achieve a geographical continuum with Muslim Turkey. In view of the Islamic Declaration analysed above which does not accept the present state of affairs in the Balkans and Turkey, and makes provision for an Islamic revolution to redress the situation to its liking, the Bosnia and Kosovo events seem only as an ominous precursor of things to come.

These concerns have been raised due to the perverse link that has been established in real politics between Muslim fundamentalist powers like Saudi Arabia and Iran who seek to further the penetration of Islam into the Balkans, against western interests, and the inexplicable rush of that same West to facilitate that penetration which is already turning against it. From the Muslim point of view, things are easy and goals are clear: to ensure the continuity of a Muslim presence from Turkey into Europe, namely to revitalize a modern version of the Ottoman Empire. True, the present successive governments of Ankara are committed to secularism of the Kemalist brand under the guardianship of the military. But as the Erbakan experience has shown (1996–1998), when democracy is allowed to operate, then the Algerian scenario may have the upper hand and an Islamist government may be elected to power that may also opt for the strengthening of the Islamic factor in Europe. Muslim fundamentalists across the world, from the Uighurs of Chinese Turkestan to the Arabs of the Middle East; from the Mujahidin of Afghanistan to the disciples of Izetbegovic in the Balkans, do not hide their designs to act for the realization of this new world order.

A summon by the Saudi scholar Ahmed ibn-Nafi' of Mecca, which was circulated to all centres of the Pan-Islamic Salvation Committee at the outset of the conflict in Bosnia, states in no uncertain terms:

> Let it be known, brothers, that life in this ephemeral world differs immensely from the life lived in keeping with the principles of jihad … Fortunate is he whom Allah enlightens in this life … by waging a jihad for Him. Following Allah's instructions, the Pan-Islamic Salvation Committee has devised a holy plan to clean the world of unbelievers. We entrust you to see to the imminent establishment of the Caliphate in the Balkans, because the Balkans are the path to the conquest of Europe.

Every individual Imam in our states, and especially Turkey, is ready to help. Know, therefore, brothers, that time is working for us. Let us help our brothers who are fighting for the holy cause in Bosnia. Let us help them for the sake of Allah, by sending them as much money and weapons as we can, by sending them new Mujahidin. Furthermore, in keeping with this holy plan, all women and children and some men must immediately be given refuge in Europe. And you, brother Muslims, must care for them as for your own, so they will spread everywhere and preach our religion, for our sake and for the sake of Allah. Brothers, give women and children refuge in each centre, collect money and weapons and send them to Bosnia. Gather Mujahidin and send them to Bosnia! This is your obligation. Help them so that Islam will spread as soon as possible ... With all your heart and soul and everywhere, fight the unbelievers! This is your duty! The Caliphate is at hand! ... May Allah reward you![77]

This appeal was by no means an isolated case. In the same month of August 1992, a poster was plastered on walls in Sarajevo, signed by the spiritual head of the Iranian Revolution, Imam Khamenei, which accused the Western nations of not preventing the genocide against the Muslims of Bosnia, due to their innate hostility to Islam, and urged them to clear the way for Iranian Mujahidin and other young Muslims to wage the war and 'drive the Serbs from this Islamic country'.[78] In Zagreb, which at the time was the ally of the Muslims against the Serbs, a local journal echoed that call:

The Muslim nation in Iran began its revolution with 'Allahu Akbar!' and succeeded. On the territory of Yugoslavia, the Serbs could not tolerate a Muslim [Izetbegovic] as the President of Bosnia-Herzegovina. Their only rival is Islam and they fear it. The time is approaching when Islam will be victorious.[79]

While the traces of Iranian and other Muslim volunteers' jihad in Bosnia were rife, Western reactions seemed more and more obtuse. Except for the theory that the US had to please Saudi Arabia as it had done during the Gulf War when it desisted from occupying Baghdad, other explanations range from sheer misunderstanding of the dangers that Islamic fundamentalism poses to the West to cold-blooded commercial gains in the short run which obscure the long-term strategic considerations. If that quandary raised many eyebrows in the West during the Bosnia War, where the US and European powers supported Bosnia at the detriment of the Serbs, so much more so for the intransigent, costly and destructive military intervention of NATO in Kosovo. As it is known, war does not determine who is right, it only determines who is left. It is time to draw the balance of who is left and what is left from that war.

The 'Good Guys' of NATO had set out, under the cover of a barrage of propaganda, to address the humanitarian problem of 'ethnic cleansing', forgetting the 'ethnic cleansing' that the Serbs had suffered over centuries in Bosnia and Kosovo. While accusing the Serbs of inflicting collective punishment on the entire Kosovar-Albanian population for the sins of the Kosovo Liberation Army, they have themselves destroyed the lives and livelihoods of millions of innocent Serbs, depriving them of bridges, potable water, supplies, municipal services, broadcasting stations and what not. And all that while relentlessly repeating in their harrowing press briefings that they held no grudge against the Serbian people, only against their leader. The real questions for the horrors of that war were never raised by NATO, and certainly never answered: What has caused the mass uprooting of people from Kosovo, including Serbs? Was it only Serbian abuses against the Albanian population, or perhaps also the fear of people who were caught in the crossfire? Why were only the elderly, women and children the ones who ran away to safety in refugee camps? Was it only because the Serbs callously imprisoned or exterminated able-bodied men, or perhaps because they were recruited into rebellious KLA troops who aided NATO's designs? Was Serbia encouraging or preventing ethnic cleansing? One day we were told that the refugees were pushed across the borders of Kosovo, another time we were told that they ran away by themselves, and yet another time we were assured that the Kosovars were prevented by the bad Serbs from crossing in order to serve as human shields. Who could take these inconsistencies seriously?

The havoc that was wreaked on Kosovo, far from settling the

issue, on the contrary, aggravated it: the Serb population was almost totally forced out of the province, and those who stayed could only do so under the protection of the NATO or UN forces. Two months after they had 'established order' there, a *New York Times* editorial had this to say about it:

> Kosovo remains lawless and violent. There are no local police, or judges ... NATO is doing an uneven and unsatisfactory job of preserving order ... Local thugs, rogue fighters of the Kosovo Liberation Army and Albanian gangs slipping [from Albania] across the unpatrolled borders, have taken advantage of the law enforcement vacuum to terrorize the Serbian and gypsy minorities and drive them from their homes ... The same violent elements also prey on Kosovar Albanians subjecting people to extortion, and potential political rivals and suspected collaborators with the previous Serbian authorities, to intimidation and murder ...
>
> NATO must rethink its overly indulgent attitude towards the KLA, which has been permitted to postpone the deadline for surrendering heavy weapons and expects to see its former fighters included in the new local police forces.[80]

One year later, in July 2000, chaos seemed to be still prevailing and the parties determined that the Kosovars want independence from Serbia, and the Serbs want to prevent it lest the Greater Albania plan comes to be implemented with the related instability in Macedonia and other areas inhabited by Albanians.[81] The UN troops are supposed to impose a 'substantial autonomy' for the Kosovars under Serbian sovereignty, but that does not seem to be in the making, but Albanians who live in Serbia Proper may want to draw UN troops across the border. Reports from the spot identify a 'Kosovo-wide problem of attacks on [Serb and other] minorities, harassment, intimidation and persecution' and the 'vicious Albania-based mafia that is spreading crime'.[82] The irony in all this is that while the problem of Bosnia remains unsettled, with the Serb and Croat entities there entertaining their hopes to join their motherlands, and the Kosovo issue festering as an open wound, NATO finds itself backing, or at least seeming indifferent to the Islamic takeover in the heart of Europe.

Robert Cohen-Tanugi, in his series of articles which has drawn world attention,[83] proposes the thesis that the US is basically interested in promoting Islamic radical states to create the 'Green Belt', loyal to it, around Russia and China, and its subsidiary, the 'Green Diagonal' designed to link Central Europe with Turkey, in order to restore the power and hegemony of this pivot of American strategy to its Ottoman times. That is the reason, he claims, for American determination to advance the cause of Islamic revival in Bosnia and Kosovo and conversely, to eliminate nationalist Serbia which stands as the major obstacle on that road. However, rising fundamentalist Islam, which is inimical to the US in particular and Western culture in general, will not necessarily play the American game and may turn against its benefactors sooner and with more vengeance that either the US or its European allies suspect.

NOTES

This was first published by the Ariel Center for Policy Research, 109 (November 2000), pp. 1–33.

1. See Lillian Craig-Harris, *China Considers the Middle East* (London: Tauris, 1993),p.275.
2. Xinhua News Agency, 20 February 1990.
3. *Patterns of Global Terrorism*, US Department of State, April 1998.
4. Policy Watch No. 296, 1998, p.3, Washington Institute, citing reports by the *New York Times* and the *Washington Times*.
5. Ibid.
6. Bat Ye'or, *The Decline of Eastern Christianity under Islam: From Jihad to Dhimmitude* (Madison, WI: Fairleigh Dickinson University Press, 1996), p.52.
7. For the details of the *dhimmi* status within the Empire, see Hans Majer, 'The Functioning of a Multi-Ethnic and Multi-Religious State: The Ottoman Empire', in Slavenko Terzic (ed.), *Islam, the Balkans and the Great Powers (XIV–XX Centuries)*, Serbian Academy of Science, Vol.14 (Belgrade: 1997), p.61ff.
8. Ibid., p.63.
9. Bat Ye'or, *The Decline of Eastern Christianity under Islam*, p.132.
10. Cited by Bat Ye'or, *The Decline of Eastern Christianity under Islam*, pp.176–7. For documents about the inequities in Bosnia against the Christian population, see also pp.421–7.
11. Majer, 'The Functioning of a Multi-Ethnic and Multi-Religious State', pp.67–8.
12. Vrban Todorov, 'The Federalist Idea as a Means for Preserving the Integrity of the Ottoman Empire', in Terzic, *Islam, the Balkans and the Great Powers*, pp.293–6.
13. *Revue de Deux Mondes* (Paris, 1876), Vol.II, No.1, pp.237–54. Cited by Jean Paul Bled, 'La Question de Bosnie-Hercegovine dans La Revue Des Deux Mondes', in Terzic, *Islam, the Balkans and the Great Powers*, p.330.
14. Ibid., pp.331–2.
15. Ibid., p.332.
16. Dusan Batakovuc, 'La Bosnie-Herzegovine: le System des Alliances', in Terzic, *Islam, the Balkans and the Great Powers*, pp. 335–43.
17. Ibid., pp.343–4.
18. Ibid., p.346.
19. Ibid.

20. A. Popovic, 'La Politique Titist envers les Religions et ses Consequences', in M. Bodzemir, *Islam, et Laicite: Approches Globales et Regionales* (Paris: 1996), pp.98–102.
21. See Raphael Israeli, 'The Charter of Allah: the Platform of the Hamas', in Y. Alexander (ed.), *The Annual of Terrorism, 1988–89* (The Netherlands: Nijhoff, 1990), pp.99–134.
22. Introduction to the Pamphlet, pp.1–2.
23. Ibid., p 2.
24. Ibid.
25. Ibid., p.3.
26. Ibid., p.4.
27. Ibid.
28. Ibid., p.5.
29. Ibid., p.6.
30. Ibid., pp.7–8.
31. Ibid., p.9.
32. Ibid., p.12.
33. Ibid., pp.14–15.
34. Ibid., pp.16–17.
35. Ibid., p.19.
36. Ibid., p.20.
37. Ibid.
38. Ibid., pp.21–2.
39. Ibid., p.23.
40. Ibid.
41. Ibid., pp.25–6.
42. Ibid., p.26.
43. Ibid., p.27.
44. Ibid., pp.27–8.
45. Ibid., pp.29–30.
46. Ibid., p.30.
47. Ibid., p.31.
48. Ibid.
49. Ibid., p.33.
50. Ibid.
51. Ibid., p.34.
52. Ibid., p.35.
53. Ibid.
54. Ibid., pp.35–6.
55. Ibid., p.37.
56. Ibid., p.40.
57. Ibid., p.45.
58. Ibid., pp.45–6.
59. Ibid., p.46.
60. Ibid., p.48.
61. Ibid., pp.49–50.
62. Ibid., p.51.
63. Ibid., pp.55–7.
64. Ibid., pp.55–6.
65. Ibid., pp.56–7.
66. Ibid., p.57.
67. See, for example, R. Israeli, 'Islamikaze and Their Significance', *Terrorism and Political Violence*, 9, 3 (Autumn 1997), pp.112–13.
68. 'The Future Saints', in Vesna Hadzivukovic *et al.* (eds.), *Chronicle of Announced Death* (Belgrade: 1993), p.46.
69. Ibid.
70. Jovan Canak (ed.), *Greater Albania: Concepts and Possible Consequences* (Belgrade: Institute of Geo-Political Studies, 1998), pp.8–11.
71. Jens Reuter, 'From Religious Community to Nation: The Ethnogenesis of the Bosnian Muslims', in Terzic, *Islam, the Balkans and the Great Powers*, pp.617–23.

72. Canak, *Greater Albania*, pp.42–3.
73. Ibid.
74. Ibid., pp.47–8.
75. Ibid., p.49.
76. Duro Fuletic, 'Consequences of a Possible Creation of "Greater Albania"', *Review of International Affairs*, L, 1085–86 (October–November 1999), p.23.
77. The hand written Arabic text of the epistle of 17 August 1992, appears in Hadzivukovic, *Chronicle of Announced Death*, p. 52.
78. The text of the summons, with Khamenei's picture, appears in Serbo-Croat, ibid., p.54.
79. Vecernui List, Zagreb, 9 August 1992.
80. *The New York Times*, Editorial, 6 August 1999.
81. See report by Therese Raphael, *The Wall Street Journal*, 7 July 2000.
82. See Flora Lewis, 'The Kosovo Mission of the UN is Left to Fail', *Herald Tribune*, 10 March 2000, p. 8.
83. Robert Cohen-Tanugi, in *Diaspora/Le Lien*, No. 112, 30 July 1999; No. 117, 22 October 1999; and No. 120, 3 December 1999.

CHAPTER FOUR

The New Muslim Antisemitism: Exploring Novel Avenues of Hatred

The old stereotypes of classical European antisemitism have been copiously replicated in Arab and Muslim writings. Recent Arab-Muslim antisemitism has taken some new forms concurrent with the enhanced antisemitic mood in the West. The main strata of inspiration have not changed substantially, and include Muslim sources, such as calling Jews 'descendants of apes and swines', and borrowings from the Christian themes of blood libel, the *Protocols of the Elders of Zion*, the world Jewish conspiracy, and the various ideas of 'poisoning'. Muslims also continue to utilize the Arab–Israeli conflict to cloak antisemitism as anti-Zionism or anti-Israelism.

What is new, however, is the operationalization of the old stereotypes into concrete acts, ostensibly aimed at countering the 'wild' and uncontrollable conduct of the Zionists and Israelis. This new operationalization of antisemitism appears in many and varied areas, some of which include:

- Using Christians who have succumbed to the *dhimmi* state of mind, both in the Middle East and in Europe, to denigrate Jews and Zionism;
- Expanding the range of hate-mongers from obscurantist clerics to large strata of mainstream intellectuals and professionals;
- Encouraging antisemitism as a legitimate tool to combat Israel;
- Conspicuously adding Holocaust denial to the old Christian themes;

- Elaborating the theme of poisoning to new levels and adapting it to Muslim notions.

The general vilification of Jews goes on unabated, concurrently with the novel manifestations of antisemitism. The demonization of the Jews naturally leads to the demeaning of anything they do, produce, or inspire – such as their movement of national liberation, Zionism, which is seen as racist and vile just as they are, or their state, Israel, which deserves elimination just as they do.

CHRISTIANS AS A TOOL

In an article in Egypt's government-owned daily *al-Ahram*, a Coptic scholar, Dr Babawi, castigated the US Congress for not stopping 'Israel's artillery attacks on the Church of the Nativity and the Al-Aqsa Mosque'. Babawi urged American Muslims and Copts to demonstrate against 'crazy Sharon, who began behaving like a madman after he was hit in his sensitive place by a bullet during the 1948 War, which left him with only one testicle, something that has affected him psychologically, and he has become a psychopath, using power to hide his weakness'.[1]

The article not only used an Arab tradition of sexually demeaning an opponent but also distorted the event at the Church of the Nativity in Bethlehem. Although Palestinians invaded the church at gunpoint, Babawi imputed the moral wrong to Israel, which tried to dislodge them from there. But no one could have missed the point: when a Copt in Egypt, a member of a persecuted minority in an Islamic country, must show that he is more Arab than his compatriots, an anti-Jewish attack was the best way to do it.

In another case, the Bishop of the Assyrian Church in Lebanon asserted that though the heads of today's Church are not Jewish, they are 'led by Jews, whose faith is inimical to God, to the people and to Christianity' – a condemnation aimed at the previous Pope's support for reconciliation with the Jews. Babawi cited Jesus as having said to the Jews: 'You are the sons of Satan, and you practice the will of Satan your father', to which they supposedly answered: 'No, we are not the sons of Satan, we are the sons of Abraham.' But he insisted: 'Had you been the sons of Abraham, you would be acting in accordance with the precepts of Abraham ... You are the sons of Satan.'[2] This delegitimization of the Jews, aimed at gaining favour with the fundamentalist Hizbullah, seemingly defies logic since the dwindling Christian minorities in the Islamic world should presumably make common cause with the Jews. The Muslims, however, pressure the intimidated Christians into justifying the hatred of the Jews.

As noted, many anti-Jewish stereotypes among Muslims are imported from Western Christianity while others are Muslim-made. The parties liberally borrow from each other through the intermediary of the Eastern Christians in the Muslim world, who are conversant in both cultures including with regard to anti-semitism. These Eastern Christians have not been affected by the Catholic Church's reformed approach to Judaism. Indeed, in passing interviews with *al-Manar* Television some Christians compared the Islamikaze[3] martyrs (*shuhada*) of the al-Aqsa *intifada* to Christ's martyrdom, even when Palestinian gunmen invaded the Church of the Nativity:

> We kneel before the Palestinian people in the Church of the Nativity. They starve and thirst, but they are steadfast ... The one who said 'I am hungry' when he was on the Cross was our Lord Jesus himself ... Our Palestinian people in Bethlehem died like a crucified martyr on the rock guarded by Israeli soldiers armed from head to toe who have no compassion, love, life, or tolerance ... The Jew has a principle from which we suffer and which he tries to impose on people, and that is the principle of Gentiles. To him, the Gentile is a slave. They give the Palestinians working in Israel only a piece of bread, and tell them: 'This piece of bread that you eat is taken from our children, and we give it to you so you will live as free men in your land, but as a proletariat and a slave in Israel, to serve us ...'. The *Protocols of the Elders of Zion* are based on this principle, and anyone who reads the *Protocols* feels that we are in this state of affairs with the Jews.[4]

EXPANDING THE SCOPE OF HATRED

In Arab and Muslim publications and media, the scope of anti-semitism has expanded beyond obscurantist clerics or fanatic nationalists to include ostensibly liberal, enlightened, and professional milieus. In this discourse, the interchangeability of Jews, Zionists, and Israelis is unmistakable. All three are alternately threatened with outright extermination. More than two decades after the Israeli–Egyptian peace treaty, the Egyptian psychiatrist Dr Adel Sadeq, who often accuses President Bush and the West of ignorance about the Arab psyche, calls for fighting Israel to the finish:

> What is happening now indicates that Israel will not exist forever. We as Arabs must know that this war will not end ... and anyone who deludes himself that that there will be peace must understand that Israel did not come to this region to love the Arabs or to normalize relations with them ... Either the Israelis or the Palestinians, there is no third option ... There are no Israeli civilians, they are all plunderers, for history teaches this. I am completely convinced that the psychological effect of the Islamikaze on the Israeli usurper will be his realizing that his existence is temporary ... Remove the Apache from the equation, leave them one on one with the Palestinian people with the only weapon being dynamite, then you will see all Israelis leave, because there is not even one Israeli among them willing to don a belt of explosives ... We will throw Israel into the sea, there is no middle ground. Coexistence is total nonsense ... The real means of dealing with Israel directly is those who blow themselves up. According to what I see in the battle arena, there is no other way but the pure, noble Palestinian bodies. This is the only Arab weapon there is, and anyone who says otherwise is a conspirator.[5]

If statements of this sort are made by mainstream opinion makers, often graduates of Western universities at the doctoral level, in such 'moderate' countries as Egypt and Saudi Arabia, how much more so by Islamic fundamentalists and other haters of Israel and

Jews. For instance, in the Egyptian government-owned weekly *October*, founded and edited by Anis Mansur,[6] one of the most virulent antisemites in the Arab world and a close associate of the late Anwar Sadat, a retired general named Hassan Sweilem had this to say:

> Throughout history, since Emperor Justinian and down to Hitler, Europe's rulers had been trying to rid themselves of the acts of violence, barbarism, corruption, conflict-mongering, and other deeds that Jews were, and still are, in the practice of perpetrating in European societies ... like, for example, their domination of monetary systems, treasuries, banks, and commercial monopolies, which has caused widespread bankruptcy and economic destruction. They also disseminate drugs, prostitution, trade in women as sexual slaves, and alcohol. They have also monopolized the gold and precious stone trade, paid bribes to rulers and extorted them throughout history ...
>
> The Jews stood behind wars and internal strife, and that caused European rulers to expel them and kill them. For example, the Crusader armies, passing through the Rhine basin on their way east, massacred them and burned their houses as an act of repentance to their God. When the Crusaders entered Jerusalem, they collected the Jews in a synagogue and burned them live. Their kin in Russia suffered a similar fate ... They were expelled from France, England, Germany, Hungary, Belgium, Slovakia, Austria, Holland, and finally from Spain, after they underwent the Inquisition trials for their conspiracy to penetrate Christian society like a Trojan horse ... The Jewish conspiracy to take over Europe generated civil revolutions, wars, and internal strife ... The Cromwell Revolution failed in 1649 in England, following the Jewish conspiracy to drag England into several wars in Europe ... Then the French Revolution broke out, which the Jews had planned, based on the first conference of their rabbis and interest-loaners that had been convened by the first Rothschild in 1773 in order to take over all the world resources ... That conference adopted twenty-four protocols, including the uprooting of the belief in God from

the hearts of the Gentiles, distracting people by distributing among them literature of heresy and impurity, destruction of the family and eradication of all morality.[7]

This article further 'credited' the Jews with: putting Napoleon on the throne and then causing his demise, the 1776 war between Britain and the nascent United States, establishing the Bank of America with a view to controlling America's wealth, and then instigating the American Civil War. Sweilem also says the *Protocols* were written in 1770 by a German rabbi, financed by Rothschild, again in order 'to destroy all governments and religions, spread anarchy and revolution, trigger wars, take over the wealth of nations, spread corruption among the youth, and control rulers by implanting in their governments Jewish ministers and advisers'. Moreover, he explains that the Jews ordered the start of the First World War, got the United States involved by spreading the rumour that an American ship had been sunk by the Germans, and, during the war, prepared the ground for both Communism and Nazism as an extension of the work of Marx and Engels a half-century earlier. Eventually Communism and Nazism confronted each other, 'exactly as the Jews had planned'. And if this was not enough, the Jews also caused the fall of the Ottoman Empire so as to concentrate wealth in their hands; and the Second World War erupted because of the constraints the Allies imposed on the Germans at Versailles – by order, Sweilem says, of the Jews.[8]

All this, from a mainstream member of the Egyptian elite. Muslim fundamentalists are even more extreme in this regard – as, for example, in the Hamas Charter.[9]

ANTISEMITISM AS A TOOL TO COMBAT ISRAEL

The above *October* article does not present historical findings for scholarly or educational purposes; instead it defames the Jews while warning of the 'dangers' they pose to the world. The implication is that the Jewish state threatens world peace and is therefore illegitimate. These allegations, some of which have been imported from Europe to the Middle East and then re-exported to the West, have become so commonplace that they are not viewed

as propaganda but rather as conventional wisdom and document-
ed history. Almost no intellectual or academic will dare to question their validity lest he be called a 'traitor' to the Arab-Islamic
cause.

Thus, forged citations and made-up 'facts', for which one could
be prosecuted in Western countries, are common currency in
Islamic countries. The misguided masses, who have neither an
interest in the facts nor a way to learn them beyond the propaganda they are exposed to, are reinforced in their antagonism
toward Israel and the Jews.

Palestinian Islamikaze bombings against Israel have often been
couched in anti-Zionist terms and justified in terms of the alleged
machinations and dangers posed by the Jews. An anonymous
Egyptian columnist, for example, like many other Egyptian pundits, specifically urged the Islamikaze to step up their operations
against the Jews, and called for more Muslim volunteers to join
them:

> with every blow struck by Al-Aqsa *intifada*, my conviction
> grows stronger that I, and those like-minded, have been
> right all along, and I am still right in my belief that the
> despised racist Jewish entity will be annihilated. Contrary to
> others, however, I am not ashamed to speak about driving
> them into the sea, to hell or to the trash heap where they
> belong ... I maintain, and Allah is my witness, that the anni-
> hilation and defeat of the Israelis, after which there will be
> no resurrection, does not require all those things. All that is
> required is to concentrate on acts of martyrdom, or what is
> known as the 'strategy of the balance of fear ...'.

Let us do some mathematical calculations: 250
Palestinians have signed up for martyrdom operations, and
it is not impossible to raise their number to 1,000 throughout the Arab world ... i.e., one *fida'i* out of every 250,000
Arabs. The average harvest of each act of martyrdom is 10
dead and 50 wounded. Thus, 1000 acts of martyrdom would
leave the Zionists with at least 10,000 dead and 50,000
wounded. This is double the Israeli casualties in all their
wars with the Arabs since 1948 [sic].[10] They cannot bear this.
There is also the added advantage, not noted by many, of the

negative Jewish emigration which as a result of 1,000 martyrdom operations, will come to at least one million Jews,
followed by the return of every Jew to the place whence he
came ...

I am signing myself up as the first martyr from Egypt and
declare that I am ready to commit an act of martyrdom at
any moment. I will place myself under the command of
Hassan Nasrallah, Hamas, Islamic Jihad and any other jihad
movement ... Never in my life have I asked Allah for money,
honour or power. All I have asked, all I ask, all I will ask, is
that Allah allow me to become a *shahid* and grant me the
honour of reaping as great a harvest as possible of Israeli
lives.[11]

This statement, which appeared in a mainstream journal in a
country that had signed a peace treaty with Israel more than two
decades earlier, did not encounter the least objection from other
writers, the authorities, or human rights groups anywhere.
Instead, it was echoed in other Islamic media. From Iran came
reports of funds raised to support Palestinian 'suicide operations'
against Israel, as well as promises from Teheran to Islamic Jihad
that its financial assistance would no longer be channelled
through Hizbullah but disbursed directly to it.[12] Israel is perceived
as a danger to the entire region, not just the Palestinians, and
Ayatollah Khomeini was cited as proclaiming that:

> the goal of this virus Israel, that was planted in the heart of
> the Muslim world, is not only to annihilate the Arab nation
> but also Islam. Therefore the solution is to annihilate this
> virus, for there is no other treatment ... The Islamic states
> and the Muslims should initiate the annihilation of this den
> of corruption in every possible way. It is permitted to use
> charity money for that purpose.[13]

Similar calls to 'annihilate the Jews' have become routine in
Muslim mosques and in the writings of Saudi and other Muslim
writers.[14]

HOLOCAUST DENIAL

Holocaust denial is not new in Muslim countries, which have sponsored lecture tours by 'revisionist historians' while also prohibiting the screening of *Schindler's List*. But recently, especially since the eruption of the al-Aqsa *intifada*, this has become a favourite pastime.

Holocaust denial assists in sustaining the long-standing accusations against the Jews, who are charged with 'cultivating that legend and turning it into a fact that ties the hands of historians'.[15] The Jews are also condemned for 'forging history', a charge that dates back to the inception of Islam, despite the 'constant refutation by scientific articles that have proved that there have never been gas chambers, or that the numbers of the dead were significantly lower'.[16] It is also claimed that the Jews actually benefited from the Second World War, since if Japan and Germany had won, the Jews 'could not have continued to blackmail the gentiles with their lies'.[17] Abu Mazen, the purportedly moderate successor of Yasser Arafat, devoted a doctoral thesis to Holocaust denial that was eventually published as a book.[18]

From denying or downplaying the Holocaust to accusing the Jews of conspiring with Nazism against their own people, as Abu Mazen and others have done, the road is short to defending Hitler against the 'offences' caused him by the Jews and their supporters. Following Western and Israeli protests to the Egyptian government about the widespread sympathy for Hitler in the Egyptian and Arab press in general,[19] the government-owned daily *al-Akhbar* relented only briefly before returning to its fascination with the Nazi despot. This time a cleric from al-Azhar University, Mahmud Khadr, titled his contribution 'In Defence of Hitler' and condemned not only Israel and the Jews but also the West:

> Hitler and many of his ministers took their own lives so that they would not have to see the faces of the old ape, Churchill, and the big bear, Stalin, who would sentence them to death with no one to defend them ... Each one of them has a right to his defence ... but Hitler's executioners took his right away and attributed to him crimes whether he

committed them or not. I do not know what would have happened to Roosevelt, Churchill and de Gaulle, had Hitler won. Perhaps the crimes for which they deserve the death sentence would have been much worse than all that Hitler had done ...

But all of Hitler's crimes and infractions were forgotten, except for the crime that was exaggerated and blown completely out of proportion, thanks to the insistence of world Zionism to continue to stoke the fire. The reason for this was the emotional need of the sons of Jacob to extort Germany and to eat away at its resources. It is amazing that Westerners, who are entitled to their own thinking, to confirming or denying anything, including the existence of the Prophets of Allah, cannot address the Jewish question, or more precisely the false Holocaust, whose numbers and scope they have exaggerated, until it has reached the level of the merciless destruction of six million Jews, only because Hitler saw them as an inferior race unworthy of living next to the Germanic race, which must rule the world ...

Anyone who knocks on this door is accused of the most horrible things, and is tried in all Western courts for anti-semitism ... for two reasons: one is due to Zionist control of thinking in the world and the degree of oppression of thought by the Zionist propaganda apparatus in those nations. No one can oppose this oppression for fear of going to prison or having his livelihood or reputation threatened ... The second is the fear that the lies of Zionism would be exposed if the subject of the Holocaust is investigated factually and the logical conclusions are drawn ...

The first dubious fact is the number of six million Jews who were burnt in the gas chambers. Did they have children or families who demanded compensation, or did Zionism see itself as their heir? If we assume that everyone had an average of five family members, this would bring the number of the Jews affected to 30 million. It is certain that many Jews escaped before the ship sunk, that many of them survived, despite the so-called extermination and burning. This would mean that the number of Jews in Germany amounted to 60 million, although the total number of Germans has never reached this many ... Even if we cross off one zero from the six million and we are left with a tenth of this number, it would still seem exaggerated and would have to be investigated.[20]

It is difficult to imagine that the writer did not verify the number of Germany's population during the war, or that most of the exterminated Jews were not German but Polish, Baltic, or Soviet, or that in many cases entire Jewish families, often over three generations, were decimated, with no heir left behind to claim damages. All these manipulations of numbers are taken from the books of Holocaust deniers and are aimed at diminishing its dimensions and accusing the Jews of inflating them. A corollary of this line of thought has been to claim that since Hitler had no reason to exterminate so many Jews, therefore he did not. But Holocaust deniers, including Arabs and Muslims, are caught in the contradiction of both lessening its numbers and citing the alleged 'threat' that the Jews posed to the Germans, hence the 'imperative' to eliminate them.

POISONING AS THE ULTIMATE JEWISH CONSPIRACY

The constant use of the *Protocols* and the blood libel in the Arab media, especially in new tele-novellas and 'documentaries' during the peak viewing month of Ramadan, creates an ambience in which any charge against the Jews is readily believed and repeated in other media as well. This is no less true in countries such as Jordan and Egypt that supposedly have made peace with Israel.

Among such claims the most virulent type deals with poisoning, and originates from the well-poisoning myth of classical European antisemitism. Arafat often accused Israel of distributing poisoned sweets to Palestinian children, or using depleted uranium in bullets so as to sexually incapacitate Palestinian fighters and thus diminish their numbers. At the height of this campaign, the Palestinian representative to the UN Human Rights Commission in Geneva, Dr Abdallah Ramlawi, said Israel had injected three hundred Palestinian children with HIV-positive serum so as to impair their reproductive organs.

When Israel sent experts to Egypt to develop high-tech

agriculture in the Nile Delta, with successful results, media reports claimed these Jews had come to Egypt, which did not need them and had sufficient agricultural know-how, only to poison Egypt's soil and destroy its age-old, sophisticated farming. Newspapers also recycled the allegation that Israel had distributed throughout the Arab world an aphrodisiac chewing gum aimed at stoking Muslim women's sexual desire so as to lead them astray.

Perhaps most notable in this regard was the accusation, initiated by Palestinians and then embellished by other Arabs and Muslims, the United Nations, the European press, and even the Red Cross, about Israel 'poisoning school girls' in the Jenin district of the West Bank. This story became a *cause célèbre* in March and April 1983, despite the fact that several investigations by Israeli and international bodies found it totally false.[21] No one outside Israel, however, criticized the Palestinians, and the other Arabs and Muslims, for this hoax, and they concluded that they could spread such fabrications with impunity. After the September 11 attack and the anthrax panic in the United States, the Egyptian scientific journal *al-'Ilm* turned the tables on America and Israel, by accusing them of committing war crimes with weapons of mass destruction:

> In the summer of 1949 cholera spread throughout Egypt, following the establishment of Israel in 1948. Egyptian documents indicate that the disease originated from Israel ... The US used germs in Vietnam and against North Korea and China ... Biological weapons research is being conducted by Israeli universities. Prior to the October War of 1973, they injected birds with germs and released them above Jordan, Palestine and the Suez Canal ... The US and Israel keep biological weapons at American bases; if they were to be used, they would destroy half the population of the area under attack. Some of this weaponry makes women miscarry ...
>
> Also, Jewish tourists infected with AIDS are travelling around Asian and African countries with the aim of spreading the disease ... It is no coincidence that the US is the only member of the UN that has not signed the agreement on punishment for the collective annihilation of people ... Israel

continues to use germ warfare to destroy the Palestinian people on its occupied land, thus challenging the international community.[22]

SUMMING UP

Antisemitic notions are so widespread in the Arab and Islamic worlds that they are taken for granted. Children are 'educated' in their light, adults with university degrees read and write about them in the press, clerics preach them in mosques, politicians invoke them in speeches, and the media generally abound with them. Antisemitism has indeed become a basic part of education and socialization in these countries. The governments, including those that have signed peace agreements with Israel, do nothing to discourage the phenomenon and often wink in approval. These expressions, including those emanating from the cultural hub of the Arab world, Egypt, are widely circulated and create a 'demand' for more.

Israel's own leniency toward this phenomenon, its failure to insist on its elimination as a condition for diplomatic exchange, contributes to its persistence. Simply demanding an end to anti-Jewish incitement in Muslim countries would not be enough; a mechanism would also be needed to monitor and curtail it. When Jorg Haider's Freedom Party joined the Austrian coalition in 2000, the Israeli government immediately recalled its ambassador from Vienna even though Haider had retracted his pro-Nazi statements. The antisemitic statements of Arab politicians, clerics, intellectuals, and pundits are, however, much more severe, prevalent, and persistent, yet Israel does not address the phenomenon seriously.

If Israel and world Jewry wish to combat Islamic and Arab antisemitism, this state of affairs cannot persist. Only if Muslims and Arabs are made to pay a heavy price for their encouragement of hatred and violence will their governments move to curb these phenomena in the education systems, media, mosque sermons, and political statements. Only the West is capable of levying such a price through pressures, sanctions, and threats, backed by action when necessary. A determination by the West to combat antisemitism in all its forms is the prerequisite for mitigating it in the Muslim world. It is primarily Israel that must insist that the West take on this role.

NOTES

This was first published in the *Jewish Political Studies Review*, 17, 3–4 (Fall 2005), pp.97–108.

1. *Al-Ahram* (Egypt), 25 April 2002 (Arabic).
2. *Al-Manar* Television (Lebanon–Hizbullah), 24 April 2002 (Arabic).
3. A term coined by the present author in his book *Islamikaze: Manifestations of Islamic Martyrology* (London: Frank Cass, 2003), from a combination of Islam and Kamikaze, designating what is commonly (and mistakenly) referred to as 'suicide bombers'.
4. Ibid.
5. *Iqra'* Television (Saudi Arabia and Egypt), 24 April 2002 (Arabic). See Memri 373, 30 April 2002.
6. For some of his most extreme condemnations of the Jews, see Raphael Israeli, *Peace is in the Eye of the Beholder* (Berlin and New York: Mouton, 1985), esp. the concluding chapter.
7. *October* (Egypt), 17 June 2001 (Arabic).
8. Ibid.
9. Raphael Israeli, *Fundamentalist Islam and Israel* (New York: University Press of America, 1993), pp.123–70.
10. In fact the number of Israeli fatalities has long surpassed twenty thousand, fourfold the author's estimate.
11. *Al-Usbu'* (Egypt), 28 May 2001 (Arabic). See Memri 224, 4 June 2001.
12. *Al-Sharq al-Awsat* (London), 8 June 2002 (Arabic).
13. *Al-Manar* Television (Lebanon–Hizbullah), 2 June 2002 (Arabic).
14. *Al-Mustaqbal* (Lebanon), 19 March 2002 (Arabic); *al-'Ukadh* (Saudi Arabia), 22 November 2001 (Arabic); *al-Riyadh* (Saudi Arabia), 22 November 2001 (Arabic).
15. *Al-Wafd* (Egypt), 13 February 2000 (Arabic); *al-Ahram* (Egypt), 19 April 2000 (Arabic); *Egyptian Gazette*, 20 April 2000 (Arabic).
16. *Al-Ahram* (Egypt), 30 December 1999 (Arabic).
17. *Al-Hayat* (London). 31 January 2000 (Arabic); *al-Akhbar* (Egypt), 26 January 2000 (Arabic); *al-Ahram* (Egypt), 18 April, 17 May 2000 (Arabic); *Egyptian Gazette*, 17 April 2000 (Arabic), etc.
18. *The Secret Ties between the Nais and the Zionist Movement Leadership* (Amman: Dar Ibn Rushd, 1984) (Arabic).
19. See Israeli, *Peace is in the Eye of the Beholder*, esp. pp.33–4, 231, 326.
20. *Al-Akhbar* (Egypt), 27 May 2001 (Arabic). See Memri 231, 20 June 2001.
21. See Raphael Israeli, *Poison: Manifestations of a Blood Libel* (New York and Oxford: Lexington Books, 2002).
22. *Al-'Ilm* (Egypt), November 2001 (Arabic). See Memri 322, 28 December 2001.

PART II

THE EMERGING PALESTINIAN ENTITY

CHAPTER FIVE

From Oslo to Bethlehem:
Arafat's Islamic Message

When town after town of the West Bank and Gaza passed into Palestinian Authority (PA) hands following the Oslo II Agreement (1995) that was designed to facilitate the transition from Israeli occupation to Palestinian self-rule, Yasser Arafat, president of the PA, began to manifest some surprising traits in his statesmanship. Most notable for someone viewed as a secular leader is his profound Islamic commitment, which harks back to his membership in the Muslim Brethren in Egypt during his formative years. The issue of Islam is of particular interest, due to Arafat's attempts to juggle between new-found pragmatism as a statesman (who has, to all appearances, chosen the road of political settlement with Israel, at least prior to the resumption of the *intifada* in the autumn of 2000), and his innate propensity for doctrinal and vindictive rhetoric. Arafat must strike a balance between his proclaimed obligation to compromise – requiring him to set aside some of his long-held Islamic convictions which had helped him mobilize Palestinian public opinion behind him – and his need to placate his most dangerous opposition, namely, Hamas[1] and Islamic Jihad (holy war), which refuse to shed the very same convictions Arafat once held, continuing instead to embrace and profess them openly.

This essay will examine whether Arafat is in fact bound by one particular set of principles (with the other being merely tactical rhetoric), and whether he espouses any particular ideology only when it appears to him at a particular time to best reflect his and his people's interest. In other words, is there a way to read between the lines of his ambiguous rhetoric and statements to gauge 'the real Arafat'? Can one predict PLO and Palestinian policies based on Arafat's patently unclear messages laced with double meanings?

THE DOUBLE-TALK OF REDEMPTION

True to his personal rhetorical tradition, Arafat pursued his Islamic discourse with eagerly receptive audiences when he oversaw the process of retrieving from Israel the West Bank towns of Jenin, Tulkarem, Qalqiliya, Bethlehem and Ramallah in late 1995 and early 1996. In the process another town, Nablus, the hub of Palestinian nationalism in the West Bank, became the focus of an anti-Israeli explosion of sentiment associated with Arafat's rhetoric of redemption. After all, 'Nablus oblige', one might say.

The abandonment by Israel of Palestinian cities to Arafat's fledgling rule was traumatic to both parties, though it had something equally redemptive about it: it gave vent to all the tensions that had accumulated during twenty-eight years of Israel's unwelcome domination. It created at the same time an ambiance of uncertainty, borne of the quasi-messianic expectation that Palestinian rule would inaugurate a new era of justice and plenty, coupled with the realization that existing social, political, and economic difficulties might seriously hamper this exciting experiment. One thing was certain: the historical scope and import of these momentous events. To rise to the occasion, Arafat had to cater to the predominant mood of excitement and hope by injecting into his speeches in practically all those cities the same redemptory themes: liberty, independence, Jerusalem as the capital, the continuation of jihad, struggle to victory.

Most of these themes are imbued with Islamic symbols and history. They are shrouded in an aura of myth, especially when Arafat himself posed, or came to be seen, as the Messiah-redeemer or Mahdi who would inaugurate this new era. Indeed, in every case when travelling to the cities in question, Palestinian crowds awaiting him clamoured cries of ecstasy upon seeing his helicopters approaching to land. Loudspeakers announced the coming of the chairman, and urged the masses to 'swear allegiance' to the president. In Bethlehem, where Arafat's inaugural visit coincided with Christmas celebrations, the entire landing ceremony, reviewing of the guard of honour, and worldwide broadcast of Christmas, were all announced over the Voice of Palestine radio and television stations as if they were all part of one great sequence.

Arafat's oratory in general leaves much to be desired. However, his habit of using repetitious phrases, easily remembered slogans, a colloquial style of speech, and popular imagery do touch deep chords in the souls of his audiences; he succeeds in creating an intimate discourse with them. He always addresses the masses that encounter him in personal terms, such as 'Brothers', 'Sisters', 'Beloved members of the family', 'Members of my tribe', etc.[2] Once he has introduced himself to his audience, he invariably invokes Jerusalem as a powerful unifying and mobilizing symbol. In every case, he lists each of the towns and villages so far 'liberated', and vows to 'march into Jerusalem' or to 'pray in Jerusalem' at the end of the peace process. He refers to Jerusalem as 'al-Quds a-Sharif' (Jerusalem the Noble), or 'al-Quds al-'arabiyya' (Arab Jerusalem), the former signifying 'all of Jerusalem' in Arab and Arafat's parlance, the latter designating East Jerusalem (the part of the city claimed by the Palestinians as their capital). Arafat also invokes the sacredness of the land. In Bethlehem, Arafat referred to 'our blessed land' which witnessed the birth of 'our Palestinian Messiah, Blessed be His Memory'. Thus, Arafat connects 'his' Palestine to the 'blessed land' with its messianic message, and then widens the scope of his Islamic commitment to Palestine to embrace Christianity as well, for the Christian Arabs of Palestine are as Palestinian as its Muslims, since Christ Himself was Palestinian. This ecumenical message, which makes Islam and Christianity (to the exclusion of Judaism) the twin divine revelations of Palestine, legitimizes Arafat as the curator and protector of the Holy Places of both faiths. It turns the PLO and its head into the representative and partner of world Christianity as well as world Islam in Holy Jerusalem. Thus Arafat tries to portray himself as a better, and more universally accepted, ruler of the city than the Israeli.

Nothing epitomized this new garb donned by Arafat better than the well-publicized and widely reported visit by his wife Suha (a former Christian who converted to Islam as a prerequisite to their marriage) to the Church of Nativity with her newborn daughter, as if to proclaim that his Islam and her Christianity were happily wed together and jointly perpetuated in the persona of little Zahwa. Of course, Arafat would not admit to this union of the two great religions on unequal terms: his wife had to convert, after all, while he did not. Their daughter is Muslim, not Christian, because she was born of a Muslim father. But his *beau geste* of extending his loving care to Christianity in Palestine immediately attracted the interpretation that he coveted and had probably intended: the Greek-Orthodox Patriarch of Jerusalem declared to a delighted Arafat on that occasion, 'Here is the successor of Sophronius welcoming the successor of 'Umar ibn al-Khattab. No one present or watching on television could miss the parallel. Reference was made, of course, to the submission of the Byzantine Patriarch of Jerusalem, Sophronius, in AD 638 to the second Caliph of Islam, 'Umar ibn al-Khattab (634–644), who conquered Jerusalem for Islam and put an end to many centuries of Christian rule. Until the Crusaders established in 1099 the Christian kingdom of Jerusalem, the city was to remain, uninterruptedly, part and parcel of Dar al Islam, the universal *Pax Islamica*. This modern-day declaration of the patriarch was so melodious to Arafat's ear that he ordered all his media to publish it in their headlines. The public learned of his command only when an ill-advised and independent-minded journalist (the night editor of the daily *Al-Quds*, Mahir al-'Alami) refused to comply, and soon found himself arrested and interrogated in the dark basements of Jibril Rajub's security apparatus in Jericho.[3] Arafat's eagerness to widely publicize the patriarch's sycophancy did not stem from his intention to humiliate the latter, nor only because he was pleased by the flattering comparison with the Great Caliph 'Umar, but because such a statement confirmed his newly acquired, glamorous image as the new 'liberator' of Jerusalem.

Thus Arafat was placed as the latest link in the chain of great Islamic liberators, which to date includes 'Umar as well as Saladin who recaptured Jerusalem in 1187 and put an end to Crusader rule there. If one bears in mind the oft-made comparison in Arab and Islamic circles between the medieval Crusader state and contemporary Israel, one necessarily comes to the conclusion that exactly as 'Umar had occupied Jerusalem by peaceful means (namely, the surrender of the Christians) and Saladin by force (by the conquest of the city and the eviction or massacre of its inhabitants), so will Arafat now repeat that feat either by accepting the surrender of at least East Jerusalem by the Israelis, or by pressing his call for jihad in order to retrieve all of it. Many

Palestinian circles (especially Muslim fundamentalists[4]) take delight in this parallel and are quick to draw conclusions from it. 'Umar and Saladin had been accepted as the legitimate rulers of Jerusalem following the oath of allegiance (*bay'a*) accorded them by the crowds. Now, as the loudspeakers were enjoining the populace to deliver the oath of allegiance to the president, the parallel became neat, complete, and inescapable. History had come full circle.

This outpouring of religiosity and Islamic symbolism by Arafat is consistent not only with his many speeches from Johannesburg to Gaza, in which Jerusalem, jihad, and other Islamic symbols have been repeatedly invoked, but also with Palestinian nationalist antecedents where Islam has played a prominent role. Indeed, since the 1920s the Palestinian national movement was headed by a religious leader, the Mufti of Jerusalem, Haj Amin al-Husseini (similar to Makarios, Archbishop of the Greek-Orthodox in Cyprus, or Bishop Muzurewa in Rhodesia). As such, it relied upon religious themes to shape the opposition to British rule and to Zionism. Moreover, in the 1930s, Izz a-Din al-Qassam, a Syrian Muslim who settled in Haifa, undertook extensive religious, political, and educational activities in northern Palestine that soon lent prominence to his leadership. He then founded a militant group, the Black Hand, as an instrument of armed struggle against both British imperialism and Jewish Zionism. Al-Qassam called openly for jihad against both until the British killed him in battle in 1935.

During the Palestinian Revolt (1936–39), the Muslim Brethren, based in Egypt, established a number of lodges in Palestine that in later years grew into a fully fledged network of the Brotherhood. The Muslim Brothers' activities later developed into a two-pronged activism (like al-Qassam's antecedent): struggle against British occupation and the Zionist menace. The 1948 War between Israel and the Arabs split the Palestinian-Arab population into an Israeli-ruled minority and a Jordanian-governed and Egyptian-governed majority in the West Bank and Gaza respectively, where the Muslim Brothers continued to swell their ranks in spite of their frequent clashes with the authorities there. The occupation by Israel of the West Bank and Gaza in the 1967 War again brought the entire Palestinian population west of the Jordan

River under Israeli rule. Paradoxically, the Muslim movements could thrive under Israeli rule, since it allowed them leeway in their overt activities so long as they did not contravene the law.

Conversely, Israel's penetration into the social, political, and economic realms of life of Palestinians contributed to the destruction of the last vestiges of their old hierarchies and loyalties, and hastened their modernization, much to the outrage (and detriment) of Muslim fundamentalists who sensed that Israel was undermining their traditional Islamic society and turning it away from Islam. The seeds of a renewed open conflict between the fundamentalists and the Israelis were thus sown in the already fertile ground of the anti-Israeli sentiment prepared by the PLO and Palestinian nationalists who had also rejected Israeli rule over them for secular reasons. Hence the eruption during the *intifada* of Hamas, which was galvanized into a zealous Islamic group (by definition) encompassing most Islamic fundamentalist currents of the day. It is worth noting, however, that latter-day fundamentalist groups did not monopolize these elements of Islam. Even mainstream Palestinian nationalism, like most local forms of Arab nationalism, have made use of Islam to characterize enemies, to imply modes of action against them, and to define the nature of the Palestinian community and its struggle, thus linking key religious and secular concepts.[5]

For example, jihad is linked with the armed struggle of the PLO – the commitment to fight imperialism linked with the fight against Zionism (itself considered to be an extension of imperialism). Both concepts are joined together in a contemporary rendition of the first historical armed entry of the West into the Muslim world since the Crusaders. When the PLO refers to its casualties as *shuhada* (martyrs), and to its guerrillas as *fedayeen* (self-sacrificers), it implies the redemption (in the Muslim sense of the concept) to be won from dying for one's homeland.[6] Similarly, the modern struggle against Jews, Zionists, and Israelis (terms often used interchangeably) harks back to the old Muslim–Jewish enmity during the time of the Prophet. Thus, when Arafat made the pilgrimage to Mecca in 1978, he vowed to liberate Palestine, including Jerusalem, from Israeli occupation. Even the secular document of the Palestinian Charter (adopted in 1964 and amended in 1968) is interspersed with concepts that can be seen as Islamic, such as sacrifice, struggle, and armed struggle; Article 16 itself refers to the issue of Palestine as a holy land with religious sites. At the Algiers Conference at which the Palestinians declared their independence (15 November 1988), Arafat referred to Jerusalem as a capital city, and he has been repeating that statement ever since.

PLO manipulation of Islamic symbols should be no surprise, for Islam is too important to Palestinian culture to ignore. However, while the PLO and now the PA handle Islam by controlling it, the fundamentalists are so passionate and so impatient that they would turn Islam into a way of life, thus challenging Arafat's secularism. So long as Arafat was struggling, like the fundamentalists, to achieve a state, he could afford to indulge in Islamic, as well as nationalistic, rhetoric, in order to mobilize the masses behind him. Indeed, Bernard Lewis has shown that Arafat's *nom de guerre* (Abu Ammar), as well as his rhetoric ('Bismillah', 'jihad', etc.), have Islamic connotations. So too have the names of the Palestine Liberation Army's regiments: al-Aqsa (refers to the mosque in Jerusalem), Hittin (Saladin's victory over the Crusaders), Ein Jalut (victory against the Mongol invasion), etc.[7] In other words, the profuse usage of Islam by Arafat has so compellingly depicted him as an Islamic leader – and not just a national leader – that he cannot disengage from that image in the process of achieving autonomy and statehood.

HAMAS CHALLENGE

During the months of negotiations leading to the Oslo Accords of September 1993, Arafat was remarkably reticent in his Islamic utterances, presumably because he had set out to attain a political-quantitative agreement based on compromise and ambiguity which otherwise might have evaded him had he insisted on the qualitative and unyielding rhetoric of Islam. On the contrary, he spoke about recognition of Israel, not denial of her rights; of the end to war and violence, not of jihad, struggle, and bloodshed; of negotiations and good intentions, not of endless *shuhada'* and sacrifice. But no sooner had the agreement been signed than Arafat was attacked by groups of his own people for having abandoned his Islamic message and relinquished the Islamic consensus that

had previously united most Palestinians. Moreover, the polarization between Arafat and his opponents from Hamas and the
Islamic jihad grew so acute, and the tensions between them esca-
lated so rapidly, that it was seen as only a matter of time before
an all-out civil war erupted.

The challenge posed by Hamas to Arafat was no mere rebellion
against his authority by an insignificant faction of the
Palestinians. Rather, it was a viable and popular alternative
offered to the Palestinian public that was just emerging from the
intifada. During that uprising against Israel, which tore apart the
West Bank and Gaza from 1987, Hamas had carved for itself an
important following in the Palestinian streets, precisely by being
more demanding, violent, and unbending than the 'National
Leadership' sponsored by the PLO. And they achieved great success, not only in fighting the Israelis and inflicting heavy casualties on them, but also in building a network of welfare and religious education institutions, in fighting crime, corruption, and
drugs, and in filling the vacuum of authority left behind by the
withdrawing Israelis. What is more, in many of the Palestinian
professional organizations (doctors, lawyers, accountants, teachers, etc.), as well as in student bodies in the universities of the
West Bank and Gaza, all of which held elections even at the
height of the *intifada*, Hamas candidates often scored more highly than PLO members, thereby enhancing the prestige of the
movement among intellectuals.[8]

The core of the Hamas programme[9] poses no less of an ideological threat to the PLO political view than the challenge of the
Muslim militants to Arafat's constituency. For while the post-Oslo
PLO is committed, on record, to negotiate and shun violence,
Hamas, like other Muslim fundamentalists, holds an unbending
view that only jihad – to liberate all of Palestine – will ensure the
victory of Allah. They have also vowed that the land must be
cleansed from the viciousness and impurity of its occupiers – the
Israelis, since only under Islamic rule is there any possibility for
other faiths to coexist. They claim that when Islam does not prevail, then bigotry, hatred, controversy, corruption, oppression,
war, and bloodshed follow, as evidenced by the existence of
Israel. Israel is hated as an occupier who, due to its Jewish constituency (described as 'the scum of the earth'), also concocts

plots to take over the world and corrupts societies from within. Hence the Muslim obligation, following the model of the Prophet, to fight the Israelis and kill them wherever they can be found, or at least ban them from Islamic lands if they refuse to submit to its beneficent hegemony.

Domestically, Hamas strives to establish an Islamic entity as part of the Islamic world that must be governed by the Caliphate. In such a state, 'Allah is the ultimate goal, the Qur'an its constitution, jihad its means, death for the cause of Allah its sublimest aspiration'.[10] Such a state is imperative because Allah had granted Palestine to His elected nation, the Muslims, as *waqf* (a holy endowment) until the end of all days. Therefore, Muslims cannot negotiate it away or strike any compromise over it, and any bilateral negotiation or international conference geared to that end is but a 'waste of time'. The only possible solution then is a *Pax Islamica* in which Islam reigns supreme and the members of the other faiths bow their heads in obedience to the generous provisions of the *shari'a* law. Jihad, the means of attaining such a state, ought not to remain a collective duty (*fard kifaya*), which would not be binding on every individual once the Muslim community as a whole has discharged it; quite the contrary, because the 'House of Islam' is aflame, it becomes incumbent upon every individual Muslim to extinguish the fire with his own bucket of water, namely, to fight jihad as a personally binding duty (*fard 'ayn*).

With such a radically different program from that of the official PLO, and in view of Arafat's inability to prove that his own version of national salvation is operative and effective, the temptation arose among Muslim militants to try the fundamentalist alternative. Success breeds success: after the Islamic revolution in Iran and the Sudan, and its near-takeover in Algeria and Afghanistan, the winds blew ever stronger in the Hamas sails. Arafat, conscious of the challenge, tried on various occasions to harness Hamas to the PLO, and of late has attempted to press them to join the system by offering them participation in the 1996 elections for the Palestinian Legislative Council. However, exactly as they had rejected his earlier proposal to join the PLO on the grounds that he was not allocating them sufficient seats in the Palestinian National Council commensurate with their real strength, they have now opposed the elections, claiming that participation would imply acquiescence in the Oslo process, which they had rejected outright.

And so, the Hamas challenge continues to irritate Arafat and to pose a mortal danger to him in more ways than one: not only can Hamas mount lethal attacks on Israel, which would force her to retaliate and wreck the Oslo process, but if they became popular enough (thanks to their stand against Israel), they may even dislodge Arafat and his Authority. Indeed, in places like universities, Muslim militants have coalesced with Habash's Popular Front and Hawatmeh's Democratic Front to win over a majority of the student body opposed to Oslo and to Arafat's policies. Arafat, either eager not to be overtaken on the right by the Islamists, or to return to his genuine self, has taken over the fundamentalists' vocabulary and jargon. True, Arafat does not openly resort to the same overtly anti-Semitic language used by Hamas and other Muslim fundamentalist groups[11] (perhaps for fear of losing his western support), but his militant Islamic message is no less acute and history-laden.

THE HUDAYBIYYA MODEL

Merely six months after the fanfare surrounding the signature of the Oslo Accords of September 1993, Arafat was on a visit to Johannesburg, South Africa, for the inauguration of President Nelson Mandela, his longstanding friend. Quite incidentally, and confident of the privacy and intimacy required for discourse with his local fellow Muslims gathered in the mosque of Johannesburg, he shared with them his thinking about the peace process that he had inaugurated with Israel, and entreated them to join jihad in order to recover Jerusalem. He also compared the Oslo Agreements to the Hudaybiyya Treaty concluded by the Prophet of Islam. When Arafat's words became known in the spring of 1994 with the release of a tape recorded by a reporter who attended that gathering incognito, a major storm swept Israel, with a part of its people feeling they had been duped at Oslo. Expectedly, the proponents of the Accords denigrated Arafat's words as insignificant rhetoric, while opponents seized them as 'proof' of his double-talk. Arafat himself, visibly shaken by the scandal that his words (meant to be uttered discreetly) had prompted once made public, explained via aides that his jihad meant 'peaceful means', and that he continued to be bound by the agreement made in Oslo.

However, careful observers in Israel and elsewhere continued to monitor his public addresses in order to determine whether his Johannesburg speech was a slip of the tongue, or part of a recurring pattern indicative of his genuine thinking.[12] This exercise has revealed that even when we do not know what Arafat says in the privacy of his councils, there is enough in his public parlance to suggest a recurring duplicity in his speeches in the Gaza Islamic College, climaxing in Bethlehem.

This is how Arafat was introduced on Palestine Television during a ceremony at Gaza's al-Azhar University on the day celebrating the *Mi'raj*:[13]

> This is the Commander, this is the man,
> His face is like a bright sunny day ...
> May Allah grant him noble qualities of manhood ...
> The leader of this nation, whom Allah watches over ...
> Allah! Allah! Allah!
> Let us see Abu Ammar lead us to jihad ...[14]
> In Jerusalem, in al-Aqsa we shall meet. [15]

And then came Arafat's turn to speak:

> My brethren, we are a sacrificing and fighting nation ... A Jerusalem *hadith* says: A group within my nation cling to my Faith and fight their enemies ... They cannot be harmed and they will win, with Allah's help. The Messenger of God asked, 'Who are they?' He answered, 'In Jerusalem ... in Jerusalem and its environs ... They stand at the forefront until Judgment Day...'.
>
> We are at the forefront, fighters at the forefront ... I said I saw a tunnel, and at the end of the tunnel are the walls of Jerusalem, with its mosques and churches ...
>
> And today, on the day Muhammad ascended to Heaven, we say: Blessed is he who goes forth from the mosque of Mecca to al-Aqsa.[16] We will enter the mosque and pray there, with Allah's help. Allah does not break his promise.

Oh Brethren, the battle is long, very long and harsh ... The Palestinian people have always sacrificed ... generation after generation. We are at a war of 100 years ... a war in all spheres: political, military, a war of history and culture, of perseverance and survival, since the first Zionist Congress in Basel ...

When the Prophet made peace with the tribe of Quraysh [at Hudaybiyya], 'Umar ibn-al-Khattab said: stop. Had we known when we acclaimed you as Allah's Messenger, we would never have fought for you'.

Umar even called it the 'despised peace'... . Our history is our best teacher, and no nation can be detached from its history ... We are a direct continuation of that nation and this land ... Bless you! Bless your struggle and your jihad on this land ... We shall press on to Jerusalem, capital of the state of Palestine ... This revolution began on 1 January 1965.[17]

Fighters in this revolution ... are the sons of Izz a-Din al-Qassam.[18] We renew our oath to the martyrs, and our oath of loyalty to Jerusalem, capital of our land in Palestine ... In the name of Allah the Merciful, we will redeem the downtrodden of the earth and make them leaders and heirs, and we will give them the land.

We will bring victory to our Messengers and to the Believers in this world and the next, thus said the Lord.

Delirious crowds shouted: 'We shall give our blood and souls for you, Palestine!' Arafat continues:

I say that all of us are made for martyrdom. Hence, I say to all the martyrs who have died, on behalf of the martyrs who still live ... that we stand by our oath to pursue [the battle] ... Be patient, our men and women prisoners, be patient, Ahmad Yasin.[19]

The same symbolism and vocabulary were repeated by Arafat in various gatherings in Gaza and elsewhere, culminating in the Christmas ceremony at the closure of 1995 in Bethlehem. Taken together with, and corroborating what had been said in Johannesburg, the following patterns emerge in his addresses:

a. Arafat purports to abide by the precedent set by the Prophet Muhammad in making the peace of Hudaybiyya ('History is our best teacher'). This means that expedient peace can be made with enemies, which can be broken when circumstances so warrant.
b. The fact that 'Umar had dubbed this peace 'despicable', even when sanctioned by the Prophet himself, could justify *a priori* its breach, again when circumstances justify.
c. Arafat learned from the experience of Hamas successes that blood-and-sweat discourses, with promises of protracted struggles and endless sacrifices, are paradoxically much more soothing, appealing and credible to the masses than empty pledges of a rosy life and easy victories. Harsh language not only justifies the martyrs of the past in this hundred-year war: it also mobilizes and encourages the new generation of *shuhada'*. The Islamic calls for jihad (and the certitude of divine retribution as a result) were found by Arafat to be more cajoling to the hearts of the populace, and he invoked them repeatedly.
d. Jerusalem is the ultimate prize, the jewel in the crown of the Holy Land. It is the prime rallying point for Muslims from Johannesburg to Gaza. For Arafat, Jerusalem is primarily Islamic and secondarily Christian (Arafat saw in his dreams mosques and churches, not synagogues). This allows Arafat to play the role of 'Umar, the Muslim leader and saviour, relegating the patriarchs of Jerusalem and the submissive Christian community to the role played by Sophronius and the Byzantines.
e. All Palestinians are potential martyrs (i.e. likely participants in the coveted jihad of liberation) and, since all are likely to swell his ranks, Arafat calls upon them to be patient. The head of Hamas, Ahmed Yasin (who had been lingering in an Israeli prison), is also one of those fighters-martyrs within the ranks, nominally under the one leader: Arafat himself. Hamas and PLO have become one.

The Prophet, 'Umar, jihad, martyrs, Jerusalem, the oath of allegiance: How do they all connect within Arafat's imagery? In order to understand the connection, the key concepts are Hudaybiyya, jihad, and Jerusalem, which have become familiar words in every Palestinian household since Oslo, especially after the speeches in Johannesburg, Gaza, and Bethlehem. Fresh from Oslo, Arafat in Johannesburg was not short of words had he wished to carry a message of peace to his Muslim audience or to convince them of his peaceful intentions towards Israel. He could have alluded to the many parallels in history, of sworn enemies who ultimately compromised and made peace. Instead, he delivered a martial speech calling for jihad, similar to the speeches reserved for Palestinian ears when urging his audiences to fight and make sacrifices. And he invoked Hudaybiyya and the other key concepts even before any substantial rift had occurred with the Israelis regarding the interpretation of Oslo or its implementation.

Why does Arafat need to stress the Hudaybiyya model? As reconstructed by eminent scholars specializing in early Islam,[20] the Hudaybiyya story unfolded in AD 628 when the Prophet of Islam, already solidly based in Medina, ordered his followers to the sanctuary of Mecca, which had become the centre of Islamic worship. However, at Hudaybiyya on the approaches to Mecca, the Quraysh tribe (originally the Prophet's own) prevented the Muslims from entering the city. An agreement was negotiated and implemented, allowing the Muslims to come to Mecca the next year. The following year in 630, the Prophet with his supporters sought to conquer the city using, as a *casus belli*, the violation by the Quraysh of one of the terms of the treaty of Hudaybiyya (one which provided not only that the parties should refrain from battle during the coming ten years but also that no client tribes of either party should attack the other's). The conquest of Mecca (called *al-fath* in Islamic tradition) involved occupation of the city as well as taking control of the Ka'ba shrine,[21] which became the central sanctuary of Islam.

While there are many unanswered questions regarding this episode, the events at Hudaybiyya have become a model for generations of Muslims and the usage (sometimes manipulation) of the model by Muslim leaders – religious and political – suggests the resilience of that precedent when brokering peace with the enemy. Sadat of Egypt needed to legitimize his peace with Israel in 1979 through the mufti of Al-Azhar, who drew the Hudaybiyya parallel.[22] Not only Arafat but others have also alluded to

Hudaybiyya; for example, the Saudi Mufti was also quoted as justifying Oslo on the same grounds.

However, of greatest interest is the application given by Arafat and others of the various aspects of Hudaybiyya to modern-day conditions, such as the negotiations leading to that treaty; the significance of the agreement per se; parallel identification of today's parties with the Prophet who signed the original treaty, 'Umar who opposed it, and the opponents with whom it was signed, then Quraysh, now Israel; and the consequences of the treaty then and now. The question of Hudaybiyya's application and consequences is of great importance because of the various existing interpretations given to everything relating to the Prophet, including his Hudaybiyya venture. For example, Islamic tradition regards the Prophet as the most accomplished of men who could do no wrong, therefore his deeds and sayings ought to be followed to the letter, almost in blind emulation. Was 'Umar, another highly adored man in Islam, wrong then when he opposed the treaty? If so, why does Arafat wish so much to be cast in his image? Or perhaps he too opposed Oslo and signed it for tactical reasons that escaped the scrutiny of his interlocutors? These are pertinent questions indeed!

When the Prophet and his seven hundred followers were militarily stalemated at Hudaybiyya, the gateway to Mecca, they tried to convey to the Quraysh that they had come only to pray at the sanctuary. When the Meccans sent a delegation to negotiate, its head reportedly denigrated the Muslim army and immediately determined that the Muslims would not be allowed to go to the sanctuary that year, apparently for fear of losing face with the rest of the tribes of Arabia if they should yield to Muslim military pressure. They also probably suspected that the ultimate goal of Muhammad was military conquest of his native city, which indeed he moved to do eight years before expiration of the ten-year non-aggression Treaty of Hudaybiyya.

In Hudaybiyya, the Prophet did not offer any tough bargaining. On the contrary, 'he made concessions which related to the very essence of his prophetic mission'.[23] For example, he omitted the *basmalah* (the ritual mentioning of the name of Allah in addresses and writings) from the text of the Treaty at the Quraysh's insistence. He also consented to return to Mecca any of the Quraysh members who would join the Prophet's faith. As a *quid pro quo*, Muhammad won recognition from the Quraysh and Mecca that his community at Medina was their equal.[24] Moreover, the Prophet was keen to avoid battle on two fronts (against the Jews of Khaybar on one hand, the Quraysh of Mecca on the other) for fear of exposing Medina to the onslaught of the one from his rear if he attacked the other in full force. Therefore, he had to make those bitter concessions as a matter of expediency until such time as he could abrogate those concessions 'for the benefit of Muslims' (as indeed they proved to be).[25]

The Prophet had first to secure his Meccan flank when he attacked Khaybar. Once Khaybar was eliminated he could then turn against the Quraysh in Mecca. The Meccans, who had signed an alliance with the Jews of Khaybar, found themselves bound by two contradictory pacts: to run to their allies' aid if attacked by Muslims, as against their new commitment to lay down their arms and avoid hostilities for the next ten years. Then the Prophet turned against Khaybar under the protection of his treaty with the Quraysh, apparently impelled by his reckoning that, in view of Jewish and Meccan sympathies towards Persia, the Sassanid defeat in February AD 628 at the hands of Emperor Heraclius had finally tilted the balance in the Muslims' favour. Hence his calculation that the time was opportune to move against Khaybar and, in the meantime, to lull the Meccans with his seemingly conciliatory stance in Hudaybiyya.[26] The destination of Khaybar was also the compensation granted by the Prophet to his followers (such as 'Umar) who had been incensed by the Prophet's concessions in Hudaybiyya and who then found consolation in massacring, enslaving, and pillaging the Jews of that imposing oasis.

In AD 630, the Prophet took Mecca and its sanctuary by assault. That conquest was consecrated by Islamic tradition as *al-fath*, literally, the opening (i.e. its opening to its new conquerors). While this was the *fath*, par excellence, all the later conquests of Islam in the Middle East were known *al-futūh* (the plural of *fath*). Another derivative connected with this is the *miftah* (key) obtained by the Prophet from the guardian of the Ka'ba whom he then ordered to open (*fatah*) the shrine. Some theories connect the *fath* with the *opening* of the sanctuary rather than with the conquest itself, while others attribute the title of *al-fath* to the Hudaybiyya expedition prior to the conquest of Mecca on the authority of 'Umar, who had reportedly said that 'there was no greater *fath* than Hudaybiyya'.

This *fath* is, in turn, connected to the oath of allegiance (the *bay'a*) given to the Prophet by his followers 'under the tree' at Hudaybiyya. There, the Prophet is reported to have had a vision in which he entered the sanctuary with his head shaved, opened it with the key, and then went to Arafa to perform rituals with the worshippers. This dream is borne out in a Qur'anic revelation:

> Ye shall surely enter the Sacred Mosque, if Allah Will, in full security, having your heads shaved and your hair cut ... He has ordained you, besides this, a speedy victory.[27]

The entrance to the sanctuary a year later for the *'umra* (minor pilgrimage) and the definitive takeover of the Shrine by Muslims two years after that are considered by some Islamic traditions as the fulfilment of the Hudaybiyya expedition.[28]

JIHAD AND JERUSALEM

The underlying justification for launching a war against an enemy is distilled by Islam in the quintessential notion of jihad. Etymologically the word may have described an intellectual striving – and by extension, also a physical striving – for a cause. In Islamic *shari'a*, however, jihad has principally one meaning: a military action designed to expand the outer borders of the realm of Islam or to protect the boundaries of Dar al-Islam (*Pax Islamica*) from encroaching unbelievers. This idea is founded on the notion that Islam is not simply one of the revealed religions but the prevailing faith, which has come to replace the other monotheistic religions. Islam constitutes the latest and consequently most valid revelation.

Islam prescribes jihad as the only valid war because the Faith by definition requires all hostilities to be directed either against unbelievers (hence the holy war to subjugate them) or against members of other faiths (including monotheistic) who do not accept the superiority and rule of Islam. The Faith is thus universal, encompassing all Muslims who are thereby enjoined not to fight against each other (internecine wars and rebellions or unrest are termed *fitna*). Thus, most wars waged by Islamic countries are usually dubbed jihad, and not only by fundamentalist groups or by religious leaders.

Theoretically, the duty of jihad is binding on the Muslim community until the entire world comes under Islamic rule. However, because most Muslim countries have desisted in practice, under various theological and pragmatic considerations, from pursuing this idea (which would otherwise have permanently pitted them against the rest of the world), jihad has been applied sporadically to describe certain wars, e.g. those against Israel, Egypt's war in the Yemen in the 1960s, the Iran–Iraq War of the 1980s, and the current wars of terror by Hamas, Islamic Jihad, and Hezbollah against Israel.

Jihad does not necessarily have to be offensive and can apply to defensive wars protecting Islamic countries against aggressors. In this regard, and certainly in the case of the Arab–Israeli wars, Muslims would claim that since Palestine is part of their patrimony, and the establishment of Israel on that land therefore constitutes aggression, it is incumbent upon them to defend their land through jihad. When at the turn of the century new winds of liberalism and reform began blowing in the Islamic world as a result of Western influence, some apologists in Islam attempted to limit jihad to its strictly defensive scope or to the extension of assistance to persecuted or otherwise needy Muslims. But again, identifying the aggressor against those Muslims remained problematic when done by Muslim interested parties. Some scholars detect a similar liberal train of thought in the early years of the Prophet's career, when he is said to have usually elected peaceful means over violence and war.[29] But the violent and war-like interpretation of jihad prevailed again when Muhammad launched his attacks against Khaybar and Mecca, and particularly after his death when Islam sprang out of Arabia and spread throughout the world via the Islamic conquests.

That violent interpretation usually continues to prevail in the modern world, especially in the jargon of the fundamentalists[30] and certainly in regard to Israel.[31] We have seen above that Arafat's repeated calls for jihad are usually focused on Jerusalem. There, jihad is referred to as a *qital* (battle), a 'struggle until victory', which demands 'sacrifices and martyrdom'. It is difficult, even if one should stretch one's imagination and generosity to the limit, to understand these words as 'peaceful'. Jerusalem as a mobilizing factor is given the role of Mecca in Arafat's use of imagery to parallel the history of the Prophet: Arafat as well stands at the gates of the sanctuary and vies to pray there, vowing to enter as the victor. That is the reason why Caliph 'Umar, who is believed to have been in Jerusalem personally, provides the crucial link between the Prophet's history and Arafat's history-making.

Arafat could make the quantum jump from Mecca to Jerusalem, and use the one in parallel with the other, due to the historical precedent established by 'abd-al-Malik, who had erected the Aqsa Mosque and the Dome of the Rock (AD 691–92) as a substitute for the Ka'ba, then under the rule of Ibn Zubayr, his rival for the Caliphate. Indeed, people who made the alternative pilgrimage there circumambulated the Rock as they used to do for the Ka'ba in Mecca. Ibn Zubayr's reaction was as staunch: he blamed 'abd-al-Malik for daring to transfer the *tawaf* (circumambulation) from the House of Allah in Mecca to the *qibla* of the Children of Israel in Jerusalem.[32]

Arafat makes efforts to exalt and glorify the religious and political status of Jerusalem in the same way as the Umayyads, who are known for their building programs in the city and sanctifying the Haram al-Sharif (Noble Sanctuary). Some scholars believe, in fact, that the Umayyads had considered Jerusalem their capital or, at the very least, made it the political and administrative centre of the district of Filastin (Palestine) in order to render it the equal of Mecca, if not its superior. We have a better understanding of present-day Muslim fears that 'Judaization' of those holy places might revive the Jewish claim to them if we add to that the fact that the Muslim rituals held at the Rock during the Umayyads 'were an echo of Jewish ceremonies' and evoked the ancient Jewish 'Temple of Jerusalem', or the 'Temple of David and Solomon' (as the 'Kings of the Children of Israel'[33]). Together with holding high the banner of Jerusalem as a holy Muslim shrine and as the capital of Palestine, Arafat would be ready to risk even open violence in order to thwart any Israeli attempt to resurrect the dead ghosts. Hence also the staunch claim advanced by

Palestinian and other Muslim clerics that Israel and the Jews have no rights whatsoever to the Temple Mount, and any idea of sharing its sanctity between the two protagonists (as in the Tomb of the Patriarchs in Hebron) is dismissed out of hand with ridicule and contempt.

But as we have seen, Jerusalem also conjures up in Arafat's mind 'Umar, who allegedly came to the city to accept Sophronius's surrender and the 'key' to the citadel without battle. Some say that 'Umar proceeded to Jerusalem from the camp town of Jabiya, in the Golan; others doubt whether it was 'Umar who accepted the surrender in the first place.³⁴ But there is no doubt that Islamic tradition took the trouble to insist that it was so, and for a reason: when Muslims arrived in Jerusalem they found a purely Christian city, with the Holy Sepulchre as the main site because it purported to have inherited the sanctity of the now-destroyed Jewish Temple. During the process of the Islamization of Jerusalem, a mosque was built on the Jewish Temple Mount. Later, when the Aqsa Mosque was built on the site, then (together with the Dome of the Rock) the whole complex came to be regarded by Muslims as the successor to the Temple: hence the *Haram*.

So, while the Christians had left the Temple deliberately in ruin, the Islamicized Mount became the destination of Muhammad's *isra'* (night journey) and the launching pad of his *mi'raj*. Tradition notes that the Caliph 'Umar went to the Temple Mount and to the Tower of David (a secondary site of Muslim ritual). After 'Umar prayed on the Temple Mount, he ordered the garbage that the Christians had deposited there over the centuries to be removed under the supervision of Ka'b al-Akhbar, a Jew who examined the measurements of the Jewish Temple and designated the exact location for cleaning. Thus, we have three authorities in Jerusalem: Islam, represented by 'Umar, the new ruler of the newly-dominating faith; the Christians, represented by Sophronius; and the Jews, represented by Ka'b. 'Umar identified on the Temple Mount the place that the Prophet had described as the location where he landed after the *isra'* and from whence he took off for his *mi'raj*. Hence, 'Umar's personal involvement in visiting the city and giving the Temple Mount its Islamic meaning satisfies the secondary question of whether he was there at all.³⁵

THE HISTORICAL REPLICA IN ARAFAT'S IMAGERY

Arafat's *modus operandi* has puzzled many observers who have been following the major milestones of this man's career and his semi-miraculous survivability. More than once, he was exposed to near-death situations: physically (e.g. attempts on his life, a plane crash); militarily (e.g. his escape from Israeli occupation in 1967, his stand in besieged Beirut in 1982, and again in Tripoli in 1983); and politically (e.g. when expelled from Jordan in 1970, from Lebanon in 1982, and forgotten in Tunis following the fiasco of his support for Saddam Hussein during the Gulf War in 1991). He was bankrupt financially and diplomatically, to the point of being thrown into the 'waste-basket of history', but for the Israeli life-buoy thrown to him at Oslo that allowed him to peak again and obtain a Nobel Peace Prize on account of the Oslo peace process.

Arafat owes his resurgence of power, each time he was considered to have been doomed, in no small measure to his duplicity. This enables him to appear passionate and pragmatic concurrently, mercurial and calculating, disarmingly naive and shrewdly plotting, furious and cajoling. At times he projects conciliation, at other times menace; he can indulge in fits of anger, and immediately after switch to excessive flowery rhetoric laced with milk-and-honey. He can promise peace and kindle the flames of war; declare his enmity to Hamas but also protect it with rage. There is no way to explain Arafat's duplicity, and the images he projects at different times, in different places, to different people, other than by the abyss constantly yawning between his self-perception as the life-long redeemer of the Palestinian people (until recently, he justified his celibacy by 'being married to the Palestinian cause') and the grim reality of extreme poverty, mounting unemployment, demographic pressures, an 'ungrateful' opposition, and the grinding helplessness and indolence encountered during his waking hours.

Arafat's moments of dream and vision carry him to the heights of the Prophet Muhammad, whose policies he purports to articulate, and of 'Umar, in whose footsteps he wishes to follow. But in his many more numerous moments of despair and frustration, he threatens, lashes out, or loses control. When the wings of vision transport him into the realm of the desirable and the coveted, then Hudaybiyya is for him the quintessence of the Prophet's diplomatic and political success; and Jerusalem the peak of 'Umar's strategic and political blueprint – in each case, political wisdom and prowess pre-empted war and violence. But when reality forces him to crash-land into the quagmire of problems which obstruct his very functioning and constrain the uplifting of his spirit, then he impatiently embraces jihad and reverts to his own true self. After all, the Prophet and 'Umar resorted to jihad when there was no other recourse – that is to say, when their enemies refused to surrender to their will.

The temptation is great to draw step-by-step parallels between Arafat as he perceives himself, and his heroes, the Prophet and 'Umar. Arafat has apparently studied in depth the Hudaybiyya and Jerusalem precedents, and endorses them as models to be emulated. How else can one comprehend his frequent references to them, in all sorts of circumstances, private and public? He appears obsessed by them and convinced they must come to fruition under him, otherwise he could not be so forceful and passionate about them. After all, history is replete with examples of nations who were at war and made peace; why did he choose Hudaybiyya and Jerusalem, of all historical accounts, to exemplify or illustrate his own situations?

The similarities between the Prophet and 'Umar's plans and deeds (as understood and preserved in Islamic tradition) on the one hand, and Arafat's utterances and behaviour (as we can best understand them) on the other, offer striking similarities:

a. Hudaybiyya was the place where the Prophet had his dream (*surat al-fat'h* cited above), took the "key," and with a shaved head entered the sanctuary in Mecca. Arafat's dream (recounted in the speech he gave in Gaza celebrating the day of *mi'raj*) also showed him the walls of Jerusalem, its mosques and churches (but of course no synagogues). One may assume that Arafat's complex about his bald head, which necessitates his perennial headgear, did not allow him to push the parallel as far as to include a shaven skull.
b. The conquest of Mecca by the Prophet (*fat'h*), or perhaps the Treaty of Hudaybiyya itself, which was also a *fat'h* by 'Umar's

own authority, compares with Arafat's Fat'h organization, of which he was the founder and the head until it became the backbone of the PLO. Admittedly, his *fat'h* originates from the acronym *hatf* (*harakat tahrir Filastin* – Movement for the Liberation of Palestine) which, when left in this order, would mean 'sudden death'. Hence the reversal of the ordering of the letters to produce the much more palatable 'Fat'h', which means, precisely, conquest for the cause of Islam, with its significance accruing from Hudaybiyya and the Muslim conquests in general. Taken together with Arafat's Islamic *nom de guerre* and the titles of his military units already mentioned above, one could understand the context in which Arafat's Fat'h came into being.

c. The Prophet had obtained the key to the sanctuary (*miftah* which accords with *fat'h*), a symbol of dominion over the place, and so did 'Umar when he received the 'key' of Jerusalem from Sophronius as a sign of surrender. The recent 'surrender' of the Greek Patriarch of Jerusalem to Arafat in Bethlehem, carried with it a symbolic yielding of the "key" of the churches of Palestine to the new master-protector of the Christians. Hence, the latter's insistence on the wide publicizing of this event.

d. The Prophet's lead at the head of his Muslim followers to launch jihad against the Unbelievers in Arabia, followed by the more extensive jihad which 'Umar conducted to expand Dar al-Islam, is continued by Arafat who incites his crowds, and is in turn incited by them, to lead them into jihad amidst shouts of 'Allah! Allah! Allah Akbar!'

e. Arafat delivered his fiery speech in Gaza on Mi'raj Day, the day on which the Prophet ascended to Heaven from Jerusalem, which was later to be conquered and consecrated by 'Umar and which will now be redeemed by Arafat, "his successor" according to the Patriarch, who himself is Sophronius's successor.

f. The Prophet made "peace" (actually a *hudna*, a ten-year armistice) with the Quraysh at Hudaybiyya, overriding the opposition of some of his most zealous followers, including 'Umar. Here, Arafat explicitly suggested the parallel in that he told his audiences repeatedly that Oslo equalled Hudaybiyya.

Since he purports to follow the Prophet, one must then assume that the counterpart of the Quraysh as his interlocutors are the Israelis. If so, this statement would have far-reaching consequences:

1. Like the Prophet who made humiliating concessions in Hudaybiyya under the pressure of circumstances, so too has Arafat. Implicit in this is the assumption that, exactly like the Prophet who knew when and how to extract himself from that humiliating treaty, so too will Arafat. This was his answer to the harsh critics among his Islamic opposition.

2. The Prophet had pledged a ten-year armistice, but, when Muslim interests so necessitated, he entered Mecca as a victor two years after he undertook that obligation. Arafat's pledge to enter Jerusalem, to pray in al-Aqsa, and to attain victory, are precisely the parallel of the Prophet's vows and deeds.

3. If the peace should turn sour (i.e. if the Israeli partners, like the Quraysh, can be accused of having violated the Treaty), then nothing binds the Palestinians, successors of the Hudaybiyya Muslims. 'Umar himself had despised that peace because of its humiliating content, while the Prophet, who had also disliked it, had the foresight to adopt it, by necessity, as a tactic. But he also knew how to rise against it and abrogate it as soon as it was expedient to do so.

4. Many western historians believe that it was the Prophet who broke the armistice of Hudaybiyya, because the Quraysh would not have dared to attack the Muslims who had become vastly superior to them militarily. Even within Islamic tradition this fact is acknowledged, together with the claim that client tribes of the Quraysh had attacked client tribes of the Prophet, thus justifying his abrogation of the Treaty. Western scholars believe that it was the Prophet who looked and found a pretext to move into Mecca. Muslim tradition contends that, of course, since the Prophet cannot be faulted, it must be the misconduct of his rivals that lay at the root of his military intervention in Mecca, in violation, as it were, of

the Treaty. But even if we adopt the Muslim view in this dispute, how could Arafat know, six months after Oslo – when everything was proceeding according to the Accords – that Israel, like Quraysh, would break her obligation to the point of justifying his jihad into Jerusalem, which he entreated his fellow Muslims in Johannesburg to join? That is unless, of course, he was looking for a pretext to abrogate the treaty, just as the Prophet did, regardless of whether or not the partner respects or violates the treaty. Or, unless Arafat was as far-sighted as the Prophet and foresaw the coming violation before it occurred.

g. Arafat's Hudaybiyya precedent was not lost on Hamas opposition, who were quick to push the parallel beyond its logic. The Prophet had temporarily appeased pagan Mecca in order to launch the onslaught on the Jews of Khaybar. But Hamas keep raising the spectre of Khaybar in their leaflets circulated in the West Bank and Gaza, one of which ends ominously with the call, *Hanat Khaybar!* (The time of Khaybar has come!). The difference is that Arafat's Hudaybiyya has not yet failed completely, and in this scenario, it is Israel who plays the role of both Mecca and Khaybar.

h. The Prophet accepted his *bai'a* (oath of allegiance) 'under the tree' in Hudaybiyya. One should note that Arafat's coming to Bethlehem and all other West Bank cities, was accompanied by calls to the populace to accord him the same *bai' a*. When they do, the parallel will be neat and complete.

We learn then that the choice of the Hudaybiyya-jihad-Jerusalem trinity by the astute Arafat is not accidental or inconsequential, but well-perceived, if ill-conceived. Arafat, true to his Muslim convictions, finds common ground between his beliefs and the deep chords that he can play to instigate massive and passionate responses among his constituencies. In doing so, he not only rallies supporters from the traditional PLO around him (i.e. those who regard him as the symbol of their national existence), but he can also cater to and forestall his Islamic opposition, who embrace precisely these very same Islamic symbols.

One may suspect that for Arafat, as for the Prophet at

Hudaybiyya, it is of greater importance ultimately to placate his constituency than to please his interlocutors through his moves towards peace. He may make concessions, which his Hudaybiyya-based worldview might regard as temporary and tactical, but when the day of reckoning comes, there is no doubt where his heart will be. Experience has indeed shown that when Arafat clamped down on his opposition it was not because Hamas acted against his and their common enemy, nor because of a disagreement on Islamic grounds. Rather, he moved against the Islamists when they posed a direct threat to his rule by creating disturbances and assembling rallies that went out of control; by denigrating him personally or mocking his visions of grandeur, and by pushing their social program to fill the vacuum left by his inability to provide security and prosperity.

The duplicity of Arafat's thinking and policy is attested by his instigation of the violent eruptions against Israel in the West Bank and Gaza in October 1996; by his release from prison of Hamas convicts; by his persistent refusal to extradite to Israel the perpetrators of murders in Israel; by his procrastination in concluding the Hebron retreat of Israeli troops; by his pitting his security chief against Palestinians who live under Israeli rule in East Jerusalem; by his reported speech before Arab diplomats in Stockholm, in which he spoke of 'the impending collapse of Israel' and of 'flooding Israel demographically to bring to its demise';[36] by the repeated declarations of Arafat and of some of his colleagues in the PLO leadership about the 'right of return of the Palestinians' (which corroborate the report about flooding Israel demographically); and finally, by the alarming press reports about Arafat's intentions to bring about a violent explosion in the territories if things do not work his way.[37] Each is an example of the duplicity under-girding his thinking and policy.

As we have seen, while Arafat pays lip-service to peace and reiterates his commitment to the Oslo Accords in interviews with Israeli and Western media, he invokes the messages of jihad, impatience, blood and sweat, Jerusalem, violence, and sacrifice when addressing Arab audiences like the Palestinians. This certainly out-speaks Hamas, who utilize the very same language, and it raises a plethora of questions about Arafat's sincerity in his purported quest for peace with Israel.

NOTES

This was first published in the *Journal of Church and State*, 44 (Spring 2002), pp. 229–48.

1. Hamas is the acronym of 'Harakat Muqawama Islamiyya' (Islamic Resistance Movement), which became the umbrella organization, created virtually overnight at the outbreak of the *intifada* in late 1987, in order to bring together all the local Muslim Associations of years past.
2. For vivid and detailed descriptions of these events, see *Ha'aretz*, 2 January 1996, sec.B3.
3. Ibid.
4. See e.g. *Al-Sirat Weekly*, 18 August 1989; see also the Hamas Charter as translated and annotated by R. Israeli, 'The Charter of Allah: The Platform of the Islamic Resistance Movement', in Y. Alexander (ed.), *The 1988–89 Annual of Terrorism* (Netherlands: Martinus Nijhoff, 1990), pp.99–134.
5. Bernard Lewis, 'The Return of Islam', *Commentary* (Winter 1976); N. Johnson, *Islam and Politics of Meaning in Palestinian Nationalism* (London: Kegan Paul, 1982), pp.8–15.
6. Johnson, *Islam and Politics*, pp.74–87.
7. Lewis, 'The Return of Islam'.
8. Incidentally, while those elections were taking place under Israeli occupation, no complaint was ever voiced regarding the 'impossibility to hold elections under Israeli guns', which would later be voiced when there was a question about general elections.
9. Israeli, 'The Charter of Allah', pp.99–134.
10. Ibid.
11. See e.g. Esther Webman, 'Antisemitic Motifs in the Ideology of Hizballah and the Hamas', *Project for the Study of Antisemitism* (Tel Aviv: Tel Aviv University, 1994).
12. For this and other videotapes, I am indebted to Mr David Ladeen and Mr Ygal Carmon of the Institute for Peace Education in Jerusalem.
13. *Mi'raj* is the ascension of the Prophet to Heaven, according to Islamic tradition. That ascension, which followed his mysterious nightly journey (*isra'*) on his winged-horse back from Mecca to Jerusalem, is yet another proof of the link of Islam with that Holy City.
14. Abu Ammar is the name of an illustrious general in the early Islamic armies. Borrowing this title as a *nom de guerre* in itself suggests Islamic thinking on the part of Arafat.
15. Palestine television, 1 January 1995.
16. Wording used in the Holy Qur'an, describing the Prophet's night journey (*isra'*).
17. Official date of the establishment of the PLO.
18. Founder of the Islamic movement in Palestine in the 1930s; he became the first martyr in modern Palestine after being killed by the British.
19. Ahmed Yasin is the founder and the foremost leader of Hamas, he has been imprisoned by Israel for his alleged instigation of murders of Israelis.
20. See W. Montgomery Watt, *Muhammad at Medina* (Oxford: Oxford at the Clarendon Press, 1956); Gerald R. Hawting, 'Al-Hudaybiyya and the Conquest of Mecca', *Jerusalem Studies of Arabic and Islam* 8 (1986), pp.1–23; Michael Lecker, 'The Hudaybiyya Treaty and the Expedition against Khaybar', *Jerusalem Studies of Arabic and Islam* 5 (1984), pp.1–11; and M. Kister, 'The Massacre of the Banu Qurayza', *Jerusalem Studies of Arabic and Islam* 8 (1986), pp.61–96.
21. Hawting, 'Al-Hudaybiyya', pp.1–2.
22. *Akhbar al-Yaum*, Cairo, 10 May 1979. The Mufti asserted in his *fatwa* that it is 'permitted to conclude peace with the enemy when Muslim interest is served. The Prophet had concluded peace with the Unbelievers of Mecca, in spite of the opposition to it, and he convinced its opponents of its validity'.
23. See Lecker, 'The Hudaybiyya Treaty', p.1. I am also indebted for this passage to my colleague Dr Ilai Allon of Tel Aviv University, who delivered a public lecture on this subject on 3 March 1992.
24. F. Buhl, cited in Lecker, 'The Hudaybiyya Treaty', p.2.
25. Muhammad Hamidullah and Sarakhsi on Shavbani, both quoted by Lecker, 'The Hudaybiyya Treaty', pp.2–4.
26. See M. Kister, 'Al-Hira', *Arabica* 15 (1968); see also 'The Massacre of Banu Qurayza', *Jerusalem Studies of Arabic and Islam* 8 (1986),

27. Sura 48 (*al-Fath*), verse 27.
28. Hawting, 'Al-Hudaybiyya', p.3ff.
29. See 'Jihad', in H.A.R. Gibbs, B. Lewis, Ch. Pellat, C. Bosworth *et al.* (eds), *The New Encyclopedia of Islam*, 2nd edn, 11 vols (Leiden: E.J. Brill, 1960–2000).
30. See e.g. Sayyed Qutb, *Ma'rakatuna m'a al yahud* (Beirut, 1986); and the Charter of Hamas.
31. See Webman, 'Antisemitic Motifs'.
32. See Amikam Elad, 'Why did adb-al-Malik build the Dome of the Rock?' in J. Raby and J. Johns (eds), *Bayt al-Maqdis*, Part 1 (New York: Oxford University Press, 1992), pp.33–57.
33. Ibid., pp.48–9.
34. H. Busset, 'Omar's image as the Conqueror of Jerusalem', *Jerusalem Studies of Arabic and Islam* 8 (1986), pp.153–4.
35. Ibid., pp.164–8.
36. *Middle East Digest* 7, no. 3 (March 1996).
37. Various articles, *Ma'ariv* (Weekend Supplement), Tel-Aviv, 1 November 1996, pp.6–7.

CHAPTER SIX

State and Religion in the Emerging Palestinian Entity

As long as the Palestinian entity existed only as a goal set forth in political slogans and to inspire armed struggles, the question of state and religion, which has been afflicting many an Arab/Muslim state, did not come to the fore as an acute problem confronting society. At most, one could observe various contending trends in a society in transition vying for different, even competing modes of life, while the issue of a predominant philosophy or ideology that would govern the body politic was pushed to the sidelines, or made subservient to the more pressing need to attain independence or to rid the Palestinians of their perceived occupiers/oppressors.

IDENTITIES IN COMPETITION

The construct 'state and religion' has connoted since the medieval wars of investiture, a confrontation between the two powerful establishments of the church and the state, in their bid to rule society. Today, this has become a competition, covert or overt, between two worldviews, aimed at converting public opinion to their respective causes and views, and forcing a decision between applying the sacral-dogmatic-scriptural in modern life, or, on the contrary, making the temporal-pragmatic-legal prevail. The 'state' part of the construct would normally base its appeal on nationalism, an essentially secular and particularistic notion, while 'religion' would claim a more universalistic approach derived from some divine authority. Hence the dichotomy between the secular-nationalistic political culture which would tend to adopt rational measures, some based on compromise and negotiations, to achieve its goals, versus the religious-absolutistic imperatives of self-righteousness and single-mindedness which often lead to extremist and fanatical behaviour.

Sensu strictu, we tend to regard nationalism as a militant political movement which articulates the link between man and a particular land, what we usually call 'patriotic feeling', in Arabic *wataniyya* (*watan* = homeland or motherland). But there are more meanings to nationalism: a policy of national independence, a policy of rescuing industry and other economic assets from the hands of foreigners (by nationalizing them), a chauvinist feeling of narrow and exclusive identity to set us apart from others, or a doctrine that lends precedence to national values over international ones and even provides a particular interpretation of national character and national values. Sometimes, this nationalism can come to be personified in the figure of a charismatic leader (e.g. Yasser Arafat).

Nationalism is also a matter of identity. Man seeks his roots – he desires to locate the origins of his being in an attempt to determine who he is, particularly in the cosmopolitan world of ours where values and consumer goods have become universalized. At times, man looks for a traumatic moment in his collective past (a revelation, a myth, a founding father, or some historical cataclysm) which helps explain how in the remote past that happening had turned an inanimate material culture, or a haphazard collection of individuals, into a culture, a religion, a history, an ethnic or national group. In the search for those links to the past, people often create their own mythology that lends depth to their history.

The Palestinian national ethos, which took shape only within recent memory, has created over the past few years a multifaceted identity that links it, on various levels, to many of the above-mentioned aspects. Indeed, the Palestinians today rewrite their history so as to incorporate in their ancestral background the Canaanites and the Jebusites.[1] They profusely use the succession of calamities that befell them in 1948, 1967, 1970, etc.,[2] to draw their ranks closer; they cultivate, like the Jews of Israel, an almost mystical connection to their land; they promote their particularistic history and culture; they are today brandishing national symbols (flag, headgear, anthem, slogans, elected institutions, stamps, passports, police, etc.) in preparation to assume the paraphernalia of full fledged independence which will bring with it sovereignty, currency, armed forces, and all the other attributes of national sovereignty. Finally, they elevate the figure of Yasser Arafat, their national symbol for over a generation, almost to the level of a cult of personality, much to the exclusion of other major personalities in the Palestinian pantheon of heroes.[3]

Most significantly, these elements appear in Palestinian writings and thinking not only as the self-defining traits of Palestinian nationalism, but also as the requisites setting them apart from, and often pitting them against, the enemy – Israel, Zionism, the Jews – because they are the ones who are perceived as posing a challenge to the Palestinians and it is to them that the Palestinians feel constrained to respond. For example, the Cana'anite claim is clearly geared to legitimize the Palestinian title to the land that has been snatched from them, as they see it, by the Zionist Jews who built Israel, who themselves based their claim on their line of descent from the biblical Israelites who had conquered the land from the Canaanites. Thus, if the Canaanites are neatly established as Palestinian Arabs, then the Jewish experience in the ancient Holy Land, based on aggression and conquest in the first place, becomes a fleeting episode in history and the Palestinians come full circle by justly (a 'just peace' based on restitution) restoring possession of the land to its original legal owners.

But then, the Canaanites were neither Arab, nor certainly Muslim. However, exactly like Sadat, who could strike the balance between his Pharaonism and his Arabism and Islam,[4] or Saddam Hussein, who claims the ancient heritage of Mesopotamia's Hammurabbi as his own but does not desist at the same time from his Iraqi, Arab, or Muslim identity, so have Palestinian nationalists learned to juggle their identities with dexterity. It is also significant that the Cana'anite antecedent is particularly popular among Palestinian Christians who, aware of the massive doses of Islam currently injected into Palestinian (and Arab for that matter) nationalism, would hark back to a non-Islamic past in which they could find solace against the pressures of revivalist Islam around them. At any rate, Palestinian nationalists, Arafat foremost among them, have discovered that old is beautiful. And so, much like the Prophet of Islam in his time, who lent depth to the history of Islam by claiming that Abraham was the first Muslim, the Palestinians today assert that their ancestry was in fact Cana'anite.

THE CONSTITUTION OF PALESTINIAN NATIONALISM

In modern times, secular Palestinian nationalism can be best captured by looking into the Palestinian National Charter, adopted in 1964 and amended in 1968, not amended again or rescinded in spite of the pressures exerted by Israel to that effect under the 1993 Oslo Accords and their aftermath. And again, the charter not only spells out the boundaries defining the Palestinians as a people and a nation with its inherent culture, ethos, ethnic affiliation, and historical specificity, but also relative to other Arabs and Muslims. And above all, the Palestinian people are called upon to crystallize their dreams and aspirations, by means of a continuous armed struggle, against a specific enemy – Zionism. In other words, the whole concept of a nascent Palestinian nationalism was made to hinge upon a dialectical struggle with its sworn enemy. This battle to the finish, as reflected in the charter, does not allow for compromise or negotiation. It vows to destroy the enemy in order to replace it with a Palestinian order, thus attaining at one and the same time the normative fulfilment of the Palestinian dream and also the realization of the Israeli political nightmare.

The Palestinian Covenant indeed traces, step by step, the contours of Palestinian Nationalism:

a. Palestine is the homeland of the Palestinians, but at the same time Palestine is part of the greater Arab Homeland and the Palestinians are part of the larger Arab Nation.[5] This means that while the Palestinians express their attachment to the land of Palestine (*wataniyya*) and state their particularistic identity, they are also aware of their belonging to a larger whole (*qawmiyya*) in terms of territory, ethno-cultural descent, historical heritage, and linguistic affiliation.

b. The covenant states that the 'Palestinian identity is an innate, persistent characteristic that does not disappear, and it is transferred from father to son'.[6] In other words, the fact that the Palestinians have been dispersed as a result of the disasters that befell them does not detract from their nationhood or their national character. Moreover, Palestinianhood is defined not only by the land ('those who lived in the land until 1947'), but also by ethnic descent ('anyone born to a Palestinian father after that, within Palestine and outside of it').[7] Outside this ethnic definition only Jews who were in Palestine 'Prior to the Zionist invasion'[8] would also be considered Palestinians, presumably a tolerated minority among the ethnic Palestinians. So, apart from this exception, Palestinian nationalism equates nationhood-peoplehood with ethnic descent.

c. If the intrinsic Palestinian character is defined along ethnic, cultural, and historical lines, the vehicle to carry them to the promised land is armed struggle waged against the external forces that attempt to thwart the realization of the Palestinian dream, chief among them are: Imperialism and Zionism.[9] This means that the outer challenges that are to be addressed are part of the defining principle of Palestinian nationalism. The nation will be galvanized by and during the struggle against the forces which stymie its emergence.

d. The outer circles of Palestinian nationalism are its Arab and Islamic identities.[10] Palestinian nationalism not only declares itself to be part and parcel of Arab nationalism in general, but also alerts the Arabs that they all face the same enemies: Imperialism and Zionism, and therefore, they should all be mobilized to push out the foreign threat. The Palestinians, however, being at the forefront of that battle, which is part of their identity, undertake to be the vanguard[11] of all Arabs in that undertaking. Islamic identity is invoked in the context of Palestine as the Holy Land, hence the urgency to restore it to Islamic hands in order to safeguard freedom of worship there.[12] Palestinians also regard themselves as part of the

Third World (the 'forces of good, progress, and peace') that they also vowed to mobilize to their cause in the unified battle against Imperialism and Zionism.[13]

e. Peculiar to Palestinian nationalism, however, beyond the outer definitions of the threatening enemies which have to be watched and thwarted, is the sine qua non assumption that the survival of Palestine and of Palestinians hinges upon the utter destruction of the Zionist entity in all its manifestations: political, military, economic, and cultural.[14] This means that, unlike other nationalisms, which aspire to independence and, when applicable, to throw the yoke of an occupier (not to eliminate him), here we see the very *raison d'être* of the Palestinian entity inherent in the destruction of Zionism.

Its resistance to alteration and amendment attests to the resilience of the Covenant as a basic constitutional document of Palestinian nationalism. Already in the Palestinian National Council (PNC) convened in Algiers in October 1988, where Palestinian independence was declared, there was talk about a shift in Palestinian orientation inasmuch as, for the first time, it supposedly accepted the notion of a two-state solution in Palestine, along the lines of the 1947 UN Resolution. However, the covenant was not amended to allow for this putative shift in Palestinian thinking. When specifically questioned about this, some participants in that PNC expressly denied that there had been any such change in the making. Indeed, according to Art. 33 of the covenant, a special meeting of the PNC was required to adopt, by a two-thirds majority, any amendment in the charter. Had the Palestinian leadership wished and/or been able to introduce such an alteration, Algiers would have been the place to do it. Instead, the Palestinians issued the Declaration of Independence, followed by a political communiqué which reiterated the delegitimation of Israel because it was founded on 'usurpation, aggression, killing, and deportation' of Palestinians.

Yasser Arafat, the head of the PLO and its symbol, made various attempts to dismiss the political character of the charter in the post-1988 Algiers conference by referring to it as *caduque* or *passé*, only to be countered by the argument that if it were so then why did not the Algiers PNC alter or abrogate it. Furthermore everyone understood the difference between a 'statement' made by a statesman whatever his stature and a resolution adopted by the institutions of the Palestinians as provided for in Art. 33 of the covenant. If a formal resolution of the PNC was required to adopt the charter how much more so when time came to repeal it? This contradiction was not lost on Israeli negotiators during the secret talks that led to the Oslo Accords in September 1993.

Indeed when Foreign Minister Simon Peres introduced the Accords to the Knesset prior to their formal signature in Washington, DC, he pledged that Israel would sign them only after the Palestinians abrogated the clauses in the charter that 'vowed to destroy Israel'. However, the Israelis were oblivious of the fact that the Palestinian covenant does not even mention the word 'Israel' (with one technical exception) much less does it openly discuss its destruction. Therefore Oslo came and went and still no amendment was brought before the PNC. Incidentally all those who had persistently claimed that following Algiers 1988 and Arafat's *caduque* statements the covenant had become irrelevant and obsolete, could not comprehend why the insistence now on the revision of that invalidated document. Be that as it may the Palestinians clung to their national constitution.

Pressed by Israel to introduce the amendments prior to the Oslo II agreements, Arafat made several deliberate steps to convene the PNC, now recognized as the sole body legally able to take such a measure. First he claimed that Israel could not possibly demand a redress while she did not allow certain members of the PNC to come to Gaza for that fateful meeting. Then when Israel reluctantly gave her assent, some of the members in question would not join the assembly either because they rejected Israel's pressure on Arafat or they thought that it was too premature to tackle that hot potato now. Lacking the legal quorum for the demarche Arafat convened the PNC in Tunis, the long-time headquarters of the PLO, but again no quorum could be assembled. Some Palestinian leaders rebuffed Israel's insistence and let it be understood that they had never promised to cancel or abrogate the covenant in the first place. They had simply discovered that such a major step on their part ought not be taken without a significant additional *quid pro quo* on the part of Israel. Oslo II came and went, and still no amendment.

Elections in Israel approached. Peres who stood for re-election understood that because of his repeated yet unfulfilled pledges to the Israeli public regarding the change in the Charter he risked his position if the razor-thin majority he enjoyed should defect to his opponent who insisted that the Charter be revised prior to any further advance in the peace process. He implored Arafat to assist him and so, out of necessity and fear lest his easy-going ally should lose the elections, the chairman finally moved decisively, convened the PNC in Gaza without encountering any difficulties in obtaining the required quorum and summarily addressed the necessary resolution. Things had changed however. Arafat was no longer willing to either abrogate the charter or even delete the articles that offended Israel. What he offered to do with Peres's tacit agreement was to promise to correct those stipulations in the document that contradicted Palestinian commitments in Oslo. So a resolution was passed at the PNC that appointed a committee to review those stipulations and to recommend a new wording that would make them commensurate with Oslo and the peace process. Arafat informed Peres in an official letter that indeed the charter had been amended in spite of the fact that it was not (at least not as yet).

Expectedly Peres hailed the move as one of the most dramatic developments in the twentieth century and his supporters in Israel boasted of that unprecedented achievement. The Israeli press was delirious praising Arafat and Peres, but little attention was paid to those who called the bluff, among them the foremost expert on Palestinian affairs, Hebrew University scholar Yehoshua Porath. Official Israeli acceptance of Arafat's interpretation backed by American and European laudatory remarks, provided the Palestinian's with a respite but not for long. The questions that continued to ring in the sceptics ears were simple:

a. It took the PNC 15 out of 33 articles of the Charter to state in detail their vow to dismantle Zionism. Why did not the Gaza PNC plainly state unequivocally that those articles were null and void?

b. The council did not decide to repeal anything specific. It did not even resolve to revise any specific clause in the covenant. It left it to the committee it established to decide what in the existing statement contradicted the Oslo Accords. If, for example, the assumption of the Charter that the Jews are not a nation and therefore did not deserve a state,[15] was not deemed as contradicting Oslo because the Palestinians made peace with Israel, not with the Jews, that clause would remain valid. Or, worse, the Palestinians could always claim that since the covenant does not mention Israel directly, there was no inherent contradiction between it and the Oslo Accords. Was that the idea?

c. The council did not impose any deadline on the committee to end its work and to recommend the new formula, if any. So while the Charter became effective immediately upon adoption back in 1964, the promise for its amendment would continue to hang in suspense *sine diem*.

In the May 1996 elections in Israel, Peres lost and his opponents won. Then the question of the abrogation or the amendment of the Charter came up again, this time with the insistence of the new government that any demarche in that regard would be made explicit, clear and public, as a condition to the continuation of the process. The protracted negotiations regarding Israel's withdrawal (euphemistically called 'redeployment') from Hebron, reintroduced the theme of the already supposedly settled question of the charter. And, lo and behold!, the Palestinians signed the agreement in January 1997 which commits them to complete the proceedings of the amendment. They recognized thereby that the process had not been brought to fruition in spite of their previous assurances to the contrary.

Right after Hebron, Arafat was quoted in a press conference[16] as questioning the need to revise and amend the Charter arguing that Israel had no right to ask the Palestinians to rewrite their constitution as long as it itself did not have one. This augured, apparently, another series of procrastinations and manoeuvres on the part of the Palestinians to avoid the issue. More importantly, it signalled Arafat's implicit admission that the Charter had never been amended since 1968, in spite of all the clamours of its irrelevance. Another attempt was sponsored by President Clinton, following the Wye Agreement of October 1998 when Arafat convened in Gaza an assembly of all popular organizations (including the PNC, but not a special meeting thereof as required by article 33), and brought to the vote the approval of his letter to President Clinton that claimed that the Charter had been amended, not the abrogation of specific articles thereof. Thus, once again, Arafat outmanoeuvred both Clinton and Prime Minister Netanyahu, but the Charter remained constitutionally unaltered. To date, the remarkable tenacity of the Palestinians in opposing any substantial amendment of any part of their basic national constitutional document goes a long way to show its centrality and immutability in the eyes of the Palestinians. It was and still is, the writ of their nationhood, dreams, and aspirations, despite, or perhaps also because of the fears it evokes in the Israeli neighbours/opponents. All the more so in the wake of the events of al-Aqsa *intifada* (since October 2000) and the Palestinian demands in Camp David (July 2000) which only confirm this hypothesis.

Certainly, the emergence of the Palestinian entity, with its attending state responsibilities over the territories and the populations under its jurisdiction on the one hand, and the rise of Islamic fundamentalism among Palestinians on the other, may change all this. For while the Islamists are posing an ideological challenge to Arafat and the PLO, it will be perhaps the demands of everyday life and the sheer necessity to work out some sort of pragmatic arrangement with Israel that will determine the survivability of the Palestinian Covenant. But until that happens, Palestinian secular nationalism, as outlined in that basic document, will have to contend with its arch rival, namely Islamic nationalism.

ISLAMIC NATIONALISM

Prima facie nationalism and Islam amount to a contradiction in terms: one is secular, the other religious; one is founded on particularism, the other claims universalism; one asserts this-worldly aspirations the other promises the hereafter. However, viewed closely, political Islam takes on some of the characteristics of nationalism: identity, attachment to the land, myths and symbols, self-definition in contrast with the others, charismatic leaders, identifying enemies and vowing to eliminate them, commitment to struggle, armed and otherwise, etc. Islam has indeed closely related, since its inception at the time of the Prophet, politics to the faith, and therefore, religion is not as antithetical to the state as it is in the West. Quite the contrary, the Muslim dogma provides the ideological underpinnings of the righteous Muslim state, and the latter provides protection to the creed and furthers its propagation.

In modern Islam we see not only the cases of Pakistan, whose founding principle was Islamic nationalism promoted by Ali Jinnah; and Saudi Arabia which stands as the paradigm of state–religion symbiosis, but we also witness many so-called fundamentalist movements, thinkers, clergymen, and even politicians, who have embraced this course. Was it not Bhutto (Benazir's father), the consummate westernized and modern Muslim, who published in the 1970s his famous article in *Foreign Affairs* upholding Islamic Nationalism? Such great Islamic thinkers as Sayyid Qutb, Mawdudi, and Khomeini have contributed considerably to viewing the modern state as compatible with Islam. Islamic mass movements in Egypt, Algeria, Lebanon, Jordan, and Palestine cannot wait to apply Islam in their politics and join the already successful cases of Iran, the Sudan, Afghanistan, and to some extent also Turkey and Pakistan. When today these movements speak in terms of Islamic nationalism, or depict the perceived enemies of Islam as a 'cancer in the heart the of Islamic Nation',[17] they clearly hark back to the pristine Muhammedan Islam and its immediate aftermath, in which state and religion were so perfectly, and harmoniously, welded together; when friends and foes were defined precisely; and the conquering, victorious and expansive Islam, led by virtuous charismatic chiefs, seemed to be the wave of the future.

ISLAMIC ANTECEDENTS IN PALESTINIAN NATIONALISM

Palestinians too are caught up in that trend of fundamentalist Islam, though this is nothing new if one takes into consideration the antecedents of Palestinian nationalism where Islam had played a prominent role. In the 1920s, the Palestinian national movement was headed by a religious figure, the Great Mufti of Jerusalem, Haj Amin a-Husseini (similar in many ways to Makarios in Cyprus and Muzurewa in Rhodesia/Zimbabwe in his fusion of secular-nationalist and religious leadership), and as such it played up in religious terms the opposition to both the

British and Zionism. In the 1930s, Izz a-Sin al-Qassam, a Syrian cleric who settled in Haifa, undertook extensive religious and political activities in Northern Palestine that soon lent prominence to his leadership. He then founded a militant group, *al-kaff as aswad* (the Black Hand) as an instrument of armed struggle against the British and the Jews in contended Palestine. He called openly for jihad against both, until the British killed him in battle in 1935.

During the Palestinian revolt of 1936–39, the Muslim Brethren based in Egypt established a number of lodges in Palestine that later grew into a full-fledged network. The Muslim Brethren in Egypt and Palestine developed a two-pronged line of activism, not unlike its Qassam antecedent: struggle against the British occupation and the perceived Zionist menace. The 1948 War between Israel and the Arabs split the Palestinian-Arab population into an Israeli-ruled minority and a majority in the West Bank and Gaza, where they pursued their propaganda and growth amidst frequent clashes with the authorities there. The occupation by Israel of the West Bank in the 1967 War brought the entire Palestinian population west of the Jordan River under Israeli rule under which they were allowed leeway in their open activities as long as they operated within the confines of the law.

On the other hand, the rapid modernization of Palestinian society, caused by the intrusion of Israel into the traditional social structures and their dismantlement, generated the outrage of Muslim fundamentalists who came to sense that Israel was undermining their traditional society through the introduction of 'Westoxicated' values. This outrage sowed the seed of a renewed open conflict between the fundamentalists and the Israelis in the grounds of anti-Israeli sentiment that had been already cultivated by Palestinian nationalists all along. Hence the eruption of the Hamas[18] during the *intifada* which has galvanized in a zealous (that is what *hamas* means) militant group, encompassing most of the existing local Muslim associations, and dedicated to raise the flag of jihad, once again, against the Israeli occupier.

It is noteworthy, however, that Muslim fundamentalists have not monopolized Islamic thinking and sloganeering. Mainstream Palestinian nationalism too, like most local forms of Arab nationalism, have made use of Islamic symbols and vocabulary to characterize enemies, to imply modes of action against them, and to define the nature of the Palestinian community and its struggle, thus linking together key religious and secular concepts.[19] Terms like jihad, *shahid*, *fidayeen*, the reference to religious sites in the Palestinian Charter as we have seen above, and the centrality of Jerusalem with its attending Islamic history and myth, all attest to the Islamic discourse that is ingrained in Palestinian nationalism. Add to that the symbolism of the usage of Islamic terms in Arafat's *nom de guerre* (Abu Ammar) and the names of his brigades: al-Aqsa, Hittin, Ein Jalut, Qadissyya, all the names of great Islamic battles (not necessarily Arab), and you have a wide sampling of the depth and the extent of Islamic hold over Palestinian nationalism.

In the 1980s, the Islamic bloc emerged as a powerful constituency in West Bank and Gaza politics boosted by the three Islamic colleges of Jerusalem, Gaza an Hebron, established in 1978. But it was not until the Intifada in late 1987 that it united its ranks and, under the new heading of Hamas, began to pose a serious challenge to the established leadership of the Palestinians, as a representative institution vying, on equal footing with the PLO, for the souls and the political allegiance of the masses. The signal was sent, loud and clear, that as against the national aspirations of the Palestinians and their ethnic-national-cultural claims, personified in and by the PLO and led by Arafat, they posited a viable Muslim alternative, which engraved its Islamic mark on Palestinian identity, and was led by another popular charismatic figure, Ahmad Yassin. Hamas was out to conquer Palestinian nationalism. The Covenant of Hamas, promulgated in the initial stages of the *intifada* (February 1988), incorporates its programme.

THE HAMAS COVENANT

The 36-article Charter of Hamas bears some interesting parallels to the PLO Charter discussed above, such as the very appellation of *mithaq* (charter), by which it posits itself as a challenge and an alternative to that of its rivals. Both documents also share an appeal to the same constituency. But it is the differences between them, some worded bluntly and uncompromisingly, others nuanced enough to soothe the ears of all Palestinian listeners, which contain the crux of the challenge:

a. While the PLO document had been deliberated, debated, argued, amended and repeatedly voted upon before it was adopted by the Palestinian National Council, the Hamas Charter was concocted by some of its leaders and only then promulgated to the public. Consequently, while the PLO Charter is considered to be a man-made political document, albeit of constitutional import, which also provides for the instrument of its own amendment,[20] the Hamas document creates the impression of reflecting universal, immutable and eternal truths that are not liable to alterations, once published.

b. The PLO Charter uses political language, though sometimes bombastic and flowery, but Hamas's Charter is wholly anchored in Islamic parlance. Not only are Islamic symbols and vocabulary often invoked, but most articles are backed by quotations from the Holy Qu'ran or the Islamic Sunna, the two sources of Islamic law that are acknowledged by most Muslim fundamentalists. The juxtaposition of the Charter's clauses with these holy texts inextricably lends to the former the sanctity of the latter.[21]

c. The PLO avoids direct attacks on Jews as such and purports to struggle against Zionism only, but Hamas unabashedly also launches anti-Semitic broadsides against the Jews, often citing such notorious texts as the *Protocols of the Elders of Zion.*[22] To them, this means that jihad is justified not only against the Zionists who usurped Palestine, but also against the worldwide evil of the Jews that threatens to undermine societies including the Islamic, in order to take them over and dominate them.

d. While also acknowledging the Palestinian particularistic aspiration to liberate Palestine (after all, that is at the top of the Palestinian agenda), Hamas regard this task as a holy and religious one, incumbent upon all Muslims of the world. Thus, while the PLO message appealed to Arab countries for support, the Hamas appeal is directed to the Islamic world at large. The very fact that Hamas declares its affiliation to the supranational movement of the Muslim Brothers and its dedication to the reconstitution of the long defunct Islamic Caliphate, indeed makes their programme universal.[23]

e. The PLO platform had committed itself totally to a political and military *modus operandi* in order to attain nationhood, and that required the definition of the contours of Palestinian nationalism as hinging on the undoing of the Zionist enemy. The Hamas Charter also outlines a socio-cultural and religio-moral mode of behaviour and action, calculated to raise Islamic consciousness and to conquer Islamic societies from within before they turn to the elimination of the enemies.

f. At a time when the PLO leadership has been attempting to adopt diplomatic means and political measures, in addition to armed struggle, to attain its goals while also securing international recognition, Hamas seems oblivious to the international community. Since the entire land of Palestine is *waqf* (Holy Endowment) given by Allah to all generations of Muslims, no one can negotiate it away. Hence, all the international talks, negotiations, and peace conferences are deemed a 'loss of time', and any intercession by foreign powers in the Arab–Israeli conflict amounts to 'Imperialism's collusion with Zionism'.[24]

g. While the PLO has envisaged institutions and civil processes to implement its platform, Hamas, leaning entirely on the Qu'ran and *shari'a* law, states its purpose to establish an Islamic state in the entire expanse of Palestine with presumably state institutions as designed by the Holy Law of Islam. Palestinian Nationalism, from this point of view, is also incorporated into the *shari'a*, as part of the revised Islamic *umma*.

THE POST OSLO POLITICAL PRAXIS

The Oslo Accords of 1993, signed between the PLO leadership and Israel, pushed the rivalry between Palestinian nationalists and Islamists from the doctrinal into the real sphere of political life. For, if during the first months of negotiations leading to the Accords, there was a similitude of commonality of fate between the two factions which sought, first and foremost, to end Israeli occupation – the signature of those agreements signalled the break which has kept them far apart ever since. Indeed, it became clear to all that the Hamas program posed no less of a threat to Arafat than the Islamists did to the PLO constituency. At Oslo, the PLO became committed, on record, to shun violence while Hamas, like other Muslim fundamentalists, continued to hold the unbending view that only jihad to liberate all Palestine could see the victory of Allah implemented.

Conforming to their platform, Hamas continued to vow that the Land, the entire Land, must be cleansed from the viciousness and impurity of the occupiers, and that only under Islamic rule is there any possibility for other faiths to exist. When Islam does not prevail, they claimed following the terms of their platform, then bigotry, hatred, controversy, corruption, oppression, war, and bloodshed prevail, as is evidenced by the existence of Israel. How, then could they accept reconciliation with the Zionist entity? They despise Israel not only as an occupier but also due to its Jewish constitution, the scum of the earth that concocts plots to take over the world and corrupt societies from within. Hence the Muslim obligation, following the example of the Prophet, to fight and kill them wherever they can be found, or at least ban them from Islamic land if they refuse to submit to its benefactory hegemony.

Domestically, Hamas strives to establish an Islamic entity, as part of the Islamic universe that must be ruled by the Caliph. In such a state, 'Allah is the ultimate goal, the Qu'ran its constitution, jihad its means, death for the cause of Allah its sublimest aspiration'.[25] This means a total rejection of civil laws, elections, and national attainment as professed by the PLO. What is more, Hamas not only continues to embrace the road of violence with regard to Israel, discarding any compromise, negotiations, or settlement with it, but seeks to turn jihad from a collective duty (*fard kifaya*), which is not binding on every individual once the Muslim community as a whole had discharged it, into a personal duty (*fard 'ayn*). In this way, the authority of the established Palestinian entity can be circumvented, and the Palestinians made individually responsible to extinguish the fire raging in the House of Islam with their own buckets of water.[26]

With such a radically different program from that of the Palestinian Authority, and in view of Arafat's inconclusive ability to prove that his formula of salvation is operative and effective, the temptation rises among Islamic militants to try the Islamic alternative. And there are role models to follow: the proven success of the Islamic Revolution in Iran, the Sudan and Afghanistan, and the brewing unrest among Muslim groups in Algeria, Egypt,

Lebanon, Jordan, Pakistan, and others, certainly pump propitious winds into the sails of Hamas. Arafat, conscious of the challenge, has tried on various occasions to harness Hamas to the PLO, and has pressed them to join the system by offering them to participate in the 1996 elections to the Palestinian Legislative Council. But exactly as they had rejected his earlier proposals to join the PLO, they have refuted the elections, claiming that by participating in them, they would acquiesce in the Oslo process which they had negated outright.[27]

And so, the Hamas challenge continues to irritate Arafat and pose a mortal danger to him in more ways than one; for not only can they mount lethal attacks against Israel, which they hope would force her to retaliate and wreck the Oslo process, but if they maintained their popularity thanks to their stand against Israel, they hoped to be able ultimately to dislodge Arafat. In some places, like universities, Hamas have indeed coalesced with other opponents of Oslo, such as the Popular Front and the Democratic Front, to win local elections for the student bodies of those institutions. This has forced Arafat to resume his rhetoric of jihad, of brandishing Islamic vocabulary and of hailing Hamas heroes as his own (e.g. Ahmad Yassin and Yahya Ayyash)[28] in an attempt to overtake Hamas on the right and prove that he is the chief of all Palestinians, including the Islamists. The latter can play the reverse card by claiming that Arafat's shameful sell-out to the Zionists was done only in the name of less than one-third of the Palestinian people residing in the Territories, while the majority of them, outside Palestine, continue to oppose him.

The struggle about the Palestinian soul and the character of the Palestinian entity is in its early stages and there is no way to predict which way it might be concluded. In all likelihood, real life will corrode the sharp edges of the seeming bifurcation between the two poles and produce some halfway modality with which everyone can live. After all, even in the avowedly civil regimes of Egypt, Turkey, and Jordan to name just a few examples, widespread lip service is paid to Islam, not just on the symbolic level but also in the participation of Islamic elements in the structure of power (more in Turkey and Jordan and less in Egypt), and in the substantive Islamic elements in legislation (more in Egypt and less in Turkey and Jordan). And vice-versa, in the Islamic regimes so far

instituted in Iran, Sudan, Saudi Arabia, and Afghanistan, a similitude of civil society, at least on the surface, is maintained: institutional and technological borrowings from the despised West,
modernization, compromises with the needs of the population, etc.

The problem is that Nationalists and Islamists, among the
Palestinians and elsewhere, sometimes speak the same language
and use the same words, but mean different things. Take, for
example, this passage from the Hamas Charter:

> Hamas is a humane movement bent on human rights, and is
> committed to the tolerance inherent in Islam, as regards atti-
> tudes towards other religions. It is only hostile to those hos-
> tile to it, or stand in its way in order to disturb its moves or
> frustrate its efforts…
>
> Under the shadow of Islam, it is possible for the three reli-
> gions: Islam, Christianity, and Judaism, to coexist in safety
> and security. Safety and security can only prevail under the
> shadow of Islam…The members of other religions must
> desist from struggling against Islam over sovereignty in this
> region. For if they were to gain the upper hand, then fight-
> ing, torture and uprooting would follow.[29]

The words for freedom and tolerance are there. But what does
that mean? Are freedom and tolerance valid when attached to the
provision of 'under the shadow of Islam'? Similarly, Arafat and
other Palestinian leaders have been committed to promoting
democracy, freedom, civil rights, and the like, but as soon as the
leader is attacked or criticized, or someone does not conform to
the personality cult he has been promoting, then the Palestinian
Authority's security forces move in and arrest the critic.[30] Any
political entity can have a beautiful 'constitution', couched in lofty
words and encapsulating the most humane and generous terms.
But is it applied in practice'? Will the one that seems to be the
most responsive to the desires of the people ultimately decide the
struggle between Palestinian Nationalism and Islamism? In Iran,
for example, the people preferred the Islamic regime to the
authoritarian one provided by the Shah and his underlings. In
practically all Islamic countries, the choice will always be
between some sort of authoritarianism and Islam.

In the competition between Islam and any other sorts of authoritarianism, Islam might emerge victorious, if only because it can be conceived as enjoying the same mantle of legitimacy that the Prophet had had, unlike the other rules which can claim none. For even if rulers pretend to have been elected to their posts, one knows exactly what those elections mean either without much competition, or under stringent controls so as to assure the results coveted by the rulers in place. So, they either perpetuate their rule by force (e.g. Assad of Syria, Saddam Hussein of Iraq), or through the mechanisms of hereditary monarchies (Morocco, Jordan, Saudi Arabia, Kuwait, the Gulf states). To acquire some legitimacy, these autocrats take on Islamic titles: 'The curator of the Holy Places' for the Saudi king, the 'Heir of the Prophet and the Guardian of al-Aqsa Mosque' for the late King Hussein of Jordan; and another, 'Descendent of the Prophet and the chairman of the Jerusalem Committee of the Islamic Conference' for King Hassan II of Morocco. Even godless Saddam Hussein announced during the Gulf War that he was adding the Islamic slogan 'Allah Akbar!' (Allah is the Greatest!) to his national flag, and his move was calculated to make his war against the Americans, the 'New Crusaders', a novel version of the war of the believers against the invading non-Muslims.

Lack of legitimacy means that someone is waiting in the aisles as an alternative to the existing order. And much like the Muslim Brothers in Egypt and Jordan, the Islamists in Algeria and the Hamas among the Palestinians, these oppositions seek legitimacy in Islam and its teachings. They may use the discourse of democracy, human rights, basic freedoms and the like, but once they come to power, like in Iran, the Sudan and Afghanistan, there is no telling how they might behave in these respects. This is the reason why Arafat hastened, with Israeli and American support, to run elections in the Palestinian self-ruling entity. At the same time everyone knew that had the Islamists participated and had they commanded a majority, the Algerian scenario would have repeated itself. Arafat did not take over power in order to hand it over to anyone else. Moreover, even according to Arafat's own logic, the elections in the territories hardly reflected the majority of the one-third of the Palestinians under his authority. The other two-thirds, whose political loyalty is difficult to call, did not express their opinions, nor were they asked to. This is also the reason why Arafat, concurrently with his official cloak as the president of the Palestinian Authority, does not relinquish the mantle of the chairman of the PLO, which purports to represent all Palestinians. His current cabinet meetings group together both the Executive Council of the Authority and the Executive Committee of the PLO – all this in the name of legitimacy, implicitly if not explicitly.

This is the reason why Arafat, together with his harsh persecution against the Hamas, not in order to please Israel but to quell their challenge to his authority, has coupled his attitude with his embracing many Hamas themes, as if to signal to the Palestinian populace that he is not less Muslim than his opposition. In January 1996, when Arafat began re-entering the cities of the West Bank that were transferred to his authority under the second Oslo Accords, he was visibly elated when he could be seen as not only regaining Arab-Palestinian lands, but also as taking control of Islamic territory. Indeed, the Greek-Orthodox Patriarch of Jerusalem, greeting the chairman at the gates of Bethlehem, declared: 'Here is the successor of Sophronius welcoming the successor of 'Umar ibn-al-Khattab!' No one present, or watching the direct broadcast on television, could miss the parallel. Reference was made, of course, to the submission of the Byzantine-era Christian patriarch of Jerusalem to the second Caliph of Islam in the seventh century, when Islam set foot in the city. That Arafat had ordered all his media to publicize this parallel became widely known following the arrest of the *al-Quds* journalist cited above.

Immediately following the signature of the Oslo Accords, and two full years prior to the rendition of the territories to his control, Arafat had begun making abundant use of his Islamic imageries to gain legitimacy among the Palestinians so as to thwart the vicious attacks against him by the Hamas and other Islamists, that he had sold out to Israel and the Americans. Shortly after Oslo, on a visit to Johannesburg for the inaugural ceremony of South African President Nelson Mandela he enjoined his fellow Muslims in a local mosque to join jihad in order to recover Jerusalem. He also compared, on that occasion, the Oslo accords to the Hudaybiyya Treaty[31] concluded by the Prophet of Islam and he mentioned Caliph Umar and Patriarch Sophronius, before the replay of their roles two years later in Bethlehem. The recurrence of the Hudaybiyya, Jerusalem, and jihad themes in Arafat's speeches to delirious Palestinian crowds, where he trumpeted the virtue of sacrifice in order to restitute the Holy places for Islam,[32] could not be accidental. Arafat knew very well the chords that he had to play on in order to instigate massive and passionate responses within his constituencies. In so doing, he not only could rally around him his supporters from the traditional PLO, who regard him as the symbol of their nationalism but he could also cater to the Islamic opposition who embraces precisely these very same Islamic symbols, phraseology, and terminology.

CONCLUSION: THE PEACE PROCESS IN-BETWEEN

The yet unsettled struggle between Palestinian nationalism and Islamism has many ramifications: domestic and external. While the way the Palestinians will choose to shape their society will certainly emerge as the Palestinian Authority acquires more power and more experience in handling its own affairs, it will remain closely intertwined with the modalities arising from the peace process between it and Israel. If the process is brought to fruition and Arafat can wave its benefits as his own doing, then his legitimacy will become ironclad and the Islamic threat might recede. If, however, the process should explode at some point then the rising Islamic alternative, which has the negation of that process at its core, might be in a position of triumphantly taking over with the vindictive grin of 'I told you!'

The peace process is crucial because it consists of negotiations in which the parties have to overcome the gap between what they regard as negotiable in a give-and-take horse-trading, and what they might deem as non-negotiable under any circumstances. Negotiable issues usually regard assets and other measurable objects, the renunciation of which means material, real estate, or monetary loss. When one senses that the sustained loss can be compensated for by other assets or, that by giving up some, one gets some, one may be inclined to negotiate and come to a compromise. That is a quantitative debate – measurable, compromisable, and therefore negotiable. When, on the other hand, the parties advance value-related arguments or claims, the debate goes one notch up. The value attached by one party to one element or another, is immeasurable and subjectively evaluated; it might be hugely significant for one but totally insignificant for the other, or equally valuable to both parties, either due to the intrinsic value attached thereto, or simply because it is so important for one party as to make the other covet it too. The contested value may be moral, cultural, or religious, and as such it becomes utterly non-negotiable. Here we enter the gate of qualitative debate.

In any process of conflict resolution, the quantitative issues would tend to be resolved first, while the qualitative ones would tend to be relegated to the end of the process. In order to reach an agreement (Oslo I and II), Israel had to pay in quantitative terms: partial withdrawal and partial independence (euphemistically termed 'redeployment' and 'autonomy', respectively), compromises on water and security, and the like. Israel, having spent many of her trump cards on this quantitative stage of settlement, has very few arrows left in her quiver for the much more difficult qualitative debate that will follow regarding Jerusalem, Palestinian statehood, the right or return of refugees, the uprooting of Israeli settlements, and any number of other intractable issues. The contradiction between the resolution of the Palestinians to ultimately arrive at their qualitative goals, and the equally rigid determination of the Israelis to foil those attempts, has caused the parties to tackle the negotiable first. So, while pragmatist Arafat is able to survive politically only as long as he delivers Israeli concessions, he might become a lame duck when Israel stops conceding, as the day of reckoning is approaching with regard to the real issues which Israel cannot yield.

Then, the turn of the Hamas alternative will come. Because, then, not only would the Islamists feel free to resume terrorism with popular support, but also they will have proven with vengeance that Arafat and his secular nationalism had failed. What is more, Hamas will certainly raise the stakes of the bargain: they will claim that Arafat's will to negotiate and compromise was at the source of the impasse. Better then to return to the infallible time and history-tested tenets of Islam, Hamas-style, which preclude any negotiation, any compromise over the *waqf* land that had been accorded by Allah to all generations of Muslims. Better die in battle while resisting the occupier, they have often said, than submit to the humiliation of lending their approval to the usurpation of Muslim land by the enemies of Allah and Islam.

In turn, with the lead of the renewed struggle against Israel having been taken over by the Islamists who do not feel restrained by the various formulations of Oslo, Islam will be strengthened at home as well. The programme of Hamas is one package: an Islamic society, governed by Islamic *shari'a* law, will also be worthy of claiming the redemption of the Holy Land from the hands of its usurpers. Such a pure society can only go back to the qualitative version of the conflict: an all or nothing choice, a battle to the finish. This trend, which has been strengthening since the outbreak of al-Aqsa *Intifada*, has pushed Arafat to sub-scribe to it, and his PLO forces (Tanzim, Al-Aqsa Brigades, Force 17) to adopt the same battle theory as Hamas, including the 'mar-tyrdom operations' where young Palestinians self-immolate them-selves in the process of massacring innocent civilians.

NOTES

This was first published in the *Journal of Church and State*, 43 (Summer 2001), pp. 423–45.

1. In addition to this prevailing theme in recent Palestinian publications, even such respect-ed scholars as San Nuseibeh hark back to this myth as if it were a fact of history. See his jointly authored book with Mark Heller, *No Trumpets, No Drums* (New York: Hill and Wang, 1993), p.32.
2. The 1948 War, which generated Israel's independence and the problem of Palestinian refugees, is often termed *Nakba* (disaster), and so is the defeat of all Arabs by Israel in the 1967 Six Day War, which ended in Israel's occupation of the West Bank and Gaza. In 1970 the PLO was forced out of Jordan (Black September), and in 1982, Arafat and his troops were expelled from Lebanon by Israel.
3. Previously prominent names in the Palestinian national struggle, such as abu Jihad and abu Iyyad or present-day Arafat aides like abu Mazen and abu 'Ala', or his opponents such as Qaddumi and Hamas leaders, are seldom mentioned in the Palestinian hierarchy of heroes. Only recent heroes who have either died dramatically (like abu Ayyash, 'the Engineer'), or do not otherwise pose an immediate threat to Arafat (such as ailing Ahmed Yassin), are occasionally mentioned.
4. See e.g. R. Israeli, 'Sadat Between Arabism and Africanism', *Middle East Review* 2 (Spring 1979), pp.39–48. See also his *Man of Defiance: A Political Biography of Anwar Sadat* (London and Ottowa: Weidenfeld and Nicolson, 1985).
5. See Art. I of the Covenant.
6. See Art. 4–5.
7. Ibid. See also Art. 7.
8. Arab literature marks the Zionist Invasion as the year of the Balfour Declaration in 1917.
9. Art. 8, 9, 10.
10. Art. 13, 14, 15, 16.

12. Art. 16.
13. Art. 22, 23.
14. Art. 22–26.
15. Art. 20.
16. See the Israeli press of 29 and 30 January 1997, notably *Ha'aretz*.
17. E.g. Sheikh Abu Sanina, the preacher of al-Aqsa Mosque, in his sermon of Ramadan, Friday, 31 January 1997. Reported by *Ha'aretz*, 3 February 1997, p.3.
18. Hamas is the acronym of *Harakat Muqawama Islamiyya* (the Islamic Resistance Movement), which became the umbrella organization created overnight at the outbreak of the *intifada* in late 1987, to bring together all the local Muslim associations of years past.
19. See Sylvia Haim, *Arab Nationalism* (Berkeley, CA: University of California Press, 1962); N. Johnson, *Islam and Politics of Meaning in Palestinian Nationalism* (London: Kegan Paul, 1982); and B. Lewis, 'The Return of Islam', *Commentary* (Winter 1976).
20. Art. 33 of the PLO Charter.
21. This system is used throughout the entire text of the Covenant.
22. See the Introduction to the Charter and Art. 17 and 20.
23. Art. 1–7 of the Covenant
24. Art. 11, 13.
25. See Art. 5.
26. See Preface of the Covenant, quoting Sheikh Amjad al-Zahawi.
27. It is noteworthy, however, that some Hamas leaders, not the most important among them and against the best advice of the leadership on the outside, have been co-opted into the legislative and executive branches of the Palestinian authority.
28. Ahmad Yasin is the spiritual head of the founder of Hamas. His physical handicap and prolonged internment in an Israeli jail have added to his charisma and appeal. Ayyash, the 'Engineer', who mounted many lethal attacks against Israel, was finally killed by the Israelis, which augmented his aura as a national hero. Both persons were lavishly praised by Arafat.
29. Art. 31 of the Hamas Charter.
30. The case of the independence-minded night editor of *al-Quds* in Jerusalem. Mahir al-Alami, who did not conform to these rules, became a *cause célèbre* in January 1996, when this otherwise respected journalist found himself arrested and interrogated in the dark basements of the security apparatus in Jerusalem.
31. Hudaybiyya was the place where the Prophet made his treaty with the Meccans A.D. 630, which aborted his pilgrimage to the Ka'ba in that year, but permitted him to come again the following year and then, under the pretext that the Quraysh had broken the treaty, he conquered Mecca. On this theme, see article by the same author in *Journal of Church and State* 43 (Summer 2001), pp.423–45.
32. See, e.g: Arafat's speech at Gaza's Al-Azllar University on the occasion of Miraj Day, broadcast live on Palestinian television on 1 January 1995.

Palestinian Women: The Quest for a Voice in the Public Square through 'Islamikaze Martyrdom'[1]

When Frantz Fanon described the Algerian struggle for independence (1954–62), he predicted that women would emancipate themselves by participating in the violence.[2] The Algerian experience remains mixed at best, as Juliette Minces' study shows.[3] In recent days Palestinian women have become 'Islamikaze' martyrs and have received much praise in the Muslim world. Will history repeat itself?

At first, acts of Islamikaze were considered rare and outlandish among the Palestinians, after they were imported from the Hizbullah, which had used them with great effect in Lebanon against the Americans and the Israelis. Then Hamas fundamentalists, a group opposed to the Palestinian Authority used the tactic, but since the outset of the *intifada* (2000) secular groups of al-Aqsa (Martyrs) Brigade, Tanzim and Force 17, elements of Fatah, the main component of the PLO, have joined them.

Islamikaze operations were praised as the ultimate weapon against Israel in particular and the West in general (hence the popularity of Bin Laden and the jubilation after September 11). The circle of Islamikaze volunteers keeps expanding. Once the exclusive domain of Muslim radicals, Islamikaze actions are now perceived in the Palestinian street as patriotic means to beat the Israeli occupier. Women and children were drawn into the activity on both sides as actors or victims. The struggle, with its multi-dimensional participants and targets, has acquired some characteristics of a total war, with an awesome impact with respect to casualties, damage, destruction and political reverberations.

The status of women in Islam has been a controversial topic for decades. Muslims point to Islamic largesse towards their women, and Western critics are horrified at what they regard as female oppression, discrimination and exclusion.[4] It is beyond the scope of this study to judge this complicated issue. Our purpose is to show the fascinating process through which Palestinian women have become Islamikaze martyrs to achieve higher status. The paradox is that– while self-immolating young women are glorified posthumously, there seems to be no change in the fortunes of the living women, just as the glorification of the dead Islamikaze males does not raise the status of the deprived youth.

PROTECTION VERSUS INSTRUMENTALIZATION OF WOMEN IN ISLAM

There has been a serious conflict in Islam about the status of women. In one pole, ultra-conservative societies such as those of Saudi Arabia, Sudan and Iran, require that their women be veiled and sheltered, either to protect them from the environing rapacious male society or from their own lust and stereotypical 'frivolity'. In Saudi Arabia and the Sudan, a male chaperone from their first-degree relatives must accompany them when they go out, but they are prevented from mixing with males or to perform tasks, such as driving, shopping or schooling which might expose them to male scrutiny. On the other hand, we watch millions of emancipated Muslim women who dress, think, behave and communicate every bit like their Western counterparts. Moreover Muslim fundamentalists who restrict women, nevertheless recognize their value in their families, raising children, and occasionally even in battle, which by definition requires mixing with males, foregoing the Islamic dress, and involvement in violence. How do we account for these contradictions?

Part of the answer lies in the concept of honour in Islam. Arabic distinguishes between male (*sharaf*) and female honour ('*ird*). As in the West, man's honour is related to the deeds he performs and image he projects. His honour is redeemable if he only applies himself to maintain it, shelter it and retrieve it when lost. The woman's honour, by contrast, refers to her intimacy, modesty and decency in dress, the preservation of virginity until marriage, gentle behaviour and keeping aloof from male society, which is corrupt by definition. If she should fail in one of those categories, her honour is forever lost. There is a linkage between the two branches of honour, however, inasmuch as the man's honour consists, inter alia, of preserving his women's honour, for letting it be smeared would inexorably expose the man's inability to protect what is his, be it women or property. That is the reason why usurpation of one's land by outsiders is often considered a violation of the honour of its owner, and then the land is said to have been 'raped', 'desecrated' or 'violated'. However, the place of the man as the protector of his woman's honour posits him in a superior standing in relation to her. For while he can act to rescue his honour, she can only prevent its loss through abstention. Hence the many intellectual difficulties one encounters in dealing with women in combat duties, especially if those who have to make the decision are Muslim fundamentalists themselves, who on the one hand cannot oppose martyrdom, but on the other hand insist on safeguarding women's honour.

After September 11, when President Bush announced a 'crusade' against terrorism, many Muslim clerics, and not necessarily the most fanatic, immediately sensed the approaching confrontation with the West in terms of jihad, in which everyone, including women, were supposed to take part:

> When the enemy sets foot on one inch of Islamic soil, we have to fight him. In this [jihad] war a son can join without permission from his father, *a wife without her husband's consent* [emphasis added], a slave without his master's agreement. Islam enjoins us to join jihad for the sake of Allah until one of two positive alternatives is gained: martyrdom or victory ... When Islam is attacked, there are no boundaries. In this case jihad is a duty binding on all Muslims.[5]

This means that for Muslims, the imperative to defend the land against the invading enemy overrides the restrictions on women's movements and cancels the chaperone requirement. Muslim women have to be protected against the onslaughts of the sceptical West that questions the humanity of Islamikaze acts, especially by Muslim women. After the onset in January 2002 of female

Islamikaze attacks against Israel, a Jordanian columnist, priding himself on the 'dignity that women enjoyed in the Arab and Islamic world', accused the Western human rights activists of 'robbing women of their rights to be human, and viewed them as bodies without souls'. He stressed that Muslim jihad fighters 'never dreamt to own a BMW or a cellular phone, and never carried makeup in their bags, but rather explosives to fill the enemy with horror'. He said that it was the West that demanded that Eastern women should become equal to men, and that that was the way the Muslim female martyrs understood equality.[6] Similarly, *Afaq Arabiya*, the mouthpiece of the Muslim Brotherhood in Egypt, accused the West of wasting money in vain, attempting to 'disrupt the consciousness of the Muslim women and make them believe that their bodies and needs were most important'. The writer, sociologist Dr al-Maghdoub, launched an all-out attack against that western intervention, which 'invokes women's liberation, equality with men, and their right to be prostitutes, to strip, and to reveal their charms', and assured that those concepts were doomed to fall on deaf ears.[7] For this sociologist, those Westernized 'superficial women' in the Muslim world served the West by

> Giving [Arab] countries their drug addicted young men and women … who have perverse [homosexual] relations, commit rape, theft, and murder … But they are still a minority, even if they make a lot of noise. The majority of young Muslims are still in good shape. It is true that they are silent, but we have seen how the silence of Wafa Idris ended.[8]

Many preachers sing the praise of Muslim women and lament the corruption the West introduces. Permissiveness has become the most negative aspect of Western society in the eyes of puritanical Muslims. Homosexuality, which in most Muslim countries is considered a crime is imputed by some preachers to the 'brothers of monkeys and pigs [i.e. the Jews], for whom, as for other Unbelievers, this is a normative pattern of conduct', and who accused the Secretary General of the UN of permissiveness in allowing prostitution which helps the spread of AIDS.[9] Permissiveness is linked to the status of women who, when liberated and westernized, become for Muslim fundamentalists the worst and most dangerous agent of social disruption. The discussion of women in the sermons of the clerics is not anecdotal as it sometimes appears in Western discourse, when suddenly interest is taken in Saudi women who are banned from corrupt and permissive ways of Western women which might wreck the entire traditional social order. For Muslim conservatives the interest of the West in the rights of women in the Muslim world signifies its determination to ruin that order by hitting it at its soft belly – its honour, i.e. the honour of the women who are dragged into promiscuity and permissive mores, and the honour of men who watch their women slipping from under their authority, exposing them as unable to protect their modesty and decency.

One sheikh, for example, said 'the woman, being a double-edged sword, can be turned into the most dangerous weapon of mass destruction', hence her being a target of most plots against the social order of the Muslim *umma*, it being understood the West is often accused of using women, the weakest link in the Muslim social chain, to detach Muslims from their faith. Under the guise of compassion, and protection of the rights of women, the West leads astray many Muslim women, who are not aware that Islam affords them a status of equality and allocates them rights and duties that 'concord with their nature and character'. Their nature and character are, of course, determined by those same clerics who say explicitly that 'permitting women to go out to the streets and rub shoulders with men, and talk in public to persons who are not their protectors, and even expose parts of their bodies that are forbidden, lead to destruction and shame'.[10]

Incidentally, the Jews take the brunt of those accusations, possibly because of their close proximity to Muslims in Palestine, and are considered as the agents of the Western drive to corrupt Muslim women. Numerous are the quotations from Muslim sources during the sermons of clerics which 'corroborate' Jewish corruption with regard to women. For example, they say that the first crime committed by the biblical Children of Israel was to let their women go out adorned with jewellery, with a view of rousing *fitna* (unrest), and were therefore punished by Allah.[11] Another preacher remarked that one could detect the clear link between the Western campaign against the 'modesty and morality of Muslim men and women, and the Jewish schemes to destroy their humanity and make them look like beasts, namely naked and exposed'.[12] Preachers draw lessons from other cultures, like the Greek and the Roman which had collapsed, in their estimate, due to 'the corruption of women in their midst'. They contend that while at the inception of those ancient civilizations women were 'modest, protected and cared about their house work, both the Greeks and the Romans were successful and built vast empires, but when their women engaged in make up and frequenting clubs and public places, those civilizations were doomed'. They infer from that example, that since the enemies of Islam wished it to collapse irretrievably, they have decided to target the corruption of Muslim women. They find solid 'proof' for their contention in the form of the 'irrefutable' Protocols of the Elders of Zion, and therefore they conclude that the 'enemies of Muslim women are the Jews, the Christians, the hypocrites, the secularists, and the utilitarian types that flock in their wake'.[13]

Imputing to the Jews the schemes to derail the Muslim woman from her traditional modesty[14] does not tell the whole story. Western women, in themselves, are to blame, for they heed the false ideas current in the West regarding the protection of women's rights, which in fact are calculated to 'push them to a sinful freedom'. According to this interpretation by the preachers, this kind of free conduct of women in the West has generated societies where 'crime is their hobby, adultery their entertainment, and murder a form of expressing anger'. This is no coincidence, in their view, in societies where 'the number of illegitimate children surpasses the numbers of those originating from legal intercourse', where women, even when married, 'do what they wish', where juvenile girls know and do more than adult married women, and where that 'ideological garbage is diffused through the media and satellite television'. They view as horrifying the sight of women 'going out of the house when they please, where they please and without permission of their husbands'. Even more horrible is the fact that 'in some households, it is the woman who establishes the rules', so much so that in many Western countries the women have grown 'masculine'. Thus, their men are emasculated to such an extent that except for their external look as men, there is nothing left to their masculinity.[15] Some clerics view Western women as a 'cheap commodity which presents herself naked or half naked to please the men', especially when they serve as maids in houses, clerks in offices, nurses in hospitals, stewardesses in flights and hotels, teachers in men's classes and actresses in movies and on television. They castigate men also for using feminine voices on radio as singers or announcers. The gloomy consequence in the eyes of those clerics is that since there are more women than men in the West, and the number of wives was unwisely limited to one, all the rest were earmarked for corruption and debauchery.[16]

Those Muslim preachers, the main shapers and controllers of public opinion in conservative Muslim societies, contrast the 'corruption' of Western women and the chastity and purity of their Muslim counterparts:

> Western women travel without supervisors and live as strangers among strangers. Thus, the enemies of Allah and of humanity have denied their unfortunate women all the fortunate components of life which make them happy, as well as their social rights, so as to condemn them to a life of corruption and destruction. And despite all these crimes, they claim that they defend women's freedom … Men have become like animals of prey who treat cruelly the weaker [women], while men regard their women like wild cats … Even Sylvester Stallone said that he had all reasons to hate women … Thus, the lot of women in Islam is far superior than Western women's, and certainly than Indian women who have to be incinerated live when their husbands die, or Chinese women whose husbands are allowed to bury them live …
>
> The West makes hollow statements regarding human rights for women by making them the equals of men, but when they leave their house they are consumed by the lie of this freedom. Public corruption grows and spreads as a result, not only to bordellos but also to hotels … dance clubs, or even on the open highway. It is no longer strange there when fathers copulate with their daughters and brothers with their sisters …

One of the mistakes committed by women is that under the pretext of fatigue, or because they wish to provoke their partners, they refrain from joining them when they are summoned to bed ... By doing so, the woman expresses ignorance, because she robs her husband from his greatest right and puts herself in jeopardy, because it is written that when a man summons his wife and she refuses, she is cursed by the Angels until she recants. Another mistake regards the service of the husband. When she fails in her duties to her husband, by disregarding his needs in cooking, washing and cleaning etc., that may be attributed to sheer laziness, and this is serious enough in itself. Service to her husband is her right and duty. Muslim women ought to treat their husband well and serve him, and this will make the husband happy and create happiness in the family ...

Another mistake is to allow into the house anyone that was banned by her husband. Husbands have the right to bring into the house only people they like, and women have to obey. She is not allowed to bring in anyone not to his liking, even if it is her relatives ... When her husband marries more wives, some women behave with extreme jealousy, ignorance and stupidity.[17]

The question of polygamy was raised again during Ramadan of 2001 and caused a storm because the 'justification' for it was not related to the doctrine set in the Qur'an, but was anchored in a series of rationalizations, harking back to other jurists. One polygamist argued, for example, that legalized polygamy was better than mass adultery. Famous Egyptian radical jurist, Yussuf al-Qaradhawi, in exile in Qatar, said:

There is no society without polygamy. Westerners who condemn and reject polygamy are doing it themselves. The difference between their polygamy and ours is that theirs is immoral and inhuman. Men in the West sleep with more than one woman, and if she gets pregnant, they deny responsibility for the child and do not support the woman financially. It is nothing more than lust.[18]

The raging sexual appetite of men is uncontrollable and

might lead them to adultery. In addition, women have men-
strual periods which in some cases last 10 days or more, and
during which their husbands cannot have sexual relations
with them. Therefore, it has been determined that a man
might have a hard time being satisfied with one woman, and
it is better to rescue him from the sin of adultery by allowing polygamy ... All women arouse a man, but not all men
arouse a woman. Even among animals, females need sex less
than males ... and they desire the male only when they want
to become pregnant, after which they lose their desire ...
Women are this way too.[19]

This view was backed by Sheikh Tamimi, the Head of the
Palestinian judicial system, who contended that unlike Western
men and women who have many lovers and mistresses, Islam
protects the women's humanity and emotions by securing for
them marriage and honour.[20] A secular lawyer concurs that it is
better to have many wives than visit prostitutes in secret, but
he also provides two more original arguments: one, if the husband travels frequently, sometimes for a few months, it is
preferable for him to take another wife than find illicit sexual
outlets; and secondly, if a man dies, his married brother can
wed the widowed wife, thus saving her and her children from
'disintegration and perdition'.[21] There are clerics who claim
that, just like men, women also can be given to a 'raging sexual desire'. But in case they are not, and their husbands cannot
be satisfied with one woman while the door to them is closed
to polygamy, then 'they will wear out their only wife with
excess of sex, or will set their eyes on other women', therefore
it is better to let them take more than one wife, as allowed by
Allah.[22] Sheikh Bitawi from the Nablus Shari'a Court, found
another justification for bigamy, to wit that 'due to the 40 days
of hiatus after giving birth, or during menstruation, men with
great sexual prowess cannot restrain themselves, and they have
the right to take another wife'.[23] Sheikh Qaradhawi also insists
that barren women give legitimacy to polygamy because a husband cannot be deprived of the children he yearns for.[24] Sheikh
Sa'id al-Jamal provides the excuse that when a woman falls ill
and can neither have sex nor do the housework, but she still is

dear to her husband, there is no choice but allowing him a second wife.[25]

Another popular justification for polygamy is demography, which is manipulated to the 'benefit' of women, inasmuch as men who wed many women as a matter of fact 'rescue' them from their celibacy, and allow them to experience motherhood, because there are more women than men. The proponents of this rationalization, like Sheikh Qaradhawi, emphasize that non-married Western women, who are not fortunate enough to embrace the Muslim solution, end up in 'licentiousness, illicit pregnancy and prostitution, which produce bastards into the world'. So, he concludes, 'maybe half a husband is better than none'.[26]

The Sheikh of Qatar, Walid Bin Hadi, basing himself on the Prophet, suggests that no rationalizations are needed and that this matter ought to be left to every man's discretion, for each has his own reasons for opting for polygamy. He argues that just as the Prophet himself had counselled 'not to ask a husband why he beats his wife', so according to the same principle, 'do not ask a husband why he takes a second wife'.[27] This state of mind allows some Muslim jurists to claim that Islam is considerate inasmuch as it restricts polygamy, because it 'only' allows four wives, following the model of the Prophet, who was the most perfect of Allah's creatures and therefore his judgment is beyond reproach. Qaradhawi again resorts to comparison with the West, from which Islam emerges as occupying the moral high ground. He says that in the sacred scriptures of the Judeo-Christian tradition, it is stated without contest or protest that David had 100 wives and 200 concubines, while his son Solomon had 700 wives. By contrast, Islam put the uppermost limit to four wives, and Qaradhawi cites the case of a contemporary of the Prophet who was married to 10 wives, but when he converted to Islam, he was enjoined to choose four of them and lay off the rest. Islam also stipulates that the four wives must be treated equally, that the man be physically and sexually capable of satisfying them all, and that he must evince his ability to protect and support his women,[28] that is to demonstrate to the world that her honour is inviolable.

And lest inquisitive minds might ask about polyandry for women, Sheikh Qaradhawi is quick to respond:

Some people say: 'why not allow women to be polygamous?'
... But we say to them that he must treat his wives equally,
and if he fears he cannot, he must be satisfied with one. How
can a woman treat her husbands equally? How can she
divide herself among them? For example, if all four want
children, who gets to have the first one?

A women could get pregnant without knowing whether the
father was Zayd or Amr. Okay, they say that today there are
laboratories to determine such things, but even if it is possible
to know who the father is, how is it possible to tell the husbands: you first, the second two years afterwards, and the third
eight years after that? Is this equality? The woman cannot treat
her husbands equally, but the man can treat his wives equally,
if he is a man of faith, morality and conscience. [29]

Dr Al-Masir, of al-Azhar University, counters the western logic of
human rights, which purports to defend the rights of married
women by denying their husbands polygamy, by positing the
right of the second and third women to be married too:

Every woman has the right to live in the shadow of her husband who will defend her purity and honour ... In the days
of the Prophet, not even one woman remained without a
husband – not a spinster, not a widow, not a divorcee ... I
ask our women and daughters not to be egotistical.[30]

Polygamy is only one of many items raised by Muslim clerics in
general, and radical fundamentalists in particular since the turn
of the twentieth century and the intensive process of modernization which exposed Muslim women to their Western counterparts.[31] For one thing, the increasing presence of Muslim women
in the public square, where mixing of genders is necessary, i.e. in
education, shopping, places of work and entertainment, has
forced Muslim jurists to tackle these issues and find answers.
Hassan Turabi, the spiritual leader of the Sudan, for example,
(fundamentalist radical as he is) has tried to address the question
of women in Muslim societies and, unlike others, approached the
matter pragmatically, and pronounced himself in favour of abolishing many of the restrictions on mixing genders, as long as

essential Muslim notions and values were preserved. Quite revolutionary is his insistence on the equality between the genders,
and his contention that it was in the Middle Ages that the *shari'a*
was made more severe and imposed restrictions on women, while
at the time of the Prophet women were encouraged to take part
in religious ceremonies and worship, of which the Hajj to Mecca
still exists to this day. Turabi's treatise on women's rights[32] not
only advocates their equality but also encourages them to work
outside the house and not be confined to their children's education. He foresees for them full integration in public life and filling
all public posts – political, elective or appointive, including the
armed forces, citing the examples of some of the Prophet's
Companions.[33] Indeed, the Islamic rule in the Sudan did recruit
women to the popular forces in order to gain popular legitimacy,
like in other revolutionary regimes in the Third World.

While Turabi remains clearly opposed to the western style of
the liberation of women, which he regards as too licentious, he is
in favour of reforming the too-strict limitations in Muslim societies: for example, not to force the veil, but enforce 'modest'
dress; to allow women in the public square, but not to exploit
their sexual attraction to sell cars and other goods. In an interview he gave in 1995, he responded explicitly to the question in
this essay, i.e. women's participation in jihad. He said:

> At the times of the Prophet ... women used to fight alongside
> with him, and were in charge of the logistics and medical
> services. There were even female Companions (*sahaba*) who
> were dispatched overseas to wage jihad and die as martyrs.
> Lately we watched in Khartum a spectacular sight, when 500
> Muslims from the entire world participated at the Popular
> Arabo-Islamic Conference, on which occasion women exhib-
> ited their military skills near the airport. Had I given a lec-
> ture on women liberation in front of all those sheikhs, none
> of them would have taken me seriously, and some would
> have even opposed me. But as they saw women riding hors-
> es, dressed in military fatigues and carrying guns, or crawl-
> ing on the ground while bomb-shells were landing around
> them, and they were singing war songs, the viewers found
> themselves joining them and repeating their words.[34]

This overstated enthusiastic call advocating women's liberation in Islam, not only was far from being implemented in the Sudan itself, but was countered by other models of Muslim fundamentalism, such as Mawdudi's in the Indian Sub-continent, and the praxis of Islamic revolution in Iran. The net result is that, by setting the high standards of the obedient Muslim woman, even when she is one of four, up against the deficient morality of the Western woman; not only are Muslim women warned not to fall into the Western trap, and the West in general is told to keep off the virtuous Muslim wives and not try to incite them to abandon their faith and submissive status. Conversely, Muslims are constantly warned by the mosque preachers against the Unbelievers' lures and customs, and urged not to follow them. Particularly targeted are the 'People of the Book', namely Christians and Jews, who are credited/accused of elaborating the trappings of Western culture that have become so attractive to the world in general and Muslim countries in particular. The inference is clear: if the Scriptuaries are inherently corrupt and the enemies of Allah, who actively seek to undermine Muslim societies and subvert Allah's, that is Muslim values, then no Muslim should approach them, learn from them or succumb to their mores. Only thus can Muslim honour, the female's, and by inference the male's, be saved.

Viewed from the Muslim woman's point of view, however, things look slightly differently, and are hardly conducive to the battle spirit that Muslim clerics claim pious women are imbued with. In the Egyptian weekly *Akhbar al-Yaum* a lengthy letter was published from an unnamed Egyptian woman, who told how it was like to be married to a Muslim fundamentalist. The Editor decided to publish it, though it was extraordinarily lengthy, after he was prodded to do so by colleagues who had 'heard similar or worse stories'. She wrote with rage, that while the Egyptian press was lauding the liberation of the Afghan women from Taliban government, it refrained from reporting on the situation of women in Egypt which was no less depressing. Excerpts from the story of her relations with her husband are edifying:

> his [pre-marital] tolerance, which had attracted me during our engagement, turned overnight into rigidity, domination

and tyranny ... A week after the wedding he asked me to sit down with him to hear his instructions:

First [he said], you must terminate all your contact with your workplace. Do not resign, just do not show up, and they will fire you, according to the law without giving you your rights, and you do not need them;

Second ... make up will not improve your appearance, so you must immediately rid yourself of all those sins [make-up] ...

Third, ... men hungry for women have become wide-spread in Egyptian society, and you are prohibited from arousing their lust. Therefore, you have to wear garments that conceal you from their adulterous eyes ...

Fourth, to expose your face and hair is a grievous sin ... you are fortunate that I can save you from the torments of Hell ... when you married a believer like me ... You must rip up your clothing, silk garments and lingerie ... You will wear the only garment a Muslim woman needs to wear, which will cover you from head to toe, and will have only one opening to allow you to see and avoid bumping into things ...

I now have many garments, all covering every centimetre of my body, and in only two colours: black for outdoors, white for the house ... In all my 25 years of marriage I knew perhaps only one week of happiness. I am the mother of six, since my husband thinks that the only reason for marriage is to increase the birth rate of the Nation of Muhammed. Were I not already 55, he would not have settled for only six children ...

My husband also forbade laughter in the apartment soon after the honeymoon, since laughter was from Satan, who aims at corrupting believing Muslims ... Imagine a house full of children who are forbidden to laugh, play or even smile ... A blind sheikh came to the house and drilled my children to memorize the Qur'an, hour after hour ... Then he demand-ed that I cover the hair of my daughters when they reached the age of 4, and dress them like me at 7. I could not remove my head-to-toe cover even in the house, lest the girls learn the bad example from me and remove it when they were outdoors, far from his watchful eyes ...

Our house has no radio or television, because they are

forbidden by Islam, as they distract children from their purpose in life ... Only recorded tapes of preachers reciting the Qur'an and commentaries were allowed, and we were made to gather and listen to them day in, day out ... When my daughter asked her father why he did not bring home the cassettes of the great preachers of al-Azhar [appointed by the establishment], my husband said that they are agents of the unbelieving government and speak its words, and therefore there was no place for their cassettes in the house ...

He thought that education was appropriate for boys, but pointless for girls ..., and after they attended an elementary religious school, he decided they should stay at home. They are ignorant of the government curriculum and hardly know how to write and read ..., though they know the Qur'an and the Hadith by heart ...[35]

A whole litany of suffering brought this unfortunate woman to the brink of committing suicide on some 20 occasions, and to a real attempt from which she was rescued, according to her own reckoning. She was particularly hurt by her son who became a harsh copy of her husband, and on September 11 came home jubilant about the horror in the US, and assuring his crying and desperate mother that he saw and knew hundreds of other people who reacted like him. She could not comprehend how his mind was taken over by violence, enmity and hatred, when he callously declared that that war would 'consume all those who are not Muslim, or do not implement what Muslims expect of them'. She lamented the 'spread of the virus of inter-religious violence in Egypt, which destroys the minds of young people', not necessarily from the deprived and disaffected social strata. That happened, she said, because many homes, like hers, were opened to fanatic preachers to brainwash the young girls and boys, something that would assuredly reflect on the next generation of Muslim terrorism, and ended with a plea to the world to realize that Egyptian women lived like their Afghani counterparts, while movements of human rights were looking on impassively.[36]

Muslim fundamentalist clerics, intent on protecting the honour of their women against foreign onslaught, sanction severe acts against them to keep them in line inwardly. The involvement of women, first as victims of terror and then as its progenitors, was discussed by Syrian-born Sheikh 'Umar al-Bakri, who took refuge in London. He advocated that 'all homosexuals there ought to throw themselves down from the Big Ben',[37] called the British MPs 'monkeys'[38] and vowed that the flag of Islam would 'fly high on Downing Street 10 and at the Elysee'.[39] He justified and defended the September 11 New York and Washington horrors, which for him came as a 'compensation for the atrocities the US had committed against Islam', and exhorted Muslims to unite and fight, sacrifice themselves and their wealth in order to gain access to Paradise and to make the difference between 'truth and falsehood, belief and heresy, oppressors and oppressed, the alliance of Satan against the Alliance of Allah'.[40] After the American attack against Afghanistan was launched, he issued a fatwa against Pakistani President Musharraf and other Muslim leaders who let their territory be used by Americans against a fellow Muslim state. In that verdict, for what it is worth, he raised, *inter alia*, many aspects of the status of women in Islam and in general, in the context of what we call terrorism and he insists on dubbing jihad. For him the Muslims who collaborated with the US were *murtaddun* (apostates), if 'at all they were Muslims to start with', and since they are involved in the war against Muslims, the sentence of *murtadd harbi* (an apostate who should be fought) applies to them, to wit:

1. His blood becomes permissible and he must be killed,
2. His marriage becomes invalid, as does his guardianship of his children and relatives,[41]
3. His property is permissible and he will not be able to bequeath it,
4. He cannot be buried in a Muslim cemetery.
5. He must be treated with animosity and hatred …
6. There is no difference between a man and a woman … The blood of a woman who is a heretic *harbiyya* is permissible, even if her fighting is limited to singing … Thus acted the Prophet against the fighting women of the Quraysh tribe. He permitted their blood and ordered them killed, although he generally prohibited killing women.[42]

This fatwa, which allowed killing Muslim women under certain circumstances, appeared under the emblem of 'The Shari'ah Court of the United Kingdom'. It was signed jointly by al-Bakri, under his title of 'Shari'a Court Judge in London', and Muhammed al-Musa'ari, the Secretary General of the Committee for Protection of Legitimate Rights in Saudi Arabia, and thus has authority and respectability. Its English version, however, was slightly different and signed by 'Muslim Jurists from Syria, Lebanon, Kuwait, the Emirates, Saudi Arabia, Pakistan, Afghanistan and the United Kingdom', with the names of the original two signatories, Bakri and Musa'ari, appearing at the bottom, with their phone numbers for further inquiries. In this version, the Qur'anic verse was added which threatened that the punishment of those who wage war against Allah and His Prophet and strive to make mischief in the land, is only this – that they should be murdered or crucified, or their hands and feet should be cut-off on opposing sides, or they should be imprisoned.[43] And the section about the women of Quraysh who were killed by the Prophet, was replaced by a paragraph that reads:

> Therefore we ask Muslims with capability, especially the armies of Muslim countries, to move quickly and to capture those apostates and criminals involved in these crimes, especially the ruler of Pakistan, King Fahd of Saudi Arabia and Rabbani of Afghanistan.[44]

The exposure of women to harrowing physical mutilation, on authority of the precedent set by the Prophet, though concealed in the English version, influenced the developing debate on the active participation of Muslim women in Islamikaze attacks as actors, or on suffering the consequences thereof as passive spectators. For, once the taboo was lifted on involving women (and children) in the course of Muslim violence during this brand of jihad, they were free to participate.

THE ROLE OF THE WOMEN FIGHTERS IN PALESTINIAN SOCIETY

These dilemmas concerning women's conduct in the public square, naturally come to the fore more acutely in revolutionary Muslim societies, such as in Algeria, the Sudan, Iran and Palestine, and by necessity produce local solutions and compromises between the various prevailing ideologies. Some Palestinian women have been quite prominent in the Palestinian national struggle, especially since the outbreak of the first *intifada* (1987–92), and then the second in 2000. They participated in demonstrations, took part in popular committees, and appeared as heroines dispatching their sons to the jihad front against Israel. Some of them, like Umm Jihad, the widow of Arafat's Deputy, Abu Jihad, believed to have been killed by Israel in Tunis, and Hanan Ashrawi, attained the rank of cabinet members in the Palestinian Authority; Ashrawi became famous as the most effective speaker for the Palestinians in the world media. Other Palestinian women, like Laila Khaled, became legends as active participants in Palestinian terrorism in the 1970s. But still, due to the strictures in the conservative circles of Palestinian society, women did not feel they got their due in terms of recognition though, as they were contributing their share to the national struggle.

Since the 1980s, however, energetic and enterprising Palestinian women, such as Sahar Khalifa, an author from Nablus, turned to establishing non-governmental associations which established research centres geared to promote the participation of women in national decision making, to provide them with educational and vocational training, and to raise their status in general within their society. Such organizations were founded in Nablus, Jerusalem and Ramallah. In 1991, for example, they held a conference on domestic violence, which attracted a wide attendance and raised the issue in public. While only a few women partook of the active national struggle against Israel, the bulk of the women's movements shifted their activity to their human and civil rights, after the establishment of the Palestinian Authority in 1994, and began lobbying for legislation to alleviate their plight. But the Authority, maybe because it considered women's equality as secondary to the national struggle, proved obtuse to their demands, and preferred to exercise a close control of those organizations rather than give them a lee-way that could embarrass the authorities in the world arena. Palestinian women ended up seeing their traditional role in the family reinforced, while their ambitions to participate in state-building and in decision-making were shelved until better days.[45] The accumulated frustration of Palestinian women, cou-pled with the other general strictures on women that apply in most Muslim societies, may have contributed to their turning elsewhere.

Hamas, which regards itself as a viable alternative to the Palestinian Authority, has been waiting in the aisles for it to trip, in order to step into the vacuum and replace it. Outwardly, it considers the entire land of Palestine, Israel included, as a *waqf* (Holy Endowment) land that has to be res-cued by jihad, not negotiations. Domestically, it turned the tenet of jihad from a collective duty (*fard kifaya*) binding on the Muslim community as a whole, namely exonerating the individuals once that obligation has been fulfilled by the state, into an individual commitment (*fard 'ayn*), binding on every person, including women. In this way, the Palestinian Authority can be circumvented and Palestinian individuals, women included, can be made directly responsible for extin-guishing the fire raging in the House of Islam.[46] The Hamas Charter devoted one of its sub-headings to 'The Role of Muslim Women', and two out of its thirty-six articles to the role reserved to women in Palestinian society, seems *prima facie* more attentive to women than the PLO and the Palestinian Authority. The latter had envisaged in the PLO Charter the institutions and processes to implement its national goals, but has been trying to achieve them by means of corrupt institu-tions and leaders, while Hamas, leaning on the Qur'an and Shari'a Law, purports to establish a righteous and honest administration that answers only to the Law of Allah.[47] It would be useful to recapitulate in full the wording of these two arti-cles.

Article Seventeen – Muslim women have a no lesser role than that of men in the war of liberation; they manufacture men and play a great role in guiding and educating the new generations. The enemies have understood that role, and realize that if they can guide and educate Muslim women in a way that would distance them from Islam, they would win that war. Therefore, you can see them expending consistent efforts by way of publicity and movies, curricula of education and culture, using as their intermediaries the craftsmen who are part of the various Zionist organizations which take on all sorts of names and shapes, such as the Free-Masons, Rotary Clubs, gangs of spies, and the like. All of them are nests of saboteurs and sabotage. Those Zionist organizations control vast material resources, which enable them to fulfill their mission amidst societies, with a view of implementing Zionist goals and spreading concepts that can be useful to the enemy. Those organizations operate in a situation where Islam is absent from the arena and alienated from its people. Thus, the Muslims must fulfil their duty in confronting the schemes of those saboteurs. When Islam will retake possession of the means to guide the lives of Muslims, it will wipe out those organizations which are the enemies of humanity and Islam.

Article Eighteen – The women in the houses and in the families of the jihad fighters, whether they are mothers or sisters, carry out the most important duty of caring for the home and raising the children upon the moral concepts and values which derive from Islam; and of educating their sons to observe the religious tenets, in preparation for the duty of jihad awaiting them. Therefore, we must pay attention to the schools and curricula upon which Muslim girls are educated, so as to make them righteous mothers, who are conscious of their duties in the war of liberation. They must be fully capable of being aware and of grasping the ways to manage their households. Economy and avoiding waste in household expenditures are prerequisites to our ability to pursue our cause in the difficult circumstances surrounding us. Therefore, let them remember at all times that money saved is equivalent to blood, which must be made to run in the veins, in order to ensure the continuity of life of our young and old.

'Lo, men who surrender unto Allah and women who surrender, and men who believe and women who believe, and men who obey and women who obey, and men who speak the truth and women who speak the truth, and men who persevere and women who persevere, and men who are humble and women who are humble, and men who give alms and women who give alms, and men who fast and women who fast, and men who watch their modesty and women who watch their modesty, and men who remember Allah and women who remember Allah, He has prepared for them forgiveness and a vast reward'.[48]

In this last citation from the Holy Book, women are compared in all regards with men, that is they can attain righteousness, exactly like men, if they pursue the Path of Allah. There are two articles about women in the Charter, certainly, but what do they say beyond the repetition of the traditional role of women in manufacturing children, educating them and preparing them, for jihad? Yes, women are obligated individually to jihad, but their jihad is to make children and raise them, namely their jihad and general status in society remain clearly subservient and auxiliary to that of men, the lip-service paid to them in the Charter notwithstanding. In other words, even the path offered to Palestinian women by Hamas, which should have seemed more attractive, because it is more equal on the face of it, turned out to be as hollow as the promises of the PLO and the Palestinian Authority. Only the avenue of Islamikaze remained, through which the self-immolating youth are not only heeded, but also become national heroes. That is the path upon which a select few Palestinian women will try to embark.

THE NEW WOMAN ISLAMIKAZE

The Palestinians have become the chief model of Islamikaze. The Palestinians have emerged in effect, not only as the most active agents in the implementation of the idea, but widened the circle of its membership beyond the few self-sacrificing radicals, into a legitimate national form of struggle in which women and children have taken the initiative. Unlike al-Bakri and al-Masri's fantasies where they articulate their wishful thinking to confront the world, bring down the West, kindle a world Islamic revolution and subvert their Western countries of exile from within, Palestinian clerics are unified by the theme of what they perceive as a concrete, daily and all-pervasive national struggle to which they provide theological responses. And once they sanctified Islamikaze as a legitimate form of struggle, indeed encouraged it, they could not exclude women and children from it. Other Muslim clerics were also dragged into the debate, but let us first focus on the Palestinian clerics' stated positions on Islamikaze, which by necessity generated the inclusion, first of individuals who did not belong to the Islamists of Hamas and Islamic Jihad, but were members of the avowedly 'secular' Fatah and al-Aqsa Brigades, and were then followed by women and children.

We have thus a new situation in which Islamikaze, though hitherto solely the trademark of Muslim radicals, and rarely at that for the daring few, has become since September 11 an acknowledged universal and common *modus operandi* by Muslim societies. On September 11 alone, nineteen self-sacrificing young Muslims died in the US; and since then about one hundred Palestinian terrorists have died in the same fashion, taking with them the lives of hundreds of Israelis. The cross-over from an extreme and unusual act to a current and routine way of action, not only necessitated the widening of the circle of volunteers within Palestinian ranks, but also engendered a new attitude towards the participation of women and children in this sort of battle. Hitherto, Muslim clerics have frowned upon active military service of women and the heads of Hamas and Islamic Jihad reserved for their women the role of educators and 'manufacturers of men', as we have seen above. The current cross-gender and cross-national universalization of Islamikaze terrorism, however, has widely opened the door towards banalization and routinization of this stunning phenomenon. Because what it takes from now on is not a trained, strong-willed and resolute fighter, with high physical skills, battlefield experience, endurance under stress and technical sophistication, but only a common person, male or female, adult or child, indoctrinated and eager to die for Allah, who knows how to push a button and evaporate instantly into Paradise.

About a dozen cases of Palestinian women who participated in

Islamikaze attacks against Israelis were recorded and document-ed.[49] In some cases the women were arrested before they could carry out their plans. In one instance (17 January 2001), a young Israeli teenager, Ophir Rahum, was lured on the Internet by a young Palestinian journalist, Amana Mona, to visit her in Ramallah, whereupon she delivered him to two Fatah men who murdered him. Other Palestinian women aided in driving Islamikaze operatives, or on lending them other logistic support. But by far the most renowned precedent-setting example of straightforward Islamikaze bombing, was carried out by Wafa Idris, a resident of Ramallah, who launched her 'martyrdom' attack in a Jerusalem street on 27 January 2002, in which one old Israeli woman was killed and ninety passers-by were wounded. To be sure, since the 1970s, when the PLO launched daring ter-rorist attacks against Israel, mainly from Lebanese territory, women had participated, were killed in their engagement with Israeli forces and then became hallowed as heroines of the Palestinian cause. But Wafa established the precedent of the first Palestinian woman who went to her death willingly and by choice. The new trend adopted by the Palestinian authorities and public at large, which runs counter to the traditional prohibition to Muslims not to take their own lives, has become an accepted, even encouraged, norm of struggle for women (and children), who were thereby put on par with men who sacrifice their lives in the same fashion.

The debate surrounding the 'martyrdom' of Wafa Idris, the first Palestinian woman Islamikaze, is in itself indicative of the new mood. Arafat's 'al-Aqsa Brigade', took responsibility for Wafa's explosion in the central street of Jerusalem in January 2002. Much of the initial debate went over her motivations to sacrifice herself, citing personal difficulties.[50] But when fellow Palestinians began to justify her act, quoting the precedents of other renowned Palestinian women-fighters, like Laila Khalid, and predicting that more women might follow suit,[51] the reli-gious aspect broke into the open. Hamas leaders said that jihad was an obligation that applied to women also, and that Islam had never differentiated between men and women in the battle-field, based on a precedent of the Prophet who used to draw lots among women who wished to join the battle.[52] Jamila Shanti, the

Head of the Women's Activities of the Palestinian Islamic Movement, concurred with the idea of equality of women in the struggle, 'provided they avoided inappropriate behaviour'. However, the women-martyrs are allowed, in her mind, to relinquish the veil for the occasion in order to 'mislead the enemy'. She believes that since the clerics share a consensus that Islamikaze operations are the highest form of martyrdom, there is nothing wrong with them.[53] The Head of Hamas, Sheikh Yassin, however, had some reservations, stating that while women had a role in jihad and martyrdom, their uniqueness warranted that they must be accompanied by a chaperone,[54] exactly as puritanical Muslims would not allow women to drive or to roam the streets unaccompanied by a brother, a father or a husband.

Yassin, bowing to operational requisites, later amended his position, realizing that the lone operation of the martyr woman would become unfeasible if she is accompanied by someone who would attract attention and might himself die in the attack. Therefore, he stated that only if the woman were to stay out for the day and the night, for operational considerations, she needed company, while if her absence was shorter, as in the case of martyrdom where she was not supposed to return, she might go alone.[55] But in a previous case of a would-be woman-martyr, arrested by Israel for attempting to blow herself up, and released after the Oslo Accords of 1993, she invoked a *hadith* where the Prophet was said to have allowed women to go to jihad even without their husbands' consent, when the land of Islam was invaded, which she thought was the case then.[56] Thus, for her, as for Yassin, necessity permitted the usually prohibited modes of behaviour. At al-Azhar University, where disputes converge in expectation for the rulings of Sheikh Tantawi, the head of that venerated institution, an internal debate ensued. While Sheikh Abu-al-Hassan decreed that the act of jihad by women against Israelis was permissible, when the enemy has 'plundered even one inch of Muslim land', in which case they are entitled to 'wage jihad even without their husbands' consent, and the slaves without their masters' permission', Tantawi ruled in favour of those acts provided they were not directed against civilians. Abu-al-Hassan also quoted precedents from the time of the Prophet when women were said to have been allowed to fight and kill enemy infidels.[57]

Although Yassin explained that women were simply not needed in the Hamas ranks of martyrs for the moment, because more male volunteers were available than his organization could absorb,[58] the debate continued to rage in the Arab world. Egypt's *al-Sha'b* glorified the woman who could teach all Arab men, rulers, princes and women, a lesson in the heroic defence of their country, in 'the battle of martyrdom which petrified the heart of the enemy's entity, and shocked the enemy with her meagre, thin and weak body … when with her all the myths about women's weaknesses, submissiveness and enslavement also exploded'.[59] In Egypt and the rest of the Arab world, words of support for Wafa Idris indeed abounded. Dr Samia Sa'd a-Din, a woman herself, proclaimed the end of gender classification in the Palestinian struggle, once Palestinian women have decided to 'write the history of their liberation with their blood, and will become time bombs in the face of the Israeli enemy. They will not settle for being mothers of martyrs any longer'.[60] Another columnist in *al-Akhbar* found it strange that while Swedish Foreign Minister, Anna Lind, was criticizing the American position [of support to Israel], Wafa carried out her act of martyrdom; for when Lind spoke up, men kept silent for fear of criticizing American policy. Thus, one brave woman spoke up while another brave woman acted.[61] For *al-Ahram* columnist, Zakariyya Nil, Wafa Idris was nothing less than a modern Jeanne d'Arc,[62] and another, 'Abd al-Halim Qandil, of the weekly *al-'Arabi*, elevated her to new heights, asserting that 'a nation who has in it Wafa Idris can never be defeated', for she became the 'most beautiful of women in the world, and in the world to come, once she rose to Heaven'. He considered her martyrdom as 'a death which instilled life' and 'a chunk of flesh and blood transformed into illuminating spirit and purity for the generations to come'. He praised her beauty when she liberated the Arabs from their sins and 'elevated the humiliated nation to Paradise'.[63] No one, however, reached the summit of praise for her as the Egyptian psychologist, Dr 'Adel Sadeq, the Head of Psychiatry at Cairo's Ein Shams University, who compared Wafa to Jesus Christ. He said that perhaps the Holy Spirit that placed Jesus in the womb of

Mary did the same by 'placing a bomb in the heart of Wafa and enveloped her pure body with dynamite', and it was no coincidence for him that 'the enemy in both instances was the same [the Jews]'.[64]

While it was to be expected that the Palestinian terrorist organizations that dispatched Wafa to her death would eulogize her in laudatory terms for her martyrdom,[65] it is much harder to explain in any rational terms the swelling support, symbolic and otherwise, that her act produced throughout the rest of the Arab world. If one can understand the political machinations of Saddam Hussein, when he decided to erect a memorial in her honour, one is aghast when a woman film-director, Dr Amira Abu-Fattuh, writes under the headline 'An Oscar-winning film':

> This is not a movie like all other movies. The heroine is the beautiful, pure Palestinian woman, Wafa Idris, full of faith and will-power. I could find no one better than she, and I could find no film more wonderful than this, that shocked Israel's heart … From Paradise where she is now, she shouts with all her strength: 'Enough glorification of the dead! Enough glorification of the victories of your forefathers!!!'. They have played their part, and now it is your turn.[66]

This short-lived but symbol-laden 'Wafa Festival', was triggered by the London-daily *al-Quds al-'Arabi*,[67] but was immediately picked up, like other sensational issues in the Arabic press, and repeated like a mantra, by Arab and Muslims writers of all political convictions. It was as if their oppressed frustration and hatred for Israel (and the Jews) regardless of the 'peace' Accords that their countries (Egypt and Jordan) had signed with Israel, at a considerable cost to the latter, were merely a new starting point to force her to disarm, to absorb attacks, at the hand of new heroes like Wafa. She was seen as 'a spark of light and hope in the midst of darkness, and courageous in deeds, not words',[68] a Mona Lisa, only more beautiful than the original, with her 'dreamy eyes and the mysterious smile on her lips', and in general 'more beautiful than any picture of a woman painted by any artists',[69] or her suitcase of explosives carried to her death as 'the most beautiful prize any woman can possibly win. Her spirit was raging, her heart filled with anger and her mind convinced by the calls of peace and coexistence'.[70] Even the horrifying detail of her act sounded like music in the ears of those columnists: 'she quietly made her decision, sought explosives, went to pray, and then chose her target carefully. She went to a big restaurant with dozens of customers. She asked Allah for a Martyr's death and victory ... she kissed the soil of the homeland and went calmly to her fate. She inscribed her name on the forehead of history'.[71] What is even more terrifying is the wish of the writer that the number of victims could have been higher, because Wafa killed 'only' one victim, an 81-year-old female passer-by in the main street of Jerusalem, but the over-enthusiastic columnist carried her in his dreams to a 'restaurant with dozens of customers'. This time he was wrong, but at other times, other females did kill dozens of unsuspecting civilians, children and entire families of customers in restaurants.

Wafa the martyr was made a model of behaviour in one Arab paper after another, by columnists of all walks and opinions, government and opposition, especially in 'moderate' Egypt, and her act of 'donning the belt of explosives and talking to Israel, America and the world, in the only language they understand',[72] was made the ideal for other youth to emulate. A female columnist, Nagwa Tantawi, dismissed Western culture and pledged victory to the superior culture of the Arabs and Muslims. She just forgot to say explicitly whether the values she was boasting about included martyrdom and wanton killing, but one could infer that from her comparison of Wafa with President Bush's daughters:

> Bush, who leads an oppressive campaign to educate the world, cannot even educate his own daughters. Note the difference between Wafa, the daughter of Arabism and Islam, and Bush's daughters. The difference is the same as the difference between our culture, based on beautiful and noble values, and on the values of homeland and martyrdom, and the materialistic culture [of the West]. This proves that whatever developments will be, victory will be ours – because we have culture and values.[73]

There was yet another, rather debasing, aspect touching upon women's position in the Islamic world, in connection with the Islamikaze acts of terror, and that was the discussion of the sexual rewards the male-martyrs were promised in Paradise, something that has no parallel with regard to the female martyrs. The rewards of the hereafter after martyrdom are the most concrete promise, indeed certainty, that pushes the Islamikaze to cross fearlessly the last obstacle of hesitation and embark on the martyrdom venture. Therefore, it is within the Palestinian community, which has trained and sent to self immolating jihad the greatest proportionate numbers of its sons, daughters and children, that these promises are most vividly described and debated, once they have become a matter of practical and close-at hand routine, and no longer of theoretical and remote theology. The debate did not begin in the aftermath of the September 11 events, but it was triggered at the end of the 1990s in the context of the Hamas and Islamic Jihad activities within Israel and against Israelis and Jews. On 19 August 2001, CBS's '60 Minutes' aired a programme on Hamas in which one its operatives, Muhammed Abu Wardeh, was asked to tell of his recruiting activities among would-be Islamikaze. He said, *inter alia*, that part of his technique was to describe to the novices the way Allah would reward them after they became martyrs by 'giving them 70 virgins, 70 wives and everlasting happiness'.[74] Embarrassed by the carnal temptations that were involved in what was to be a pure act of self-sacrifice for the sake of Allah, Muslim leaders in the West (not in the Islamic world where this doctrine enjoys widespread currency), raised questions about the accuracy of the translation of the interview and tried to discredit CBS, accusing it of 'fabrication' and defamation of their faith, and demanding retraction and apology.[75]

The controversy centered around the translation of the *houriya* term, which all conventional interpretations, including the Muslim ones as we shall see below, are proud to render as 'virgins', usually with the epithet of 'black-eyed', while some Muslim organizations in the West insisted that it was a metaphoric appellation of 'angels' or 'heavenly beings'. While it would have been much less important to focus on sexual

fantasies of the killers than on their horrific acts of indiscriminate killing among the innocent, the newsworthy sexual controversy persisted nonetheless. To counter those denials,
Sheikh Palazzi, an Italian Muslim leader, gave references in the
Qur'an as well as in Islamic tradition (Sunna or Hadith) where
the doctrine of the 72 (not 70) 'black-eyed' 'wives' is elaborat-
ed in rich and plastic detail,[76] and took the other Muslim leaders in the West to task for their ignorance of the sources.
Among Muslim clerics in the Muslim world, by contrast, there
is no equivocation, things are clearly and unabashedly stated.
In response to an Australian Muslim query about the reward of
female martyrs in Paradise, in comparison with the males who
got the black-eyed virgins, the Deputy Director of the authoritative Al-Azhar University, Sheikh 'Abd al-Fattah Jam'an
responded:

> The Qur'an tells us that in Paradise Believers get the black-
> eyed, as Allah [namely the Qur'anic text] has said: 'And we
> will marry them to the black-eyed'. The black-eyed are
> white and delicate, and the black of their eyes is blacker
> than black, and the white [of their eyes] is whiter than
> white. To describe their beauty and their great number, the
> Qur'an says that they are 'like Sapphire and pearls',[77] in their
> values, in their color and in their purity. And it is said of
> them: 'They are like well protected pearls in shells,[78] that is
> they are as pure as pearls in oysters and are not perforated,
> no hands have ever touched them, no dust or dirt adheres
> to them, and they are undamaged.' It is further said: 'They
> are like well-protected eggs,[79] that is their delicacy is as the
> delicacy of the membrane beneath the shell of an egg.' Allah
> also said: 'the black-eyed are confined to pavilions,[80] that is
> they are hidden within, save for their husbands ...'.
>
> Most of the black-eyed were first created in Paradise, but
> some are women who acceded to Paradise from this world
> and are obedient Muslims who observe the words of Allah:
> 'We created them especially and have made them virgins, lov-
> ing and equal in age.' This means that when the women of
> this world are old and worn out, Allah re-creates them after
> their old age into virgins who are amiable to their husbands;

'equal in age' means equal to one another in age. At the side of the Muslim in Paradise are his wives from this world, if they are among the dwellers of Paradise, along with the black-eyed of Paradise …

If a woman is of the dwellers in Paradise but her husband in this world is not among them, as in the case of Asia, the wife of Pharaoh, she is given to one of the dwellers of Paradise who is of the same status. Regarding the woman who was married to more than one man in her lifetime, and all her [former] husbands are dwellers of Paradise, she may choose among them, and she chooses the best of them … Thus, it is known that women in Paradise also have husbands. Every woman has a husband. If her husband in this world is a dweller of Paradise, he becomes her husband in Paradise, and if he is an Infidel, she is given to one of the dwellers of Paradise who is suited to her in status and in the intensity of his belief.[81]

CONCLUSIONS AND CONSEQUENCES

The centrality of martyrdom in Palestinian life after the outbreak of the September 2000 (al-Aqsa) *intifada* is reflected in Palestinian writings, broadcasts, the written media, leaflets, audio and video cassettes. They extol acts of Islamikaze, sanctify their perpetrators and cause families who have sacrificed a son to pledge the souls of the rest of them for the sake of Allah. Wasn't it Arafat himself, who in the heat of the battle against Israel coined the war-cry 'We are coming to Jerusalem, as martyrs in the millions'? But measured in terms of a breakthrough in the status of women in Palestinian society, there does not appear any achievement to boast about.

The petrifying idealization of violence and death expanding to ever wider circles under the instigation of the Palestinian leadership, is rooted in the wide-ranging and all-encompassing theology that lays at its base; in the embrace that non-radical Muslim groups have given to this ideology in order not to be seen as lagging behind their radical rivals in the national struggle; and in the callous modes of behaviour adopted by the Palestinians, which lend legitimacy to the application of the Islamikaze ideology aimed at turning it into a horrifying and matter-of-course routine.

On the theological level, the Chief Mufti of Jerusalem, Sheikh 'Akrama Sabri, an Arafat appointee who criticized the Muslim authorities who did not approve of Islamikaze attacks, meant Sheikh Tantawi of Egypt and a Saudi Mufti who had prohibited such attacks in general, and then limited the prohibition to only innocent civilians. According to the Palestinian Mufti, the rulings of those clerics were the result of international pressure, and admonished 'those who do not have the courage to speak the truth, to remain quiet and not say things that create confusion'. He added that 'resistance is legitimate, and those who give up their lives do not require permission from anyone', and that 'we must not stand in the way of the *intifada* and jihad. Rather, we must stand at their side and encourage them.' When asked whether no differentiation should be made between civilians and fighting personnel, he clarified: 'Who is civilian and who is military? There have been many more Palestinian civilians than fighters killed in the *intifada*, school children whose bodies were torn to pieces, pregnant women who were prevented from reaching hospitals, and many times both the mother and child died.'[82]

If this is the position of the highest cleric in the Palestinian Authority, how much more so for Hamas, which often virulently accuses the Authority of 'collaborating' with Israel against the martyrs?[83] The mouthpiece of Hamas, *al-Risala*, sees the struggle waged by the jihad martyrs as a clash of civilizations:

The starting point of Islamic civilization is the basic fact that the *umma* is guided in all its deeds by the divine Straight Path, which constantly oppresses the natural propensity of humans towards evil … Conversely, their [Western] civilization, was not blessed by that enlightened aspect, which should have oppressed their desire to control others and to rob their resources … Therefore, violence has come to characterize Western civilization throughout its history … Let us respond to some of their false accusations that they try to market …

They accuse us of violence. For example, they take the rapid Islamic conquest of many countries, by the force of the sword in their view, to be the best evidence of violence in Islam. Our response is that the only way to explain the

Islamic conquests is that they were in implementation of Divine Will, which charged the Muslims with the responsibility to disseminate it, in consequence obliging Muslims to transmit that message to those who did not receive it yet. When that message reaches non-Muslims, they only face two choices: either to convert to Islam or pay *jizya*[84] to the Muslim government, which today may be interpreted as taking up civil obligations [under the Muslim state].

As to conquest by the sword, Islam does not resort to that means unless it feels impelled to remove obstacles in the way of the Divine Message ... If no obstacles are put on Islam's road to deliver that Message, it would not use the sword. History proves the peace-loving nature of Islam. Caliph 'Umar captured Jerusalem peacefully, and the inhabitants of the conquered countries were acculturated to the Islamic *umma* and enjoyed the same rights and duties. Muslims did not go to those countries as colonialists who oust the native inhabitants and replace them, as America did with the Indians and Israel with the Palestinians. When Muslim armies conquered Samarkand, its inhabitants applied to the Muslim judge, claiming that they were not given the choice between conversion, paying the *jizya* [i.e. *dhimmitude*], or waging war [to the finish] that the Muslim conquerors had customarily accorded to others. Thus, the Muslim judge had no option but to order the Muslim armies to evacuate the city ... How can one then say, that Islam is a violent civilization?

Conversely, Western civilization was profoundly influenced by [Roman] civilization which sanctified force and used to throw gladiators to the arena to fight each other or be swallowed by lions, in order to satisfy their own inferior bestial instincts. The characteristics of this civilization consist of oppressing the other and robbing his resources. It is known for its egotism and arrogance towards the weak. Many wars broke out only to enable it to lay its hand over more wealth. The peak of its appetite was evinced in its kindling two world wars within a quarter-century, in the latest of which nuclear bombs were used that annihilated hundreds of thousands of people.[85]

This view of the Islamikaze by intellectuals, professionals and journalists, often at the hub of supposedly moderate and pro-Western Arab societies, has a great impact on their crowds through the press and talk-shows. No words of condolence for the victims are expressed, and victims then adopt harsher measures of defence to bring more destruction and bereavement, including the loss of young men and women to Palestinian audiences who applaud Islamikaze acts.

Incapable of matching the technological superiority of the West, on which they depend much to their chagrin, they despise it culturally and claim to have an edge. And if they cannot face the humiliation of technological inferiority, they would use the ultimate weapon of Islamikaze to terrify western populations with their own women and children participating in that chilling national endeavour.

Ironically, the attempt of Palestinian young women to make their voice heard could be counter-productive. Their struggle could attract outside sympathy and help, but the indiscriminate killings of other women (and children) might estrange potential Western sympathizers. The Muslims who encourage the women are also those who would deny them the equal status sought.

NOTES

This was first published in the *Journal of Terrorism and Political Violence*, 16, 1 (Spring 2004), pp. 66–96.

1. The term Islamikaze, which combines Islam with Kamikaze, has been coined by this author in his article 'Islamikaze and their Significance', *Journal of Terrorism and Political Violence*, 9, 3 (Autumn 1997), pp.96–121.
2. Frantz Fanon, *A Dying Colonialism*, cited by Juliette Minces, 'Women in Algeria', in L. Beck and N. Keddie (eds.), *Women in the Muslim World* (Cambridge, MA: Harvard University Press, 1978), pp.159–71.
3. Ibid.
4. Examples of both poles can be seen in the thirty-three articles in Beck and Keddie's book cited above. It is also instructive to look at the chapter on women in Ibn Warraq, *Why I am not a Muslim* (New York: Prometheus, 1995), pp.291ff.
5. Sheikh abu al-Hassan, the Head of the Fatwa Council, 18 October, 2001. Extracted from the al-Azhar Internet site by Memri 28, *Terror in America*.
6. *Al-Dustour* (Jordan), 5 February 2002.
7. *Afaq Arabiya* (Egypt), 7 February 2002.
8. *Al-Quds al-Arabi* (London), 8 February 2002.
9. www.alminbar.cc/alkhutab/khutbaa.asp?mediaURL = 5473, accessed 1 February 2002.
10. Ibid.
11. Ibid. See also Sura XVII, verse 4. Muslim preachers routinely accused the Jews of spread-

ing corruption in the world citing the biblical stories of the Jewish women who adorned themselves with jewellery, associated with the worship of the calf when Moses was on Mount Sinai receiving the Ten Commandments from God. The credibility of the Qur'an is supreme, being itself the Word of Allah, while many passages of the Bible were forged by Jews, according to Muslim belief, it is the Qur'anic text which prevails. Surat, *The Children of Israel* says in effect, in its verse 4: 'And we decreed for the Children of Israel in the Scripture: Ye, verily will work corruption in earth twice, and ye will become great tyrants.'

12. www.alminbar.cc/alkhutab/khutbaa.asp?mediaURL= 1620, accessed 5 June 1999.
13. www.alminbar.cc/alkhutab/khutbaa.asp?mediaURL= 1628, accessed 22 May 1999; and www.alminbar.cc/alkhutab/khutbaa.asp'lmediaURL = 2699, accessed 13 June 1998.
14. Ibid.
15. www.alminbar.cc/alkhutab/khutbaa.asp?mediaURL = 4096. No date.
16. www.alminbar.cc/alkhutab/khutbaa.asp?mediaURL = 1069. No date.
17. www.alminbar.cc/alkhutab/khutbaa.asp?mediaURL= 1633, accessed 1 May 1999; and = 4461, 4 September 1999.
18. *Al-Jazeera* Television (Qatar), 30 December 2001.
19. Ibid.
20. *Al-Quds* (Palestinian Authority), 8 March 2001. See also Sheikh Bitawi, in *al-Ayyam* (Palestinian Authority), 12 August 1999.
21. *Al'Awda* (Palestinian Authority), 1 May 1998.
22. *Al-Quds* (Palestinian Authority), 17 April 1998.
23. *Al-Ayyam* (Palestinian Authority), 12 August 1999.
24. *Al-Jazeera* Television (Qatar), 30 December 2001.
25. *Al-Quds* (Palestinian Authority), 17 August 2001.
26. *Al-Jazeera* Television, 30 December 2001.
27. *Al-Ra'y*, (Qatar), 5 January 2002.
28. See note 26.
29. Ibid.
30. *Akher Sa'a* (Egypt), 6 December 2001.
31. See, i.e. B. F. Stowasser, 'Liberated Equal or Protected Dependent?: Contemporary Religious Paradigms on Women's Status in Islam', *Arab Studies Quarterly*, 9, 3 (1987); Ann Mayer, *Islam and Human Rights: Traditions and Politics* (Westview Press, 1991); Nahid Toubia (ed.), *Women in the Arab World: The Coming Challenge* (London: Zed Books, 1990); Beck and Keddie (eds), *Women in the Muslim World*; and, more recently, Mareike Jule Winkelman, 'The Construction of Female Identity in Muslim Modernity', *Newsletter of the International Institute For the Study of Islam in the Modern World (ISIM)*, September 2001, p.4; Martin van Bruinessen, 'Islam, Women's Rights and Islamic Feminism', *ISIM*, September 2002, p.6; and Amir Weissbrod (ed.), *Turabi: Spokesmen of Radical Islam* (Hebrew) (Dayan Center for Middle Eastern and African Studies, Tel Aviv University, 1999).
32. Hassan Turabi, *Women in the Teachings of Islam* (Arabic), cited by Weissbrod, *Turabi*, pp.53ff.
33. Ibid.
34. Weissbrod, *Turabi*, pp.55–6.
35. *Akhhar al-Yaum* (Egypt), 29 December 2001.
36. Ibid.
37. *The Times*, 9 September 1996, and the *Guardian*, 9 September 1996.
38. *The Mercury*, cited in http://artsweb.bham.ac.uk/bmms/sampleissuejan2001.asp.
39. *Le Monde*, 9 September 1998.
40. *AFP*, Paris, 14 September 2001.
41. Even in relatively moderate Egypt, whose regime is one of the closest to America in the Muslim world, a case became a *cause célèbre* recently, when an outspoken woman writer, Nawwal Sa'dawi, who criticized the *hajj* to Mecca as an act of paganism, was declared heretic by Islamists, and her husband was ordered to divorce her. Previously, an academic

from Cairo University, Dr Nasir Hamid abu-Zeid, who had been equally accused of heresy, was ordered to divorce his spouse and created a worldwide outrage. He exiled himself to the West rather than submit. For this note, I am indebted to my colleague, Dr Rivka Yadlin.

42. www.obm.clara.net/shari'acourt/fatwas/fs3.html.
43. Sura 5:33.
44. See note 23.
45. 'Women, Gender and Politics', in A. Sela (ed.) *Political Encyclopedia of the Middle East* (Jerusalem: Jerusalem Publishing House, 1999), pp.795–800.
46. See the Preface to the Hamas Charter in R. Israeli, *Fundamental Islam and Israel: Essay in Interpretation* (New York and London: University Press of America, 1993), pp.123, 125.
47. R. Israeli, 'State and Religion in the Emerging Palestinian Entity', *Journal of Church and State*, 44 (Spring 2002), pp.240–1.
48. Qur'an, Sura 33:35 (Alahzab the Clans).
49. See the Israeli Government's *The Involvement of Arafat, Palestinian Authority Senior Officials and Apparatuses in Terrorism Against Israel, Corruption and Crime*, compiled by Minister Dani Naveh, released in April 2002, pp.46–7.
50. See *al-Sharq al-Awsat* (London), 2 February 2002; *al-Ayyam* (Palestinian Authority), 31 January 2002; *Kul al-'Arab* (Israel), 1 February 2002.
51. *Kul al-'Arab*, 1 February 2002.
52. *Middle East News Online*, 28 January 2002; and *al-Sha'b* (Egypt), 1 February 2002.
53. *Al-Sha'b* (Egypt), 1 February 2002.
54. *Al-Sharq al-Awsat* (London), 31 January 2002.
55. Ibid., 2 February 2002.
56. *Al-Sharq al-Awsat*, 31 January and 2 February 2002.
57. *Afaq Arabiya* (Egypt), 30 January 2002; *al-Quds al-'Arabi* (London), 31 January 2002.
58. *Al-Sharq al-Awsat*, 31 January 2002.
59. *Al-Sha'b*, I February 2002.
60. *Al-Akhbar* (Egypt), 1 February 2002.
61. Ibid.
62. *Al-Ahram*, 2 February 2002.
63. *Al-'Arabi* (Cairo), 3 February 2002; and *al-Quds al-'Arabi* (London), 4 February 2002.
64. *Hadith al-Madina* (Egypt), 5 February 2002; and *al-Quds al-'Arabi* (London), 6 February 2002.
65. *Al-Ayyam* (Palestinian Authority), 1 February 2002.
66. *Al-Wafd* (Egypt), 7 February 2002; *al-Quds al-'Arabi* (London), 8 February 2002.
67. *Al-Quds al-'Arabi* (London), 28 January, 2002.
68. *Al-Wafd* (Egypt), 3 February 2002.
69. *Al-Ahram* (Egypt), 10 February 2002.
70. *Al-Dustour* (Jordan), 24 February 2002.
71. *Al-Wafd*, see note 31 above.
72. *Al-'Arabi* (Egypt), 3 February 2002; *al-Quds al-'Arabi* (London), 2 and 4 February 2002. See also *al-Ahram* (Cairo), 3 and 5 February 2002; *al-Wafd* (Egypt), 1 February 2002; *al-Gumhuryya* (Egypt), 31 January 2002; *Sawt al-Umma* (Egypt), 3 February 2002.
73. *Al-Wafd* (Egypt), 3 February 2002; and *al-Quds al-'Arabi* (London), 4 February 2002.
74. Cited in print by Memri (Washington and Jerusalem) 74, 30 October 2001, article by Yotam Feldner.
75. Ibid.
76. There are no less than six references for the virgins and the black-eyed in Paradise that are mentioned or hinted to in the Holy Qur'an, and massive elaborations on those brief references in the vast literature of the *hadith*, Palazzi specifies that those women are available not only to martyrs but to any Believer who accedes to Paradise.
77. Surat *Al-Rahman*, verse 58.
78. Surat *Al-Waqi'a*, verse 23.
79. Surat *Al-Safat*, verse 49.
80. Surat *Al-Rahman*, verse 70.

81. Cited in Memri 74, 30 October 2001.
82. *Al-Hayat*, 7 December, 2001, cited by *Ha'aretz* (Israel), 9 December 2001.
83. A leaflet distributed in the streets of the major Palestinian cities on 27 November 2001, accused the Palestinian Authority of exchanging intelligence with Israel and bringing about the liquidation of many jihad fighters. Citing a verse from the Qur'an (17:18), the statement promised that its 'truth would smash the Authority's lies', and that the latter would literally be sent to Hell.
84. The *jizya* was limited to the Scriptuaries (Jews and Christians), while pagans were subjected to the sword. The payment of *jizya* symbolized the subjugation of the *dhimmis* to Muslim rule, and in return for it they received protection from the Muslim state, the assumption being that no other state was legal.
85. *Al-Risalah* (Palestinian Authority), 11 October 2001.

PART III

THE PALESTINIAN ARABS OF ISRAEL

CHAPTER EIGHT

Arabs in Israel: Criminality, Identity and the Peace Process

Criminality among 'Israeli Arabs', or 'Palestinians in Israel' as they often prefer to call themselves, has reputedly been higher than in the general public in many areas of 'crime'. According to police statistics cited below, the rate of criminality among Arabs amounts to double their rate in the general population (32 per cent compared with 18 per cent). Add to that the high proportion of children among the Arabs and the correspondingly low rate of adults, and you reach an even higher rate of adult crime. This state of affairs, which will be described in detail in the following pages, derives from the idiosyncratic position of this population which has been torn between its country (Israel) to which it owes loyalty as citizens, and its people (the Palestinians) with whom its country has been at odds for half a century. For Arabs in Israel, now totalling about 18 per cent of its population, are caught in four concentric circles of identity: Israeli, Palestinian, Arab and Islamic (in their majority),[1] and they often experience a greater pull towards one of the latter than towards the first.

The current peace process, which has perhaps somewhat blunted the enmity between Israel and the Arabs in general, has on the contrary sharpened the hostility of certain extremist Muslims and some radical Palestinians towards Israel. Hence, the assumed mix of mitigation of the anti-Israeli sentiments on the one hand, and their aggravation on the other. Arabs in Israel, depending on the strength of their leanings towards one or another of their identities which in itself is often directly linked to the fortunes of the peace process, are presumably also caught in these confusing dilemmas and, therefore, are seen as zigzagging between one position and another. One of the best indices of

these attitudes of Arabs in Israel towards their country is the rate
of criminality and the varieties thereof among them.

CRIMINALITY AND IDEOLOGY

Criminality is defined as an offence punishable by law. Although
crime is usually viewed as an evil, one can imagine contexts in
which it would be considered as positive and desirable when it
accomplishes national, ethnic or religious goals. Certainly, while
in the eyes of the state judiciary crime is absolute and punishable,
it can very well be relativized in the eyes of its perpetrators, when
their social/national/religious group upholds or even hails their
acts, which then become laudable.

Much has been written about political crime in general.[2]
Indeed, in the context of the Israeli Arabs, crime can be divided
into common and ideological or political. Common crimes are
those shared by the general criminal public in Israel, Jews and
Arabs alike. But even here, there are shades of differences which
would depend on the individual criminal's motivation. For example, if an Arab murders a fellow villager, this would usually be
treated as a family or clan feud, or an act of felony against one's
fellow man. But when the Arab kills a Jew, the doubt, where
there is no certainty, creeps in about whether the 'nationalistic'
element did not play a role. A Jew and an Arab can commit the
same crime, sometimes even collaborating in its perpetration,
but, while a common robbery of a bank, for example, would be
nothing extraordinary in the eyes of a Jewish criminal, it may
acquire in the mind of the Arab an 'anti-Israeli' or 'anti-Zionist
establishment' connotation, which would, in consequence, even
lend a sort of justification to the act.

Even more problematic is the category of 'soft crimes' (to dis-
tinguish from the aforementioned 'hard crimes'). Soft crimes are
those which do not necessarily involve loss of life or inconven-
ience to individual victims (such as theft). For example, illegal
construction, document forgery, contravention of law in daily
life, smuggling and tax evasion are all violations of the law which
can be explicitly perpetrated against the others' system, the alien
establishment, the Zionist entity or what have you. Therefore, it
becomes justifiable, at times even laudable, in the Arab community,

while it is condemned by the legal authorities. Moreover, while a Jew who would perpetrate the same crime is seen by the Israeli public as a 'mere' criminal, Arab criminals of this sort would in addition be suspected of ideological and political crimes.

Ideological or political crimes are quite another category, not only due to their relativity in the eyes of their beholders, but also because, in the context of Israel, they can be differentiated into nationalistic and religious crimes. They both manifest themselves in the same fashion: murder ('killing the enemy' in the eyes of the perpetrators), bombing, burning fields or forests and the like, spying, inciting, lending a hand to saboteurs, violent demonstrations, etc., civil disobedience, tax evasion and the like, with the clear purpose of hurting the 'Zionist enemy'. However, the motivations of their perpetrators vary: one is driven by the urge to identify with other Palestinians/Arabs, and therefore this urge may be toned down by hopeful events or developments; the other is moved by religious devotion which knows no boundary and is not likely to be mitigated by the peace process. Sometimes it is quite the contrary. Often the two brands of motivations are woven into a powerful religio-nationalist fabric of hostility towards the state – Israel. In all cases of this sort, the perpetrator of the crime (with or without quotation marks), unlike the common criminal, does not purport to draw any personal material benefit. On the contrary, for the sense of satisfying his ideological urge, he stands to lose, to be arrested and prosecuted by law.[3]

ROOT CAUSES OF CRIMINALITY

Criminality among Israeli Arabs, both the political/ideological and the ideologically-connected part of the common crimes, has been inexorably linked to the fortunes of the Arab–Israeli conflict in general, especially the Palestinian aspect thereof, on the one hand, and the inner developments of the Arab community within Israel on the other.

When the State of Israel was established in 1948, the Arab population constituted about 18 per cent of the total (156,000 out of 872,000). That means that in spite of the rapid growth of the Jewish population, due mainly to the huge waves of *aliya* (immigration) in the 1950s, 1960s and 1990s, the proportion of

Arab citizens of Israel has been sustained throughout, and it is likely to rise when the *aliya* waves to Israel recede, as the pool of potential immigrants dries out. Among these Arabs, some 80 per cent are Muslim (14 per cent of the total), the rest being Christian and Druze.

The question of demography is crucial because, as we know from experience in Israel and other places,[4] the larger the minority the more vocal and demanding it can become. And when its ever higher expectations[5] are not met by the host culture, it may turn violent and question the very foundation or at least the nature of its state.[6] Evidently, the rejection of the state's basic policies may engender violence and degenerate into 'criminal' acts, at least from the viewpoint of the majority.

Important milestones in the development of the consciousness of the Arab population in Israel were:

a. The removal of the military government regime on the Arab minority in 1966, which signalled the legal equalization of the Arabs with the Jewish majority. This seemingly positive step in itself was pregnant with far-reaching implications. On the one hand, the Arabs became conscious of their new, more liberal and freer status, but paradoxically it also brought into focus the huge socio-economic gap between them and the Jewish majority.

b. Cultivation, by Israel, of the Arab semi-autonomous educational system bore fruits in the long run, insofar as the Arabs became accustomed, with state approval and support, to a different set of values, language, thinking and identity than the ones upheld by the Jewish majority. This, reinforced by the Arab abstention from serving in the Israeli Defence Forces, admittedly the most powerful factor of integration in Israeli society, encouraged the growth of the 'otherness' of the Arabs and brought ever closer the feasibility of delegitimizing the Jews, the 'establishment', and of committing 'crimes' against them.

c. The 1967 war, which occasioned the social reunification of Arabs in Israel with their Palestinian brethren in the West Bank and Gaza, also alienated the Israeli Arabs further, in an interestingly paradoxical way: Israeli Arabs found themselves much more developed, educated and wealthy than their poor kin in the Territories, but this encounter of unequals, far from alienating them from each other, on the contrary created sentiments of sympathy, commiseration and active support for their less fortunate brothers. Those years also witnessed the rise of Palestinian nationalism, personified by Yasser Arafat, the head of the PLO. Since more countries recognized the PLO than entertained relations with Israel, and a world consensus, made up of the Eastern Bloc, Islamic and Third World countries, coalesced with the Arabs against Israel, Israeli Arabs could easily envisage their country losing legitimacy to the PLO. This trend, which came to its apex in the UN 1975 Resolution which equated Zionism to racism, did little to reinforce Israeli Arabs' loyalty to their country and a lot to uphold their Palestinian identity.

d. From the mid-1970s onward, Israeli Arabs moved one notch up the scale of disapproval of their country of citizenship, by either approving of, or participating in, violent demonstrations of their bitterness, frustration and aspirations. First, the Arabs mounted some underground organizations (like the Sons of the Village), then launched a series of violent gatherings which, while immediately responding to the confiscation of Arab land by the Israeli government, certainly were also used as a conduit to channel all the accumulated rage and growing alienation from Israel. It is no accident that not only did Land Day become an annual commemoration day which mobilizes all Israeli Arabs, but it also serves as a common denominator, drawing closer together the Palestinians on both sides of the erstwhile 'Green Line'. Israeli Arabs rewarded their Palestinian brethren in the Territories for their solidarity while they, in turn, fully mobilized to support the *intifada*, the uprising of the Palestinians in the Territories which broke out in December 1987. At first they were hesitant and diffident to join openly and violently, but they made clear where their hearts were and soon fully tapped their resources to supply their brethren with money donations, food, medicine, demonstrations of support and condolence visits to families of Arab victims (not Israeli or Jewish victims of the same incidents).

e. The Israeli national elections of June 1992 brought full circle these trends of socio-political differentiation with Israel. These elections showed to the local Arab population, which had been accustomed to the democratic process and brought up to believe in its electoral strength, that in a situation of deadlock among the Jewish electorate, they could determine the shape of the Israeli government and exercise their power of leverage to extract from it many of their wishes. Conversely, by proving that they were uniquely concerned with their ethnic benefits, and that they remained opposed to the Israeli national ethos (*aliya*, settlement, strong military), they also exposed themselves to sharp criticism by the Jewish majority to the effect that they want their share in a state they do not support. They also exposed the Labour government they upheld by their votes to ever sharper broadsides of the right-wing opposition, to the effect that it was not legitimate since it relied on anti-Jewish, in fact anti-Israeli members of Parliament.

f. The peace process, embraced by Israel's Labour government, is vehemently encouraged by the Arab votes in the Knesset, and was the *raison d'être* of the Labour–Arab coalition. However, while the Labour government regarded its razor-thin majority, which could only survive due to Arab support, as legitimate in the democratic game in order to achieve the lofty goal of peace, opponents of that government pointed to Israeli Arabs' zeal to push Israel to relinquish its security and other assets in favour of the Palestinians so as to weaken Israel and correspondingly strengthen their Palestinian kin.

These momentous developments in the Israeli-Arab milieu have shaped a remarkably vivid, creative, well-led, self-confident and for the most part well-off Arab society in Israel. It is today widely different from its genesis in 1948, and much more articulate than its pre-1967 or pre-1987 antecedents. Most of its members were born in the State of Israel and, despite their self-imposed segregation, Israeli culture and values have rubbed off on them. Even if only a small minority of these Arabs openly voices hostility to Israel and draws question marks on its legitimacy, and even though it entertains in its midst many different, at times contradictory, interests, it is safe to assume that, as far as criminality is concerned, most Arabs are probably still law-abiding today.

However, the built-in characteristics of this rapidly changing society and the trends it has been adopting in recent years point in the direction of an increasing problem of law enforcement in their midst in the years to come. Unresolved contradictions between majority and minority in a multi-ethnic and multi-national society, when allowed to mount to the surface, can wreak havoc, as the case of the former Soviet Union well and tragically illustrates.

What are these contradictions which, in the immediate future, threaten to raise the level of 'criminality' among Israeli Arabs and, in the long run, unless addressed now, to dissolve the very fibre of the state and society?

We have already analysed the question of the rising separate Palestinian identity among Israeli Arabs. Their self-identification as 'Palestinians residing in Israel' and their reluctance, even outrage, to be dubbed 'Israeli Arabs', is significant in itself, insofar as it became universally accepted among them. Advocates of this Arab behaviour tend to dismiss it as a differentiation between 'civil identity' (Israeli) and 'national identity' (Palestinian), while others regard it as a process of rapid alienation from the State of Israel and substitution of a Palestinian identity for the Israeli one.[7]

Be that as it may, it is clear that this double identity in a situation of as yet unresolved conflict has already produced the following irreconcilable problems which are pregnant with a potential of 'criminality':

A. The growing Palestinian identity of Israeli Arabs has definitely brought into question among them the validity of a Jewish state. The reasoning is crystal clear: if the Arabs in Israel are no longer an ethnic, linguistic or cultural-religious – but a national minority (Palestinian), and if Israel is indeed a democracy as it claims to be, the inescapable conclusion is that Israel is not, indeed cannot be, a Jewish state. Since it belongs to all of its citizens, who are divided between nationalities – Jewish and Arab, then it cannot be but bi-national. This is no mere rhetoric: Israeli Arabs who advance that claim pursue their argument that since Israel's

Jewish symbols are alien to them, and specifically Jewish laws are discriminatory against them, they ought to be altered to elicit their consent. If Israel does not concur, it may become justifiable to struggle by democratic means first, then to use other means, until it acquiesces in the new state of affairs.

True, Arab leaders in Israel, while softly voicing support for this view, are reluctant as yet to turn it into their central political platform, for fear that the Jewish majority public in Israel might be outraged against it. But the undercurrent professing this trend is clearly identifiable and growing. It is only a question of time until it breaks into the open.

B. Arabs demand complete equality with Israeli Jews. 'Equality' has become a major rallying slogan in some Arab parties in Israel and it found considerable appeal in Israeli government circles, which can neither deny the existence of discrimination in Israeli society nor resist the pressures to remedy it. In fact, the Labour government elected in 1992 invested in 'gap bridging' projects more than any previous government, in order to bring Israeli Arabs to a par with Jews in the domains of housing, education, employment, budgets, etc. The higher the achievements of Israeli society in general and the faster the rise of its standard of living, the more pressing the Arab clamouring for equality.

But 'equality' has not produced the hoped-for decrease in the feelings of frustration and alienation. Quite the contrary, the larger the budgets the Labour government disbursed for its Arab citizenry, the more vocal became the Arab outcry. 'Not enough', they said. Paradoxically, as the government responded to Arab needs, the latter felt 'vindicated' in their grievances about discrimination. And, aware of the former's dependence on them for its very survival, they could afford to press more and so get more proof of their claimed discrimination.

At the same time, however, Arabs are aware that equality is a buzz-word for privilege. For, while they insist on equal rights, they are still reluctant to share equal duties with the Israelis, including military service or some other sort of national service. And so they want to have a full share in an establishment, the philosophy of which they reject, with whose goals many of them cannot identify and by whose laws, obligations and aspirations some of them would not abide. In the widening gap between what they are prepared to do for the country and the expectations from them to be more forthcoming, resides the potential for conflict which may break into the open in the future.

C. The Arab demand for equality is complemented by their growing insistence on autonomy in various spheres, primarily education and culture. They aspire, for example, to establish an independent educational system where they would determine the contents and the structure of the cultural luggage they wish to bequeath to their children. One can easily envisage how this cultural autonomy, once attained, could further widen the yawning gap between the majority and the minority, and produce more alienation and potential for criminality.

To date, except for some enclaves of the Islamic movement (see below), which collect moneys and finance a whole set-up of social welfare activities, most Arab communities in Israel remain heavily dependent on the government for their budgets and therefore are unable to carry out their aspirations of autonomy any time soon. But, in view of the institutional autonomy that they have been erecting for years (e.g. the Committee of Arab Mayors and the Follow-up Committee, made up of Arab mayors and Knesset members), time will come when these aspirations will be fulfilled, followed by claims for economic and even territorial autonomy. From there, a short step will lead to Palestinian *irredenta*, open struggle against the Israeli authorities, underground activity, etc.

D. The process of alienation of Israeli Arabs from their country has gathered a further impetus from the deep and wide current of Islamization which has been sweeping Arab society in Israel[8] and elsewhere. This current, which has been institutionalized within the 'Islamic Movement', is much akin to the Muslim Brothers in Egypt and elsewhere[9] in its aspiration to apply the *shari'a* (Islamic law) in all aspects of personal, communal and national life. This movement, like its counterparts in other places, tends to crystallize around charismatic figures of sheikhs who amass power and influence through their scholarship, simple demeanour, accessibility to the masses and forceful leadership by their personal example.[10]

Several of these young, deeply venerated and widely popular leaders have taken over local mayorships in several Arab townships in Israel. The members of the Islamic Movement, led by these tremendously popular sheikhs, have embarked on recreating a Muslim society within Israel and have in fact turned many of the localities under their jurisdiction into Muslim enclaves. Their statements and actions,[11] which at times openly delegitimize the State of Israel[12] and mock its Jewish nature[13] or its ideology,[14] and their open utterances of support to the Hamas and the *intifada* against Israel[15] are barely short of incitement and encouragement of crime, especially of the ideological/political type.

This Islamic Movement, not unlike its sister organizations in adjoining countries, has embraced a multi-stage program of action[16] which includes first a spiritual rebirth, usually connected with a return to piety, observation of the refinements and tenets of the faith and a gradual weaning from social and moral wrongs (such as alcohol, crime, drugs, etc.). This stage is usually followed by, or goes concurrently with, a wide-ranging program of the community, by the community and for the community, to improve the socioeconomic standards of its membership in the fields of welfare, health and education. In so doing, the Muslim community is mobilized and accustomed to refer to its spiritual guides as a substitute for all other religious and temporal leaderships and social frameworks (family, party, local government, the mosques, and other traditional or present-day forms of authority). This is much akin to the Muslim Brothers in Egypt, who act in a quietist fashion, accumulate a vast pool of popularity and goodwill among their prospective constituencies, and get ready for the day when they can fully bloom into the open political field.

The third stage, which may be accompanied by the use of violence, strives to establish a Muslim state. This has been the case in Iran, the Sudan, Afghanistan and Algeria, and to a certain extent in Jordan and Lebanon, Pakistan and among the Gama'at in Egypt. In Israel, the Islamic Movement has gathered enough steam and popularity to embark on this third stage. But the strength of the Israeli state, which allows the movement much more leeway than most Islamic countries would; and the extremely tough competition the Islamists face from secular-modernizing Arab-nationalistic parties within Israel, have hitherto hindered its impetus.

E. This round-up of built-in conflicts within Israeli society cannot be complete without a few words on the rapid process of urbanization within the Arab community. Not only do Arab villages develop into townships with many of the (good and bad) characteristics of urban agglomerations, but growing numbers of individuals and families have been settling down of late in mixed Arab Jewish cities such as Haifa, Acre and Jaffa. This process is not massive as yet because, after all, most Arab villages are located within one or two hours' drive from a major urban centre. But in the long run, if and when this process gathers momentum, new foci of friction between Jews and Arabs are likely to emerge, especially in places where the Arab minority becomes so large as to be perceived as a threat to the local Jewish majority.[17] In view of the wide gaps separating these two competing, immensely self-confident cultures, clashes are bound to occur when differences, and then struggles, about the character of the common locality turn into violent eruptions, possibly pregnant with criminality.

Urbanization may affect criminality for yet other reasons. As everywhere else, urbanization generates the dismantling of traditional social frameworks and the pulverization of conventional norms. Immigration to the cities is bound to create marginal groups whose social, cultural and economic differences with the affluent majority may become so large as to increase alienation, frustration and crime. Intellectuals and middle class Arabs who succeed economically in the mixed cities but are excommunicated by the Jewish majority, may likewise translate their frustration into nationalistic/religious alienation and extremism.

THE ISRAELI–PALESTINIAN PEACE PROCESS

What does the current peace process, started in Oslo in September 1993, do to the trends outlined above? The question is valid because, on the one hand, one might surmise that, with the end of the Israeli Palestinian hostilities, the reasons for ideological/political crimes among Israeli Arabs are bound to recede; similarly, frictions between them and the Jewish society, which are based on socio-economic differences, would disappear in view of the expected wide distribution of prosperity that is to descend upon the country as the fruit of peace. On the other hand, one cannot escape the fact that concurrently with the recognition by Israel of Palestinian nationalism, the Arabs in Israel, who are similarly and equally Palestinian, have pushed their claims for being accepted as a national minority within Israel. This implies that Israel would turn into a bi-national state, ironically the very hindrance that the Israeli Labour government of 1992–96 was citing as a reason for its hastening a settlement with the Palestinians, in order to avoid such a claim. Rising Palestinian nationalism within Israel, coupled with the separate existence of a Palestinian state, may in turn engender not only criminal-prone ideological antagonism between Arabs and Jews in Israel, but also produce close cooperation between Israeli Arabs and their compatriots in Palestine, in fields such as joint theft and robbery and drug traffic, with the Israeli Arabs providing 'expertise' and familiarity with the local scene, and the Palestinians providing cover, shelter, a market for the stolen property and, ultimately, a refuge from the pursuit of justice. Brought to fruition under conditions of mutual support and a common ideology, this would be the stuff which encourages the growth of *irredenta* towards Israel or parts thereof.

Hints to possible developments in that direction already exist: car theft in Israel has increased dramatically since the Oslo agreement, with stolen cars ending up in the autonomous regions of the Palestinians. Even before the Oslo Accords, the Arab minority in Israel had already set a pattern of criminal behaviour that was quite different from common criminality of the general public, especially after the outbreak of the *intifada* in December 1987. Before the *intifada*, in spite of the contradicting long-term interests between the Jewish majority and the Arab minority in Israel, and the high rate of alienation among the Arabs, the latter usually refrained from ideologically-motivated acts of sabotage, with the exception of some notorious incidents of this sort which became *cause célèbre*. Arab criminals, although they 'specialize' in such contraventions as illegal construction or other 'soft' crimes, tax evasion or traffic accidents and driving license counterfeit-ing,[18] as a rule they acted like, or in collaboration with, their Jewish compatriots to cover the whole span of criminality: drugs, robbery, theft, murder, etc.

What is even more disturbing is that the Arab sector was found, already in 1987, as evading social security payments by a huge population (it paid only 40 per cent of dues), in spite of the fact that full benefits in childrens', old-age disability and other allowances were received.[19] According to press reports, the year 1996 was to be characterized by wide-ranging raids by the tax authorities against sectors of Israeli society, mostly reputed for tax evasion, notably Arab contractors.[20] This means that tax eva-sion has become endemic as part of Arab white collar crime against the State of Israel.

Since the outbreak of the *intifada*, however, there is a notice-able use of ideologically-induced crime among the Arabs, by all appearance out of identification with their rioting brethren in the Territories. In 1989, for example, in the area of northern Israel alone, the number of such illegal acts of all sorts doubled com-pared to 1988 (989 versus 446), including ninety-two cases of 'incitement to rebellion' (compared with thirty-seven the previous year), 109 cases of throwing rocks against Jewish traffic (com-pared with twenty-five), ninety arsons (compared with thirteen), 387 cases of general disturbance of public order (compared to 342) and nineteen cases of Molotov cocktails against passing traf-fic (compared to two in 1988).[21] At least in 196 of these cases, which included illegal raisings of the PLO flag, the perpetrators were dubbed as 'Palestinian nationalists', others were Muslim fundamentalists. Many of these criminal activities received praise and support from the outside. When a large arson ravaged an Israeli forest, words of encouragement were sent to the 'blessed hands who set fire to the forests of Palestine [not Israel, of course] thus causing the enemy millions of dollars of damage and the loss of decades of effort'.[22]

In March 1988 the Israeli security apparatus arrested a group of youth from Umm al-Fahm, the hub of Muslim fundamentalism in Israel, who clandestinely held ammunition and explosives that they had illicitly collected from training areas of the Israeli Defence Forces. It could not be ascertained whether this secret organization necessarily emanated from the Muslim movement in Israel, but it is evident that the open endorsement by this movement of the *intifada* has created an atmosphere of permissiveness among Arab/Muslim youth, to strike at the heart of the 'Zionist enemy', which also happens to be the legitimate ruler of their country.[23] Police statistics also reported a rise in white collar crimes during that period, such as tax evasion and counterfeiting of driving licenses, which could be interpreted as part of the rebellion against state authority and of the building of counter-state institutions by the Muslim movement.

Nevertheless, the rate of political or ideological criminality among the Arabs of Israel remained far lower than that of the Territories. For one thing, most Arabs in Israel fear that attempts to resolve their problems violently might backfire on them and engender the loss of whatever gains they have accumulated over the years in the political, social and economic domains. One might also point out in this regard that the very diversity of ideological views among the Arabs of Israel (secular, religious, Communist, etc.) and the communal tensions between them (Muslims, Christians, Bedouins, Druze) has in itself prevented so far the rise of a common front for a violent struggle against Israel.

When the Oslo Accords were signed in 1993, the widely-held assumption was that the establishment of a Palestinian autonomy in the Territories would satisfy the Arabs in Israel who would then turn to full integration into Israeli society and economy, and begin to partake of mainstream political activity in the country. This would, in turn, reduce the tension between Jews and Arabs in general, and bring to a halt hostile Arab acts against Israel from within. However, the reality where PLO rule is challenged by extremist movements, such as the Democratic Front and the Popular Front, or by Islamic rejectionists such as the Hamas or the Islamic Jihad, who have their counterpart among Israeli Arabs, raises many questions about this initially optimistic expectation.

Some members of the Islamic Movement in Israel criticize the Peace Accords as insufficient, and are likely to join hands with their like-minded kin in the Territories. This reality will become particularly sensitive and explosive if the permanent settlement between Israel and the Palestinians, which is to be negotiated in the future, does not lead the Palestinians towards their coveted goal of a Palestinian state with Jerusalem as its capital.

But even in the interim period of the autonomy, there are indications of an increasing collaboration between Israeli Arabs and their brethren across the border. This has been occasioned by the pattern of Israeli settlements in the Territories which dictates open boundaries between Israel and the Territories on the one hand, and the accessibility of the autonomy to Arab markets at large, on the other. Add to that the easy and unhindered access (when no closures are imposed following acts of terrorism), aided by family and partnership ties, of the Palestinians in the Territories to their kin in Israel, and the inability of the still inexperienced Palestinian police to tightly control the territory under their jurisdiction, and perhaps even some complicity between police and criminals,[24] and you have a recipe for increasing collaboration between Arab criminals of both sides of the Green Line which is likely to drive upward the rate of criminality in Israel.

Statistics released by the Chief Police Statistician,[25] comparing the year 1993, which preceded the Oslo Accords, and 1994, which followed them, reveal many important trends, some expected and some rather surprising, in the criminality rate among the Arabs in Israel. These statistics can easily be misread or manipulated, especially because the thin line separating regular crime from ideological crime is often blurred and hard to detect. Police statistics do differentiate between the two kinds of crime, but very often it is hard to tell one from the other, and therefore one ought to read the figures with great circumspection. The figures also provide us with a control group, the crime rate among the Jewish public, in order to facilitate the computation of the relative rate of criminality among the Palestinian Arabs in Israel. Comparisons are also suggested between Israeli Arabs and Palestinians in the Territories, but since political-ideological matters did prevail in the Territories in the period under consideration (1993–94) and law enforcement there was far less strict than in Israel, they are for the most part irrelevant to the present study. They will be mentioned only when they are deemed necessary to understand the other data.

The gravity of criminality among the Arabs in Israel can be graduated into the five categories mentioned below. Expectedly, there is a reverse correlation between gravity and the number of violations: the more serious the violation and its punishment, the less perpetrators are ready to venture into it. The base of the pyramid consists of the most widespread soft crimes, while the apex describes the rarest hard crimes. Thus, the pyramid of violations might look as follows:

Terror
against persons   a

Violence against   b
property

Illegal acts of protest   c

Criminal activity with
ideological justification   d

White collar crime
with ideological justification   e

a. *Anti-personnel terrorism* includes assassinations of Israeli citizens (civilians and soldiers), through the throwing of Molotov cocktails, shooting, knifing, with ideology supplying the rationalizing/justifying underpinnings. This category also covers collaborators of terrorists, arms dealers and smugglers, and membership in terrorist organizations.
b. *Terrorism and violence against property* (private and particularly public). This form of crime again uses ideological justification/rationalization to burn fields, forests, cars and other properties; to destroy or harm plantations, orchards, agricultural machinery, construction sites, industrial means of production.
c. *Illegal protests* means illegal incitement, road blocks, attacking police and disobeying their orders, throwing rocks, mounting riots and illegal demonstrations, and raising the PLO flag (when it was forbidden by law).
d. *Criminal activity* includes thefts of cars, breaking into houses and cars, sexual assaults against Jews, all of which can be and often are justified/rationalized by ideological/political argu-

ments.
e. *White collar crime* also is often ideologically bound, insofar as it can justify/rationalize economic crimes, tax evasion, intentional bankruptcy, forging permits, illegal construction and the like as acts of delegitimizing the state authorities.

Regular Crime

The most striking datum in this category is that the rate of criminality among Arabs in Israel is considerably higher in certain areas than among the general population. It is hard to determine whether this is to be imputed to the root causes described above, specifically the state of deprivation of the minority and the bitterness arising therefrom, or to a mood of disengagement from the Zionist regime which lacks legitimacy in their eyes, and therefore does not have to be obeyed. But be that as it may, the figures are illuminating both on the unchanging score and on the vacillating score between the pre- and the post-Oslo period.

Murder: twenty-nine cases of murder (four of them 'ideological') were registered among Arabs in Israel in 1993, and twenty-two one year later. These figures compare with forty-two and fifty-four (two of them 'ideological') respectively in the Jewish sector. Taking into consideration the fact that Arabs constitute only 18 per cent of Israel's population but commit about 50 per cent of the murders, this means that their rate of crime in this category is about twice that of the general population. Murder attempts show an even more dramatic gap between the two populations: thirty-eight (two ideological) and forty-five (seven ideological), for the years 1993 and 1994, respectively, in the Arab sector, compared with almost identical figures in the Jewish sector: thirty-seven (one ideological) and forty-seven (one ideological). This means that in this category, the criminality rate among the Arabs is four times as large. There may also be significance to the fact that in the murder attempts category the number of cases dubbed by police as 'ideological' rose from two (before Oslo) to seven after Oslo.

Assault and injury: Here, too, the number of Arab cases mounts to about half the Jewish cases (329 vs 656 in 1993; 451 vs 746 in 1994). This means that the rate among the Arabs is about twice that of the Jews. Among these cases, none is cited by police as 'ideological' in the Jewish sector, while in the Arab sector 'ideological' cases rose from five in 1993 to ten in 1994. In fact many more cases out of the total may be imputed to ideology.

Drugs: In the consumption of drugs, Arabs compare with Jews (1,301 cases vs 4,514 in 1993; and 1,193 vs 4,607 in 1994). In drug traffic, Arabs are 'credited' with almost half the volume of trade (800 cases among Arabs in 1993 vs 1,920 cases among Jews; and 628 vs 1,565 in 1994). This can be explained by the facility the Arabs have in contacting and contracting other Arab traffickers, both in the Territories and along Israel's borders with Egypt and Lebanon.

Car thefts: Unlike other categories of crime (such as robbery, theft, break-ins, etc.) where Jews and Arabs match each other's skill and motivation, it turns out that in car theft the Arabs far surpass the Jews. Between two thirds and three fourths of the cases are attributed to Arabs in Israel (908 out of 1,293 in 1993; 855 out of 1,242 cases in 1994). This is easily imputable to the stolen car traffic across the Green Line to the West Bank and Gaza, where cars are either put to use under forged plates or dismantled and sold as spare parts. This is corroborated by another statistic from the police report to the effect than among Israeli Arabs there were in the same periods 278 and 156 cases of theft of parts of vehicles, as compared with 413 and 304 in the Jewish sector and 740 and 483 by the Palestinians in the Territories. This overall drop in car and spare parts theft by perpetrators of all categories may be attributed to the rising effectiveness of the Palestinian police as the year 1994 unfolded.

Since the establishment of autonomy, many cases are known of cars taken over by the Palestinian Authority police. As for thefts of property from parked cars, here too the Arabs account for about 50 per cent of the cases (1,663 out of 3,671 in 1993; and 1,170 out of 2,773 in 1994).

Arson: Here too the Arabs account for about 50 per cent of the cases (167 out of 375 in 1993 and 155 out of 311 in 1994). However, while in the Jewish sector there were 'only' two cases of 'ideological' arson in 1993 and none in 1994, the Arab sector accounts for sixty-two and nineteen cases, respectively. Incidentally, the corresponding figures in the Territories for the same periods are 617 and 504 cases, many of them the burning of Israeli cars, as compared with only ten and eighteen cases attributed to 'criminal' motives there.

Agricultural theft: This is very peculiar to Arabs both in Israel and the Territories. This category, which indicates the huge gap in technology and productivity between Jews and Arabs, includes theft of agricultural implements and products. Here the Arabs far surpass the Jews even in absolute terms: 240 vs 179 cases in 1993 and 202 vs 127 in 1994. That means a ratio of about 6:1 in agricultural thefts. This figure is further enhanced by the agricultural thefts perpetrated in Israel by Palestinians from the Territories: 498 in 1993 vs 394 in 1994.

Ideological Crime

We have already referred above to some facets of regular crime which may also be interpreted as 'ideological', notably arsons and sabotage, protest activities, and even economic crimes which, by definition, do not bring with them any direct benefit to the perpetrators. There are, however, other categories of crime which are par excellence ideological. We will cite a few of them:

Illegal road blocks: Demonstrators who want to make a point or to protest against something or someone may obstruct traffic by building a road block made out of rocks or burning tires and the like. This is done by Jews and Arabs alike, and it has to be interpreted as 'ideological', since no personal material gain is pursued by the perpetrators. Against seven cases perpetrated by Jews in 1993 and eight in 1994, Arabs in Israel are 'credited' with eight in 1993 and thirteen in 1994. These figures compare favourably with twenty-one cases in the Territories in 1993 and twenty-eight in 1994.

Rock throwing: While in the Jewish sector five cases of stones thrown against Arabs were registered in 1993 and seven cases were reported in 1994, the Arabs in Israel committed 133 cases in 1993 and 174 in 1994. Of course, compared with the *intifada*, where specialized rock throwers perpetrated thousands of acts every year, these figures seem rather moderate. But it is noteworthy that during the years under study, even in the Territories, the recorded number of cases has dropped considerably and became almost equal to that of the Arabs in Israel: 148 in 1993 and 192 in 1994.

Incitement: Police recorded only eight cases of 'incitement' by

Israeli Arabs in 1993 and even less (two) in 1994. But judging from the equivalent figures in the Territories (nine and five, respectively) it is evident that written and many oral incitements are not included in police statistics. Of the cases of incitement against Israel in the Palestinian press, in Hamas communiqués, in Friday sermons in mosques, and in political speeches, many are beyond calculation, both in the Territories and among Israeli Arabs.[26] Another category of 'incitement to rebellion' is perhaps the answer to this lacuna. Police listed twenty-five cases of this kind in 1993 and eighteen in 1994, compared with six and nine, respectively, in the Jewish sector.

Hoisting the PLO flag: Until the 1993 Oslo Accords, dealing with the PLO or its symbols was considered a crime in the Israeli penal system. While in 1993, seventeen cases were recorded among Israeli Arabs (compared with one case among Jews), in 1994 the figure dropped dramatically to four and equalled the four cases among Israeli Jews. It turns out that in spite of the Accords, this contravention of the legal code was not removed from the list in police statistics.

Molotov cocktails: Only one case was registered in the Jewish sector, compared to sixteen cases among Arabs in 1993 and twenty-four in 1994.

Spying and treason: Five cases were recorded among Jews in 1993 and three in 1994, almost identical to the number of Arabs who committed the same felony: eight in 1993 and two in 1994.

CONCLUSIONS AND PROSPECTS

What are we to learn from all this? Where are these developments likely to lead? Of course, as the cliché goes, it will all depend. On the morrow of the signing of the Oslo B agreement (September 1995), which extended Palestinian autonomy to much of the West Bank, while there was some optimism regarding the attenuation of the Israeli–Palestinian conflict, one has to bear in mind that this was no more than an interim accord which was to be reopened for negotiation. Therefore, the conduct of Israeli Arabs, criminal or otherwise, will necessarily be moulded by the developments within the Palestinian autonomy and in its relations with Israel and, more importantly, by the prospects of producing a permanent settlement to the liking of the Palestinians, i.e. a full-fledged Palestinian state.

During the interim stage of autonomy, if the Palestinian institutions grow satisfactorily, and the local police succeed in containing terrorism against Israel, this atmosphere of calm and state-building might have a beneficial, quietist effect on Israeli Arabs. In this case, the latter would concentrate on their internal problems of equality and integration within Israeli society, their standard of living would continue to rise, the tension between them and the Israeli majority might recede and so would the rate of criminality among them.

If, however, the strife continues within the autonomy, between supporters of Arafat and his opponents, this might reflect directly on its relations with Israel. Arafat's rivals would continue, then, to mount terrorist activities against Israel, aided and sheltered by the ten cities in the West Bank and Gaza under PLO jurisdiction, where Hamas and Islamic Jihad members might simply melt into the generally sympathetic population and pursue with impunity their acts of sabotage. Such a turn of events would of course embitter the relations of the autonomy with Israel, put a hold on the negotiations of a permanent settlement, and turn the Israeli Arabs against their country, with all the correlatives of ideological criminality involved.

The negotiations for a permanent settlement, while in themselves likely to shake the fledgling Israeli–Palestinian relationships, due to expected disagreements on such vital issues as Jerusalem, the right of return, a Palestinian state, water, the Israeli settlements, and any number of road mines of this sort, will be a time bomb for Israeli Arabs as well. Every discord, let alone deep crisis or unmitigated recriminations announced by one of the parties, can only create an atmosphere of bitterness, distrust and doomsday, where Israeli Arabs hardly find their place, being innately closer to their brethren in the conflict. When brought to its extreme, this mood may engender Arab crime against Israel, especially on the part of Muslim fundamentalists who would then be 'vindicated' when pointing to Israel's 'obduracy' as a sign that a settlement is not in sight.

If negotiations come to a happy end, two scenarios can be envisaged. either all is agreed and well, and the Palestinian authority will establish a Palestinian state where democratic institutions might operate smoothly; in this case the lure of living under Palestinian rule might encourage some Israeli Arabs to undertake *irredenta* activities and demand their annexation to Palestine. Or, if things go wrong and the Palestinian authority, as it does today, deals heavy-handedly with its citizenry, then, paradoxically, the Arabs of Israel might come finally to the conclusion that a liberal democratic Israel is a better place to live than an autocratic Palestine. Their attitudes towards Israel might then be mitigated with all the expected consequences on criminality, ideological or otherwise.

All these scenarios have to be re-examined in the event Muslim fundamentalists take over in Palestine or constitute a major component of its rule. In this case, in spite of the three generation acculturation of the Arabs in Israeli society and adopting many of its liberal democratic values, the very existence of a Jewish state in the heart of the Arab Islamic world might always give messianic hopes to fundamentalist groups that one day, somehow, the Zionist entity might be overcome and Palestine revert to Islam. These trends, which already exist in the margins of Arab society in Israel, may, in due course and under circumstances described above, bloom into a full-fledged clash between them and their country.

These speculations about possible scenarios which may unfold in the future should not obscure the fact that in view of the permanence of the root causes of criminality, and of the built-in contradictions between Israel's host culture and the Arab guest culture, the existing rates of criminality are already indicative of a trend, which may be blunted or boosted, depending on the future of the relations between Israel and the Palestinians. This trend notwithstanding, it is essential to avoid sweeping generalization because the one year statistics following the Oslo Accords have revealed mixed findings which may be interpreted one way or another. On the one hand, there were some serious increases in criminal activity among Israeli Arabs since Oslo, such as stone throwing, Molotov cocktail throwing, drug trafficing and road blocks. Most of these acts, which can be dubbed 'ideological crimes', may reflect either opposition to the peace process, due to its deficiencies in the eyes of its beholders, or a rise in Palestinian

Muslim self-identity which refuses to act against the 'others' in order to stand clear from them.

But, on the other hand, there was a temporary drop in car thefts following Oslo, as well as a decrease in arson, drug consumption, hoisting PLO flags, etc. Each of these categories calls for a different interpretation:

a. Car thefts rose to a peak in the months preceding Oslo or immediately following it, as thieves were pressed to intensify their activity before the forthcoming Palestinian authority might thwart it. Therefore, the year following Oslo, having passed the peak of the preceding years, seemed relatively easy on car theft. Another possible explanation is that during 1994, Palestinian police accumulated experience and were better able to enforce the law and block car traffic across the border from Israel, which rendered car theft too risky and unworthy an enterprise.
b. The decrease in drug consumption is imputable first and foremost to the Islamic movement which has eliminated this vice among many of its constituents. One could almost suggest a formula which says: religious revival = drop in drug consumption.
c. Flag hoisting, once becoming non-antagonistic to much of Israel's public opinion, is either not accounted for by police as severely as prior to Oslo; or, since the contravention is no longer enforced by police, it has lost much of its provocative appeal in the eyes of its perpetrators.

In May 1996, following murderous attacks launched by Palestinian terrorists against Israeli civilians, and the earlier than scheduled elections, a right-wing government was installed in Israel, much to the chagrin of the Arabs in general and the Israeli Palestinians in particular. For not only were they no longer needed to sustain a coalition, and hence their power of leverage blunted, but they feared that the slowdown of the peace process might complicate their situation, halt or reverse the many accomplishments they had achieved under the Labour government and even marginalize them. As far as criminality is concerned, new dilemmas faced the Palestinian population of Israel: if they should raise their voices of criticism of the new government, they might arouse against them the new majority on which they depended for budgets and other perks, and push their rank-and-file to illegal acts bordering on crime. Worse, if they should adopt a quietist approach in order to traverse this difficult period, they would betray their commitment to their Palestinian brethren with whom Israel is pursuing negotiation willy-nilly.

Four years after the Oslo Accords (1993), three years after the post-Oslo period surveyed in this article (1994) and nearly two years after the change of government in Israel which followed (1996), trends remain in flux. A much longer lapse of time is needed to evaluate the potential of criminality of Arabs in Israel in light (or obscurity, as the case may be) of the developments in the peace process. It is safe to assume that as the Palestinians cross their transitional stage from a divided people in a divided land controlled by others to a united country where they assume self-rule, their patterns of behaviour will be moulded and will in time help shape the modalities of Arab behaviour within Israel. But it is already evident that, in spite of the efforts made by the Likud government to maintain the advances in Arab society within Israel in the fields of education, development and equality in general, the deadlocked peace process with the Palestinians will have a far-reaching effect on the radicalization of Israeli Arabs and on the rate of ideological criminality among them. If car theft, for example, is an indication, it has risen sharply in the past two years, with the connivance and at times active participation of Palestinian police and notables.

Arabs in Israel live in a society ten-fold more economically and technologically advanced than the Palestinian entity taking shape in their neighbourhood. They have grown accustomed to its liberal regime, its freedom of speech and association, its democracy, its plural party system and other trappings of democracy yet to be adopted by the emerging Palestinian entity. These are precisely the characteristics that arouse the wrath of Muslim fundamentalists, who regard Westernization as anathema and Westernized societies as their sworn enemy. Therefore, while Westernized Israeli Arabs, aided by peace between Israel and Palestine, are likely to shed much of their potential for ideological crime against Israel (we call that Israelization) or if, on the contrary, Islamization or Palestinization gains ground among Israeli Arabs, aided by successful Muslim revolutions in adjoining countries (Jordan, Egypt and Lebanon) or in Palestine itself, then Islamized/Palestinized Israeli Arabs might become the spearhead of the Arab/Islamic world against Israel. The rate of criminality among Israeli Arabs today will then fade in comparison with what is to come.

NOTES

This was first published in *Journal of Terrorism and Political Violence* (Spring 1998), pp. 35–59.

1. See R. Israeli, 'On the Identity Problem of Israeli Arabs', in A. Hareven (ed.), *One Out of Six Israelis* (Hebrew) (Jerusalem: Van Leer, 1981), p.175.
2. See, e.g., M. Amir, 'Political Crime and Common Criminality: Some Preliminary Considerations', *Violence, Aggression and Terrorism*, 1, 4 (1981), pp.371–402.
3. Ibid.
4. See, e.g., R. Israeli, *Muslims in China* (Curzon 1980), chs.1–3.
5. E.g., see Gilles Kepel, *A L'ouest D'Allah* (Paris: Seuil, 1994), pp.205ff.
6. The Tamils in Sri Lanka are also a case in point, as are the Kurds of Iraq.
7. See the Jerusalem Centre for Public Affairs, 'Report on Law Enforcement among Minorities in Israel in the 21st Century' (Hebrew), June 1993, pp.6–7. This author was a member of the team which wrote the report.
8. See R. Israeli, *Muslim Fundamentalism in Israel* (London: Brassey's, 1993).
9. See, e.g., E. Sivan, *Radical Islam* (New Haven, CT: Yale University Press, 1985); J.P. Peroncel-Hugoz, *The Raft of Mohammed* (New York: Paragon, 1988).
10. See, e.g., Israeli, *Muslim Fundamentalism in Israel* (note 8), esp. chs.1–4.
11. Ibid. see esp. chs.2, 5, 6.
12. Ibid., pp.41–2.
13. Ibid., pp.41–4.
14. Ibid., pp.41–7.
15. Ibid., pp.43, 45, 47–8.
16. For details, see R. Israeli, 'Muslim Fundamentalists as Social Revolutionaries: The Case of Israel', *Terrorism and Political Violence*, 6, 4 (1994), pp.462–75.
17. See, e.g., Louis Wirth, 'The Problem of Minority Groups', in R. Linton (ed.), *The Science of Man in the World Crisis* (New York: Columbia University Press 1957).
18. Already in 1978, stupefying data to this effect came to public attention when the Financial Commission of the Knesset called upon the tax authorities to tighten their control over the Arab sector in Israel in view of massive tax evasions by individual businessmen, which was more than double the national average. Part of the problem was the reluctance of the authorities to act as severely as they would in the Jewish sector, e.g. through confiscation of property, for fear of violence and unrest. Additionally, Arabs having large families legally applied for tax exemptions, which in turn decreased even further the rate of tax payment among them; *Ha'aretz*, 25 Dec. 1978.
19. *Ma'ariv*, 26 Aug. 1987.
20. *Ma'ariv*, 7 Nov. 1995.
21. *Ha'aretz*, 13 March 1990.
22. *Al-Islam wa-Filastin*, 30 Oct. 1989, p.l.
23. *Ha'aretz*, 20 March 1988.

24. There is widespread evidence that cars stolen in Israel by Palestinian thieves have been put to use by Palestinian police.
25. Statistics were handed to this author, at his request, by the Chief Police Statistician. They cover the periods Jan.–Dec. 1993 and Jan.–Dec. 1994. I am indebted to the Police Headquarters and to the Chief Statistician for their forbearance in the face of my insistent, repeated and detailed requests.
26. The Muslim Movement in Israel publishes several organs which systematically denigrate the Jews, deny the Holocaust and view the rehabilitation of Islam as the supreme ruling principle. See Israeli, *Muslim Fundamentalism*, pp.38–48.

CHAPTER NINE

Muslim Fundamentalists as Social Revolutionaries: The Case of Israel

I. APOLOGIA

Muslim fundamentalist movements throughout the Islamic world and beyond have been branded as 'obscurantist', or 'terrorist', or a 'threat' to the world, mainly due to some of their violent activities which have captured the imagination of the Western world. Indeed, shootings of Western tourists in Egypt, or dagger attacks against Israelis in Israel and its administered territories, as well as violent rhetoric by some Muslim radical leaders, or the sabotage of the World Trade Center in New York, have come to dominate the Western view of fundamentalist Islam. Little is projected or widely known in Western public opinion about the domestic programmes of Islamization advocated by these movements within their own societies, which purport to revolutionize them in accordance with their oft-repeated slogans: 'Islam is the Alternative', 'Islam is the Solution', or 'Islam is the Truth'.

The Muslim movement in Israel, which has acquired importance in the late 1980s, is a case in point. Although it officially controls only a fraction of the Arab minority in Israel, it has become popular and appealing in the 1990s. This is due, partly, to the Muslim fundamentalist wave which has been sweeping the area; partly as a consequence of the collapse of Communism and the ensuing decline of the Communist Party among Israel's Arabs. Also important are the recent rise of Islamic radical movements among the Palestinians: the Hamas and the Islamic Jihad in the territories, and the Muslim Brothers, under various appellations, among the Palestinians who now constitute the majority of the inhabitants of Jordan. While other studies of Muslim fundamentalism among Israeli Arabs address themselves to various aspects of this movement's genesis, growth and political impact,[1] the present study proposes to limit itself to the great social upheaval that the Islamic movement has produced in its wake.

II. IDEOLOGY AND PRAXIS

The social revolution generated by the Muslim movement in Israel not only encompasses practically all domains of the everyday life of the Muslim-Arab population, but also purports to create new frameworks and infrastructures for the future, and has been providing the ideological religious underpinnings for such an endeavour, with the clear purpose of winning the entire Muslim population in Israel to its side. To examine the extent, the depth and the scope of the Islamic impact, it is necessary to refer not only to the ideological rhetorics but also to its application in real life. It is proposed to gauge the rhetoric-versus-action formula in the following categories or in combinations thereof:

a. The Islamic Movement versus tribal organization;
b. A new charismatic leadership versus the traditional notables;
c. Autarchy versus the old patron–client relationship;
d. Voluntarism versus resigned dependence on the powers that be;
e. Self-cleansing versus crime-ridden groups;
f. Islamization of society versus the modernizing pull;
g. Public welfare awareness versus traditional individualism and family-orientated activities;
h. The active status of women versus passivity in the past;
i. Politicization, mobilization and self-assertion versus apathy and resignation;
j. Alienation from the host society, anti-establishment propensities and alternative anti-state 'enclaves' of Islamic existence.

1. Identity, Leadership and Social Organization
The watershed which marked the development of Islamic fundamentalism among Israeli Arabs was the 1967 Six-Day War. As in the rest of the Arab world, a paradoxical process set in: a deep sense of humiliation, but also an ironclad resolve to seek redress

by identifying the illnesses that had affected Arabism and Islam, and then to strive to find a remedy and apply it vigorously. Islam was believed to be the panacea in many circles in the Islamic world. The renewed encounter between Israeli Arabs and their brethren across the 'Green Line' in the territories newly occupied by Israel lent a new impetus to this trend among the Arabs of Israel. For in the West Bank and Gaza, which had been administered by Jordan and Egypt respectively since 1949, Islamic associations, notably the Muslim Brothers, had remained solidly rooted within Palestinian society.

As always, quasi-messianic movements of this sort depend on charismatic leaders, pioneers who show the way and sweep the masses behind them. The founder of the Islamic Movement in Israel, an old supporter of the Rakah-Communist Party, was a 'born-again' Muslim, who in the mid-1970s joined the ranks of disillusioned Muslim youth. Sheikh Abdallah Nimr Darwish was in 1979 a leading member of 'Usrat-al-Jihad' (the Family of Jihad) which undertook acts of economic sabotage against Israel.[2] All members of the group were arrested, but then released when they undertook to act only within the confines of law. The Sheikh had studied, in 1969–72, at the Islamic Institute in Nablus, and began to teach Islam upon his return, imploring the Believers to return to the Faith. Many educated people and intellectuals became fascinated by his charisma, as did others who were practically illiterate or criminal and who viewed Islam as their personal way back into society.[3] Others may have later been drawn into the Sheikh's orbit by the apparent success of Muslim movements in Iran, Lebanon, Egypt and elsewhere.

The Sheikh's organization took on the name of 'Islamic Youth', but by creating this new grouping the young Sheikh unwittingly broke away from the existing order and suggested an alternative method of social organization. In so doing, Sheikh Abdallah acted not unlike the Prophet Muhammed, who had installed the *umma*, the congregation of all Muslims, as a substitute for the primeval ties of the individuals to their clans and tribes, pending the conversion of entire tribes to his cause. Disaffected elements in society, such as drop-outs, addicts, criminals, or independent thinkers who could no longer bear the shackles of their traditional and authoritarian clan notables, sought and found solace in the emerging brotherhood of fellow 'born-again' Muslims.[4]

This pattern was followed by other leaders of the same calibre and mettle, like Sheikh Ra'id in Umm al-Fahm,[5] Sheikh Sarsur in Kafr Qassem,[6] Sheikh Rayan in Kafr Bara,[7] or Sheikh Khatib in Kafr Kanna.[8] All in their twenties and thirties when they took the leadership of their local Islamic movements, they brought to their villages welfare associations which sought to step into the social and cultural vacuum left by the lack of socio-economic involvement by the Israeli government in their particular village.

Their Islamic message soon found a tremendous appeal among day workers who commuted daily to Tel Aviv and who endured daily humiliation in their encounter with Israeli prosperity and cultural assertiveness. Their message also appealed to the youth who were seeking new directions and new answers, and to professionals who were in search of new channels for their nationalism or new definitions for their identity. The movement appealed as well to the rank and file who observed with admiration and pride the welfare, development and cultural projects that the Muslim movement began undertaking in their home village.

As the physical and spiritual accomplishments of the movement shone, the traditional organizations of the kinship clans and political parties were dwarfed and made obsolete, almost irrelevant. Sheikh Ra'id of Umm al Fahm is a case in point.[9] His opponents in the village claim, not without reason, that his dramatic takeover of the mayorship in 1989 had been preceded by twelve years of systematic Islamic *da'wa* (propaganda), judiciously planned and executed among the population, and coupled with a variety of social services conducted for the benefit of the entire deprived population of his townsmen. By colouring with Islam their populist and hopeful platform, the fundamentalists under Ra'id presented their opponents of the Communist Party as 'godless' or 'anti-religious', thus making a vote for them tantamount to harming the Faith itself.[10]

Just prior to the elections, Ra'id was taken to court by his opponents in the Communist Party who contended that instead of printing his full name on the voting tickets, he contented himself with his first name, Ra'id, and his father's name, Salah. The Sheikh belongs to the Mahajneh clan, one of four in the village, and all candidates to elections have always stated their family affiliation. But the Sheikh rebelled against this convention because he needed to identify himself as a candidate representing *all* local inhabitants and not only his clan. He lost in court, and he was ordered to add his clan name to his voting slips, but his message was not lost: a break was effected with the past. The Muslim candidate was no longer propelled by his clan, which sought support from the other large families, but ran on an Islamic platform which by definition sought to rally the support of all Muslims. He got 80 per cent of the vote in his village. The resounding message of Islamic identity, which now transcended tribal affiliations, indeed won over six mayorships to the fundamentalists in the 1989 local elections.[11]

The acceptance and legitimation accorded the Muslim fundamentalists as such generated a snowball effect. For not only were the movement's leaders recognized as effective mayors, but due to their populist bent, which was undiminished by their power, their popularity kept growing. When one walks into Umm al-Fahm City Hall, one is amazed by the accessibility of the Mayor: no secretaries in between, no pomp and ceremony. One simply walks into the Mayor's office and finds him grappling with his timetable, his telephone calls and the many citizens who come to ask for help, advice or redress. When he walks (not drives) the streets of the town, he has time for everyone he encounters, exchanges a hug, a smile, a pat on the shoulder with fellow-townsmen, and hurries to supervise in person the school system, the home for the aged, the hospices, the dispensary and the cleanliness of the streets. Never in other Islamic countries, or in Israel for that matter, has one seen a mayor of a town this size (30,000 people) conducting himself, interacting with other people, and devoting all his self to his public duty, in this simple, direct, warm and selfless manner.[12]

No wonder, then, that when the new brand of socio-religious leaders took local initiatives well before they were elected, in order to resolve local problems of youth delinquency, economic backwardness, lagging development, poor education, primitive public works and the like, they *ipso facto* accumulated a vast pool of goodwill on the part of the population which came to acknowledge not only their care and concern, but also their leadership and *savoir-faire*.

This leadership also provided the ideological underpinnings for their new social organization. No longer was this only a collective of local notables who tackled questions of social welfare and immediate material want, but a dynamic group of visionaries who had a long-term vision of what they wanted: to turn their society into an Islamic one.[13] Here is how their message is defined by their organ:

> Our programme has clear stages and well-defined steps. We know what we want and we know the way to get there .... Our goal is the Muslim people and the Muslim person, thereafter we act so that our message would get everywhere to every home. We want the banner of Allah to flutter again proudly over the lands that used to constitute part of Islam at any time in the past[14] and where the voice of the muazzin could be heard praising Allah ... We want our call to reach everywhere and to be heard by all people of the Universe. Every-one of our steps has its means and ramifications, but we are reluctant at this point to elaborate anymore.[15]

By merging their social programme with personal piety on the individual level on the one hand, and the religio-political mission of the collective on the other, the Islamic movement in fact proposes an all-encompassing vision of life and commitment, within which a Muslim can live and with which he can identify.[16]

2. Self-Help as a Key to Self-Fulfilment

As conventional wisdom would have it, the rise of Islamic fundamentalism is due primarily to economic deprivation.[17] This approach, which has been almost universally adopted by scholars of Islam as well as by politicians and policymakers,[18] suggests that if one throws a few dollars and cents to a fundamentalist group, the latter would forgo its religious 'fanaticism' and come back into line with society. Not only is this view of the fundamentalists inherently denigrating (who else would sell out his ideas and beliefs for economic reward?), but it lacks foundation in reality. The case of the Islamic movement among the Arabs of Israel proves this point, even when wealthy countries like Iran and Saudi Arabia, both fundamentalist, or the far-from-disadvantaged leadership of the Islamic movements elsewhere (Muslim Brothers, Hizbollah, FIS, etc.) fail to do so. Leaders of the Islamic movement in Israel like to boast that 'while others shout slogans, we act'.[19] Indeed, they have an impressive record of achievements to their credit, beyond the missionary work of returning lost souls to the fold of Islam. Their accomplishments include a remarkable infrastructure of social services which, like the Muslim Brothers in Egypt and the Hamas in the territories, have coupled broad organizational work with doctrinal activities in order to widen their public appeal and win over a solid constituency.[20]

The parade of success began a long time before the Muslim movement took over six local councils in 1989. At a time when despair and abandon had gripped most of the Arab villages in Israel, the only hope was offered by the Muslim movement. The new Muslim leaders realized that in order to achieve credibility among the masses and gain their support, they must adopt the principle of self-reliance. As part of their missionary activity, they extolled, not unlike the Hamas, the merits of *zakat*, the alms giving which forms one of the Five Pillars of Islam.[21] And like the Prophet in his time, the leaders of the Muslim movement created a communal treasury in order to provide for the needs of the disadvantaged and the disaffected, thus enabling them to join in a newly organized community. The model of the Prophet in instituting *zakat* and in turning it into a religious duty was transposed onto their own environment where alms giving had become a matter of personal charity and was no longer considered, in practice, as a mandatory tenet. The Muslim movement revived that obligation, which is anchored in ancient Islamic society, and imposed it quite successfully. In allocating the *zakat*, the Muslim movement requested only 2 per cent of an individual's income and were prepared to accept payment in kind as a contribution towards the fulfilment of that tenet. Their readiness to accept smaller payments, building materials, skilled labour, heavy equipment or even manual work as contributions was a sign of their flexibility. The end result was a universalization of the *zakat*, each according to his capacities, which in turn became a mobilizing factor in society, once the positive fruits of the proceeds became evident.[22]

The pioneer of this stunning turn about was Sheikh Kamal

Rayan of Kafr Bara, who had initiated a five-year pilot project before it became a model to be implemented elsewhere. When the 25-year-old Rayan took over the mayorship of his village, there was only one main street leading to the mosque. All the rest were improved alleys. The elementary school did not have enough classrooms or toilets. The water network was a patch-work of plastic pipes winding up and down over hundreds of yards from the house of the father to the houses of his sons. Electricity was supplied in the same makeshift fashion; sport facilities or game grounds were considered an unattainable dream. There were no medical facilities and anyone who needed the slightest treatment had to go to the nearest Jewish town.[23]

But when Rayan launched his Islamic group in the village in the early 1980s, he began organizing his fellow villagers not only to study the Qur'an, but also to volunteer for public works. With the benefit of hindsight, there is no question that it was the mobilization of the local population to help itself that differentiated Kamal's preachings from those of other political parties, and paved the road to his election. Within his first term of office a fully-fledged modern water network with a storage pool and a pumping station was built, electricity supply was regularized, four new classrooms and new toilets were installed at the school, a full-sized soccer field was built, and alleys and roads were paved and lined with sidewalks, trees and flowers. A new public park and a vast cultural centre were opened, a new clinic offered medical services six days a week, and six sheltered bus stops were erected. The young Sheikh concedes that his budget does not exceed the low budgets that have become the norm in Arab villages and which amount to no more than 25 per cent per capita of the standard norm of budgetary allocations in Jewish towns and villages.[24]

How did he do it? Here is an example. In 1985 the Planning Authority of Israel gave permission for a new cultural centre which should have cost $350,000. Rayan applied for financial assistance to the Israeli government and to other public foundations, but to no avail. But then, a young and popular local activist of the Islamic movement died suddenly of heart failure, and the enterprising mayor declared a fundraising campaign to build the centre in memory of the deceased youth. Building materials were purchased with some $40,000 raised in cash. Masons and builders from the Muslim Movement membership volunteered their services. Altogether, 1,000 tradesmen and labourers worked in shifts around the clock, and in eighteen days and nights the building stood erect. The pool of volunteers was made up of those faceless and anonymous multitudes whose wives and daughters wear the long grey-coloured traditional dress and head scarves which hide their hair from indecent exposure. The men have beards and dress in Western attire, just like the mayor. In 1989 Kafr Bara returned Rayan to a second term of office by comfortable margins.[25]

This example was followed by youth organizations of Muslims practically everywhere among Israeli Arabs.[26] All that one has to do is to watch the metamorphosis of the towns and villages that have come under the sway of fundamentalists. The towering Islamic Centre in Umm al Fahm, the mainstay of Islamic fundamentalism in Israel, is another case in point. In contrast with the battered, neglected and decrepit town that the fundamentalists found when they came to power, the luxury of the Islamic Centre looks out of place. It is an enclave within the society that they laboured to convert to their cause. It illustrates what the fundamentalists are able to do, and the heights, material and spiritual, to which they are able to lift their constituents, if their word is heeded. It also illustrates the fact that mobilization of existing resources was the challenge of the new Islamic leadership, not the traditional supplication of government and institutions to raise the needed funds.[27]

3. Re-Islamization and Recruiting the Margins

The traditional rule of the notables in the Arab society of Israel had marginalized some of its most vigorous and dynamic forces – youth and women – and driven into public oblivion the less fortunate and the disaffected who reminded society of its failures by the mere fact of their visible existence. To be a criminal, or a drug addict or, Allah forbid, to distance oneself from tradition and the mainstream, were phenomena that Arab society wished neither to see, nor to hear; it elected to look the other way, or to sweep such misfits under the rug, pretending they did not exist. These were, to a large extent, taboos.

Under the impact of the Israeli host society, but even more so under the pressure of the Islamic movement, what used to be marginal shifted to the centre: youth and women became mainstream in the Islamic movement; criminals and disaffected social groups gained and retained its attention; taboos were lifted on the public agenda, and even statements against Israel, which Israeli Arabs in general were wary to avoid, erupted into the open without fear. A society that was tranquil, low-key, homogeneous, conservative and patriarchal suddenly burst into a bustling, multifarious, assertive and youth-oriented new world. Instead of the superficially relaxed, resigned and easy-going atmosphere, one can now sense tension and bitterness; the Arab population was diffident, conscious of its majority-turned-minority status; now in the fundamentalist circles, it is cultivating a self-confidence born out of the self-imposed quasi-isolation from the Jewish state of Israel.

The key to this change lies not only in the mobilization of the hitherto remote and irrelevant strata of society and the rise of Palestinian nationalism, but also in the re-Islamization of society as a whole and the new value systems and pecking order emerging from it. If we can say that old Imams in the traditional order or clan-heads-turned-politicians called the rules of the game previously, now it is the young sheikhs who double up as politicians and lay leaders, who count among their constituents and vocal supporters low-born elements in the margins of society, and who determine the public agenda. And their agenda is Islam. Sheikh Ra'id of Umm al-Fahm credits himself and his colleagues in the leadership of the movement for the long, arduous and frustrating task of shifting the interest of the youth from matter to spirit, from the here-and-now to the hereafter.[28] They believe that their success emanated from their convincing their constituency that 'everything comes from Allah', that 'neither Marx nor Sartre' could provide the answers to existence or man's place and mission in the world.[29] The Sheikh insists that the return to Islam is part of a universal trend which came to the fore with the collapse of Communism and the rebuilding of churches in the Eastern bloc countries.[30]

Soon after he came to power, Sheikh Ra'id focused on the re-Islamization of his microcosm in Umm al-Fahm.[31] Today, at the gate of the local high school, boys and girls exit and walk home separately, and leaders of the movement are talking about separating the sexes in the classroom. Cafés have closed, in part

because of the banning of alcohol, in part because their customers have returned to the fold of Islam. The local soccer team,
dressed in training suits, pray to invoke the grace of Allah before
each game. When friends visit, the women are herded into separate rooms, while the men sit together in the large and hospitable
living room. Many people pray five times a day and those
employed in Jewish factories have requested prayer breaks as of
right. Local *zakat* committees provide the financial and religious
underpinnings for activities in villages not yet under the movement's elected leadership. But in Umm al-Fahm, where the movement has succeeded, these activities are co-opted and led by the
local municipality.

The most outstanding programmes implemented by these
charity committees are the Islamic work camps, which channel
the Islamic fervour of the fringes into constructive activities
which, in turn, enhance the movement's image and lend to it an
aura of activism and enterprising initiative. In 1986, one such
camp built in Umm al-Fahm a public library, a mosque and shelter for visitors to the town's cemeteries. They built and paved
roads, refurbished existing mosques and schools and installed
lighting for a basketball court. As the movement grew, a broad
range of activities benefiting the disadvantaged were adopted in
education and welfare. In cases where heads of poor families
were drug addicts or criminals, and aid could not be disbursed to
them for fear of misuse, funds were paid directly to stores which
provided the families with food. The *zakat* committees also provide funds for tutoring weak students, university scholarships,
and even study abroad. They also use their funds to support local
sports, male singing groups, and Islamic theatre; teach classes in
religion at local mosques; publish books and leaflets; and promote Islamic practices and ritual among all strata of society.

The metamorphosis in Arab villages is readily visible: mosques
are full of worshippers, especially youth; young men grow
beards, the hallmark of Muslim Brothers; between prayers hundreds of youth attend Islamic extra-curricular education; young
people dress modestly in the streets; and in many villages alcoholic drinks have disappeared, replaced by stands displaying and
selling religious literature and pamphlets.[32]

In the villages not yet under Islamic rule, Muslim associations

act like shadow governments, stepping in to provide services and
public works that the legally established municipality, belonging
to the Israeli order, is unable to fulfil. These activities and the
leadership' s impeccable reputation for modesty and incorrupt-
ibility have turned the Israeli establishment into a shadow government, far and remote, having little or no impact upon the lives
of their constituents. The leaders of the movement insist that
these changes must be effected smoothly, through preaching and
persuasion, but it is evident that when the leaders of the movement 'recommend' that all women dress in the modest Islamic
way, or that alcohol be banned in cafés, non-conformists would
be ostracized in such an environment. Even the intelligentsia,
who has adopted over the years many of the ways of Israeli-
Western society, has come under the sway of Islam. Many of
these educated people, who used to pioneer the way of modernization, now find modern up-to-date interpretations of the tenets
of Islam and follow them willingly.[33]

Not unlike other fundamentalist movements, the Muslim
movement in Israel stresses the role of women, due to their exclusive function in bearing and rearing children, in spreading the
message of Islam among other women, and in building and maintaining the nuclear family.[34] The Hamas Charter devotes an entire
chapter to women (Articles 17, 18) specifying their role in 'manufacturing men' and educating the younger generation.[35] Women
preachers assemble thousands of women in their gatherings and
many young women elect to study at local Islamic colleges to join
the ranks of the *da'is* (preachers) in the cause of Allah. In their
sermons they stress modest dress, namely that only the hands and
the face should be exposed and the rest of the body must be covered. Under the Islamic environment that has been gaining
ground in Israel, Muslim (and sometimes even non-Muslim)
women in Arab villages are taught to conform. Moreover, tran-
scending their marginality of years past, women now participate
in the vanguard of the re-Islamization wave.[36]

III. FROM SOCIAL TO POLITICAL REVOLUTION

There is little doubt that the Islamic movement in Israel, like its
peers elsewhere, has succeeded in forging a new society born out

of ideological purism and social puritanism. These fundamentalists are insistent and militant in their demand for total and immediate conversion of society to their line, because they can easily show that the general environment in which they live is corrupt and degenerate. They can also attack the existing educational system as defective, since it encourages apostasy rather than belief, and therefore as subversive, destructive and unreliable in bringing about a spiritual and social turnabout. They claim that the ultimate goal of the West and Israel is to undermine and weaken Islam.[37] By contrast, their holistic brand of Islam, with its socio-cultural strictures, offers an alternative which, if implemented in letter and spirit, provides all relevant answers to the pressing problems of the day.

The popular fundamentalist leaders are authoritarian to be sure, but they are also accessible to the people, modest in their demeanour and lifestyle, sometimes even ascetic. Their message to the masses is not soft, materialistic, cajoling, this-worldly and immediate, but rather spiritual, exciting, exacting, promising little and demanding a lot, shifting the emphasis to the hereafter. The fascinating paradox is that they seem to appeal much more with their hard and counter-current message than the established old-fashioned leaders and notables, with their flurry of praises and rosy rhetoric. In the eyes of these transformed masses, it is evidently preferable to share in a crude and modest egalitarianism, led by the example of their fundamentalist leaders, than watch a corruptive wealth unevenly distributed or disbursed to un-Islamic purposes. It is perhaps part of human nature that, in time of distress, it pins more hope on a difficult road which promises an ultimate way out, than on the illusion of quick shortcuts which lead nowhere. This deep psychological understanding of the masses is what permits the fundamentalists to break through into society and profoundly transform it.

The intriguing question is whether the social revolution already underway will stop there, or whether it will bring in its wake a political revolution transforming the existing Islamic enclaves within Israel into pockets of irredentism and bases of military activity against the state. Judging from the fact that the revival of Islam in the Arab world has been inextricably tied to the Arab–Israeli conflict, and that the higher the profile of Islam, the more virulent the anti-Israeli sentiment one detects among Israel's Muslim rivals (not only Arabs), the answer seems clear. But a closer look at the Islamic movement in Israel nevertheless reveals nuances emanating from the dual, and often contradictory, nature of this community: Israeli citizens on the one hand; adepts of the universal Islamic movement, on the other.

The Muslim movement in Israel, as elsewhere, has in effect been taking political stands on all major issues,[38] mainly because of its decision not to leave the political arena exclusively to its rivals, the Communists or the vestiges thereof. At the beginning of its activity in the early 1980s, the movement catered to the overwhelmingly pro-PLO stance among Israeli Arabs and was wary of immediately identifying explicitly with its sister organization, Hamas in the territories, when it came into the open in 1987. However, the prolongation of the *intifada*, in which Hamas had been gaining prestige and scoring points among the Palestinian public on the one hand, and the tremendous success of the Islamic movement in the February 1989 elections in Israel on the other, have apparently strengthened the more radical elements within that movement. Apparently upstaging the more conciliatory head of the movement, Sheikh Darwish, the young mayors unabashedly stress their Islamic commitment much more and come dangerously close to the Hamas line of argument.[39]

Already in late 1988, the first indications of that shift were noticeable in *al-Sirat*, the main organ of the movement, when an editorial stressed that 'the Palestinian people have hoisted the banner of Jihad in order to die for the sake of Allah'.[40] It does not take much daring or imagination to conclude that since the members of the movement considered themselves both Palestinians and Muslim, they would have no qualms to join in their brothers' endeavours if and when the circumstances so allow. More accusations were heaped against Israel, their country, in terms that would have perhaps justified legal steps against the movement. In the aftermath of an arson attack on a mosque in Israel, blame for which was, expectedly, laid at Israel's door, *al-Sirat* wrote:

> Satan had advanced the claim of the superiority of his Nazi race over the human race. Now, his disciples profess the superiority of a certain race over all the rest. Satan has

indeed found disciples of flesh-and-blood who are implementing his doctrine faithfully. Anyone who respects himself ought to stand up against Satan and his army; the caravan of Belief alone, when united, is able to undo their schemes.[41]

Such statements and others which carry even more vitriol[42] come dangerously close to inciting revolt against the Israeli authority. It has become conventional wisdom in the literature of terrorism and extremist political activity that delegitimation of your opponent is the first step toward resorting to violence against him. If this is so, and in spite of the skilful way the leaders of the movement have learned to skate to the brink, and avoid overstepping the boundaries of legality at the last moment, it is doubtful whether the masses, once incited and indoctrinated in this way, would not be swept into negative action beyond the control of their leaders.

NOTES

This work is based principally on three years of fieldwork in several Arab villages and on the movement leaders' writings, pamphlets and speeches. This was first published in the *Journal of Terrorism and Political Violence*, 6, 4 (Winter 1994), pp. 462–75.

1. See, e.g., R. Paz, *The Islamic Movement in Israel following the 1989 Israel Elections* (Hebrew), (Tel Aviv: Dayan Center, 1989); R. Israeli, *Muslim Fundamentalism in Israel* (London: Brassey's, 1993); and Th. Mayer, *The Muslim Awakening in Israel* (Arabic), (Nazareth, 1986).
2. For the entire story of Usrat al-Jihad, see Mayer, *The Muslim Awakening*.
3. Ibid.
4. See Israeli, *Muslim Fundamentalism*, pp.54–61, 120–6.
5. For details, see ibid., pp.35–8.
6. Ibid., pp.51–4 and 120–6.
7. Ibid., pp.61–5 and 120–6.
8. Ibid., pp.67–70 and 120–6.
9. See R. Israeli, *Fundamentalist Islam and Israel: Essays in Interpretation* (New York and London: UPA, 1993), pp.95–122.
10. See Atallah Mansur, *Ha'aretz Daily*, 6 March 1989; and Gideon Samet, ibid., 20 Oct. 1989, p.35.
11. See Paz, *Islamic Movement*.
12. Personal observations made during a day spent with the Mayor in June 1993.
13. See Israeli, *Muslim Fundamentalism*, p.111ff.
14. A clear message meaning that Palestine (including Israel), which had constituted part of Dar-al-Islam since it was occupied by Caliph Umar in the seventh century, must return to Islamic hands. For that matter, Andalusia and Southern France must undergo the same process of 'reconquista'.
15. *Sawt al Haqq wal-Huriyya*, 29 Dec. 1989.
16. Israeli, *Muslim Fundamentalism*, pp.111–19.
17. See, e.g., E. Sivan, *Radical Islam* (New Haven, CT: Yale University Press, 1985); G. Kepel, *La Revanche de Dieu* (Paris: Serial, 1990); H. Dekmejian, *Islam in Revolution* (Syracuse, NY: Syracuse University Press, 1985).

18. Several Israeli, American and Arab leaders have repeated this proposition of late, in the context of the Middle East peace process.
19. Sheikh Darwish and other leaders in the movement often make this remark in the speeches.
20. See Israeli, *Muslim Fundamentalism*, pp.88–144.
21. See R. Israeli, 'The Charter of Allah', in Y. Alexander (ed.), *The 1988–9 Annual of Terrorism* (Dordrecht: Martinus Nijhoff, 1990).
22. For this point, see Israeli, *Muslim Fundamentalism*, pp.130–8.
23. Ibid., pp.132–3.
24. Ibid., and pp.61–5.
25. Ibid.
26. Personal tours of these villages effected by the author during 1986–93.
27. Israeli, *Muslim Fundamentalism*, pp.133–4.
28. See interviews by Marc Duvoisin, *Philadelphia Inquirer*, 23 March 1989, pp.16–17; A. Maniur, in *Ha'aretz*, 10 Oct. and 15 Oct. 1989.
29. Ibid.
30. Ibid.
31. Ibid. and personal field observations by the author. See Israeli, *Muslim Fundamentalism*, pp.130–5.
32. Ibid.
33. Ibid., pp.134–5.
34. Ibid., pp.137–8.
35. See Israeli, 'Charter of Allah' (note 21).
36. See Israeli, *Muslim Fundamentalism*, pp.137–8. See also laudatory words by female readers of *al-Sirat* about spreading the use of Islamic dress among the female Muslims of Haifa University. *Al-Sirat*, June 1986, p.52. See also I. Lapidus, *Contemporary Islamic Movements in Historical Perspective* (Berkeley, CA: University of California Press, 1983), p.27.
37. E.g., see *al-Sirat*, June 1986, pp.11–13.
38. See, e.g., Israeli, *Muslim Fundamentalism*, pp.88–119.
39. Ibid., pp.111–19.
40. *Al-Sirat* monthly, Nov. 1988.
41. Ibid., Dec. 1988.
42. See Israeli, *Muslim Fundamentalism*, pp.38–48. See also the citation of a fundamentalist leader on p.173.

CHAPTER TEN

The Anti-Millennium:
The Islamization of Nazareth

On 21 December 1997, just four days before Christmas, Muslim zealots fenced in the area at the foot of the Basilica of the Annunciation in Nazareth, declared it *waqf* land (a Muslim holy endowment), erected a large tent as a provisional mosque, and demanded the construction of a permanent mosque with a towering 86-metre minaret. Two months earlier, during the Jewish High Holidays, two car bombs were activated by Muslim citizens of the state of Israel in the heart of the cities of Haifa and Tiberias. Are those events inter-connected? In other words, is the takeover of Nazareth by Islamists a follow-up of the violent acts of terrorism by the same fundamentalists? The violent riots of the 2000 *intifada*, where the Israeli Arabs, led by Islamist elements, joined the violent demonstrations of the Palestinians against Israel, tend to answer those questions in the affirmative.

The conflict which pitted Nazareth's Muslim majority (70 per cent) against its Christian minority (30 per cent) was only the tip of a growing enmity between the two communities during the past decades. As long as nationalist Arab groups within the city had been able to live under the uniting umbrella of the Communist party, which had ruled the city for decades, questions of religion and communal rivalry had been set aside. But with the decline of the communists and other Arab nationalists headquartered in the city, new groups began to emerge, the most important of which are the Islamists. This reflected the demographic transformation of Nazareth, known for its Christian holy sites, into a Muslim city where local Muslims sought to dominate.

The process of the Islamization of Nazareth has been gradual. Some time after the establishment of the State of Israel in 1948, the traditional Christian majority came to be balanced by the Muslims, mainly due to the influx of refugees who had sought shelter there when their villages were destroyed during the war. Subsequently, the more Westernized and better educated Christians bore fewer children while their Muslim compatriots continued to have large families. As the millennium approached, highlighting the Christian history of the city, the Muslim majority decided to intervene by scuttling the elaborate festivities planned by the Israeli government and the Municipality of Nazareth, headed by its Christian mayor. As part of this effort they sought to construct a mosque which would tower over and dwarf the Christian Basilica of the Annunciation, the largest church in the city.

The Islamists' take-over of Nazareth has also been inexorably linked with the mounting anti-Israeli moods in the city as in other parts of the country where Muslim fundamentalists are in power, notably Umm al-Fahm, the largest Muslim town in Israel. Not that before the Islamic takeover there was any great love for Israel in that hub of Arab nationalism which was nurtured by the Communists and their various successors (the Rakah and then the Hadash Party); but, as highlighted in the October 2000 riots of the Israeli Arabs, Muslim fundamentalists in their midst contributed, to a great extent, to the violence of the confrontation. In that sense, the loss of the Christian grip in Nazareth also signifies, to a large extent, the dwindling of Israel's power and authority there.

THE COMMUNIST ERA IN NAZARETH

Until the mid-1970s, municipal government in Nazareth was dominated by local parties associated with the ruling Mapai party and its derivatives, whose power was based on family connections. These parties were so incompetent in administrative and urban governance that in 1974 Prime Minister Golda Meir appointed a commission of inquiry which recommended the dismantling of the city council and placing city affairs in the hands of an appointed commission manned by officials of the Ministry of Interior.

However, in the municipal elections of 1975, the first where the mayors were directly elected, Tawfiq Zayyad, a Muslim and the rising star of the Communist party (thereafter Rakah and then Hadash), who headed a local list of his own creation – the Nazareth Democratic Front – garnered a stunning 70 per cent of the vote. His victory, and the establishment of the first communist-led city administration in Israel, created apprehension in the Israeli government which regarded Rakah as an enemy. In consequence, the Ministry of Interior refused to co-operate with Zayyad, probably hoping that his isolation would bring about his downfall.

The Democratic Front led by Zayyad, with the backing of his new city council, revolutionized city politics and the city administration, and was re-elected by a landslide in 1979. At that time, Ramiz Jeraisi was elected deputy mayor and would become the actual city Manager while his boss was engaged in national politics as head of the Hadash party in the Knesset. Jeraisi, a young (27-year-old), educated engineer, was a Christian. The charismatic Zayyad became, in effect, the 'foreign minister' of Nazareth, inasmuch as he could lobby government offices, and negotiate with other parties and government ministers on behalf of the city's interests as well as those of all Arabs in Israel. During the nearly two decades that Zayyad served as a powerful spokesman for Nazareth and the Arabs in Israel (until his tragic death in a car accident in 1994), his loyal and devoted deputy, Jeraisi, took care of the affairs of the city.

Zayyad was easily re-elected in 1983 and Hadash held a majority in the city council (eleven out of seventeen seats). Just before the elections, the party journal, *al-Ittihad*, published his powerful poem lauding the 'Great Egyptian Crossing' in the October 1973 war, a demonstration of Arab nationalism for which the Arab voters rewarded him. Zayyad's success in local politics spilled over into national politics when, in the general elections of 1984, more than half the Arab population of Israel voted for Hadash, and the new Committee of Heads of Arab Councils (CHAC) practically adopted the Communist platform at Zayyad's instigation.

Zayyad was also the engine behind the organization of annual summer camps used to mobilize Arab youth for the party. Each year thousands of volunteers, including some from the West Bank and Gaza and even from abroad, would participate in maintenance work throughout the city, mending fences, paving roads, and refurbishing schools, mosques, and cemeteries. Local contractors, as well as the city, donated machinery and materials as well as skilled labour. After the day's work, the participants were given lectures that stressed the importance of volunteer work for the Arabs and for strengthening the links among the Palestinian people. The local Arab press reported extensively on the camps, emphasizing the point that despite discrimination suffered by the Arab towns and villages in terms of state government funding, Hadash was there to compensate for this with its spirit and organizational abilities.

The demise of the Soviet Union, followed by the Gulf Crisis of 1990–91, threw the communists into disarray. Zayyad, who continued to be personally popular in Nazareth, had difficulty adapting to the new reality. In the wake of the embarrassment caused by the Iraqi invasion of Kuwait and the pro-Iraqi stance adopted by Yasser Arafat, Zayyad declared that the invasion of one Arab country by another had to be pushed aside in the face of the much larger concern about the return of American imperialism to the Middle East. While grassroots support for the communists began to drop significantly, compared with their heyday in the 1970s and 1980s, the mayor of Nazareth remained a pivotal figure in Arab politics in Israel.

When Zayyad died in the prime of his career, his deputy and fellow party member, Jeraisi, was elected by the Democratic Front's majority on the council as the new mayor. Yet, however talented he was in dealing with city affairs, he had neither the stature nor the religious affiliation that would make him acceptable to the rising new power of the Muslim fundamentalists in city politics. Zayyad, the previous long-time mayor, had been a Muslim and, in spite of his communist 'heresy', no one could challenge him due to his popularity in Nazareth during the preceding twenty years. With Zayyad now gone, the Muslim political activists in Nazareth sought to crystallize their constituency not only in support of the Islamic party lists but also in opposition to the discredited Communist party and its new chief – the Christian Jeraisi. The Islamists would henceforth set Nazareth on a course of collision not only with their Christian fellow citizens but also with the state of Israel.

THE RISE OF THE ISLAMIC MOVEMENT

By the time of Israel's municipal elections of 1989 it had become evident that the nascent Islamic movement in Israel had turned its focus from the religious-cultural pursuit of 'born again' Muslims into a religious-political organization intent on seeking power as a way to implement its programme. Five Islamist mayors were elected, including Sheikh Ra'id Salah as the mayor of Umm al-Fahm, the largest Muslim town in Israel. Forty-five Islamic movement councilmen were also elected to various town councils, including Nazareth.

This shift in Arab politics also affected Nazareth quite deeply. Even though the Islamist candidate for mayor, Umar Shararah, was defeated by Zayyad, he nevertheless succeeded in gaining a majority of the vote in the Muslim neighbourhoods. Zayyad was re-elected only due to his personal popularity and the rallying of the Christians in towns around the communist Democratic Front in an effort to block the rise of the Muslim fundamentalists, who elsewhere in the country coupled their ascendance to power with vicious anti-Israeli propaganda.

In consequence of the demise of the Soviet Bloc and of Communism worldwide, the national elections of 1992 in Israel saw a sharp decline in support for the communists throughout the country. The Islamists, as a sign of their non-recognition of the Jewish State of which they were citizens, shunned the elections. It is assumed that since the voter turnout among Arabs shrunk from about 73 per cent in 1988 to about 70 per cent, the Islamists, who did not participate in the general elections for ideological reasons, made that difference. Nevertheless, Zayyad was re-elected to the Knesset at the head of Hadash, which still received close to 50 per cent of the vote in Nazareth, despite the general losses of the party in the city and countrywide. In the local elections of 1993, voter turnout jumped to 90 per cent as compared with 70 per cent in the national elections a year earlier. This is seen as evidence of the Arab view of their local authorities as arenas in which they can vent their political concerns. The Hadash party continued to dominate local Arab politics despite its sharp losses in the national elections. In 1993 the party won twelve mayoralties down from fifteen in 1989, but in Nazareth it registered gains, mainly due to Zayyad's stature. At the same time, the Islamic Movement maintained its strength with five mayoralties and fifty local councilmen countrywide.

THE MARGINALIZATION OF THE CHRISTIANS

The Christians in Israel, in general, and those of Nazareth who had been the champions of the Communist party in years past, in particular, could not help seeing the writing on the wall: their political status was slipping and the rise of the Muslim fundamentalists began to pose a direct threat to them. This generated a loss of self-confidence in their future as a minority within the Arab minority in the country. Even though the more moderate elements within the Islamic Movement in Israel heralded the 'links of fraternity between Muslim and Christian Arabs', the Christians were not particularly keen to find themselves living under the strictures of Islamic Shari'a rule that would relegate them to the status of *dhimmi*[1] should its political platform come to pass. True, they were not immediately exposed to the formal change of their status as long as Israel's laws protected them, but they could learn from the example of Umm al Fahm that once Islamists took over, they could enforce local by-laws prohibiting liquor, separating the sexes in co-ed education and imposing modes of dress and dietary laws that were unacceptable to them.

In 1992, the Islamic Movement organ *Sawt al-Haqq wa-l-Huriyya* (Voice of Truth and Justice) carried an attack against the respected Arab-Christian journalist Atallah Mansur for a series of articles in the Israeli daily *Ha'aretz* that he had published criticizing the moral conduct of some Islamist leaders.[2] He was accused of harming Islam, diffusing lies, and violating the integrity of Muslim fundamentalists and Muslim women. He was condemned as a racist and a war-monger who sowed discord among the Arabs of Israel. Mansur sued in a court of law and was compensated for the libel, but the Christians in general continued to sense that the State of Israel, as a democratic state, ought to prohibit by law incitement against them. The Christians simply ignored, or were not aware of, similar incitements against Jews, which were published in the official organs of the Islamists in Israel such as Sawt al-Haqq and went unpunished by the authorities.

Attacks and condemnations of Christians (and Jews for that matter) are also heard in mosques, sermons, and publications of the Muslim Movement. On the eve of the Id al-Ad'ha festival in 1996, that is the major festival in the Islamic calendar, the Feast of Immolation, otherwise known as the Feast of the Qurban or the Great Bairam, on the tenth day of Dhu'l Hijja, a leaflet was distributed in Umm al-Fahm which accused local youth of improper behaviour 'mimicking that of Jewish and Christian Unbelievers'. A copy of the manifesto reached Nazareth and caused outrage there, which was reflected in the local press such as *al-Sinara* and *Kul-al'Arab* owned and edited by Christian families. Yet, in response, far from counter-attacking, the Christians reacted like a *dhimmi* people, singing the praises of the Muslim majority under whose mercy they were reduced. They protested that they were as good as any other Arabs, pointing to their contributions to Arab culture and history, which only encouraged additional onslaughts upon them.

In June 1996, an Arab-Christian psychology student surveyed high school students in Nazareth on questions regarding the identity of Christians in Israel. The questionnaire he circulated among students at the Baptist school in Nazareth, which had been completed by other Christian students in other towns in Israel without problems, triggered a sudden storm of controversy that was widely echoed in the Arab and national media including the Islamic *Sawt al-Haqq*. Again, in a sycophant manner, even the Christian writers who tried to fend off the Muslim (and some Christian) attacks heaped blame on their co-religionist, who was accused of 'sowing the poison of racism and division between Arab Christians and Arab Muslims'.[3] The school authorities were also blamed for permitting the circulation of the questionnaire.

Another case in point was a conflict around land ownership in Nazareth, which was to become the antecedent of the much larger dispute that was to erupt in 1997–99. During Zayyad's term as mayor, a mosque was built without the requisite city permit at Nabi Sa'in, the location of the tomb of a local Muslim saint, which dominates the city from the surrounding heights, in close proximity to a Christian monastery. The illegally constructed mosque later received a retroactive permit when the city leaders realized that their intervention would kindle a clash with the Muslim

majority. The growing Muslim Movement in Nazareth then proceeded to claim that an adjacent 213-dunam (c.50 acres) area
was *waqf* (holy endowment) land, while the municipality insisted
that it owned the property. The local Christians feared that
Muslim claims to property that was not theirs, under the pretext
of it being *waqf* land, was but a stratagem to pursue the take-over
by Muslims of the Christian City of Nazareth. At the same time,
the Muslim success was evident in that neither the Christian
minority nor the Israeli authorities were up to meeting the challenge raised by the Muslim Movement. The Christians, due to
their dwindling numbers, did not want to further raise the
Muslims' wrath against them, and they were unable to arrest that
process. The Israeli successive governments were unwilling to
clash with the Muslims of Israel in general.

Although since the inception of Israel in 1948, and in spite of
the massive immigration of Jews to the land, the Israeli authorities and public viewed with a sense of alarm the rapid demographic growth of the Arab population in the country, no government devised any plan to either integrate that population wholly
so as to blunt its hostility, or to set it apart and separate from it.
All successive Israeli governments have been attempting to manage the internal conflict between Jews and Arabs rather than
solving it, with the result that the situation kept worsening. To
this decaying state of affairs there were three major considerations:

- The Arabs of Israel had ceased since the 1970s, by reason of
their contacts with other Palestinians in the Territories under
Israel, to identify themselves as a religious-ethnic-linguistic
minority in the Jewish state, and began to clamour for the recognized status of a national minority, which if accorded to
them would have turned Israel into a bi-national state.
- The Arabs of Israel being Palestinians, tended to identify with
their people rather than with their state, thus resuscitating
suspicions among the Jewish majority about their loyalties. A
double loyalty, which may be an acceptable state of affairs in
any pluralistic country which has no enemies and is in a state
of peace, becomes problematic when hostilities still exist
between Israel and other Arab countries, notably Palestinians,

as the violent events of October 2000 have dramatically and sadly shown.

- In spite of the vast immigration of waves of Jews to Israel, which have increased the country's population tenfold (from 600,000 in 1948 to 6 million in 2000) in 50 years, the Arab-Palestinian minority has increased by the same proportion due to internal growth and constitutes now a hefty 20 per cent of the total. Again, in a normal situation, where citizens are equal and feel for their country regardless of their ethnic affiliation, this would not matter. But in view of the compressed hostility among the Arab population, which carries a huge potential of explosion and violence – as recent events have demonstrated – a rapid demographic growth of the discontent minority sets the country off on a Bosnia-like course.

In spite of the writing on the wall which every Israeli saw, most of all the successive governments of Israel, the political system of the country that has never given any major party the requisite majority to rule, obliged the major parties to seek partners wherever they could find them: the right wing was more inclined to woo the Jewish religious parties while the left opted to lean on the Arab parties in times of need. In either case, the government in place, which could not afford to alienate the Arab constituency or would not simply adopt policies that were not consistent with basic rules of democracy, survived its term without tackling the issue and passed the hot potato to the next. The result is that both Palestinian nationalism, which is bolstered by the unending Palestinian–Israeli dispute, and more so the rise of Islamic fundamentalism among Israeli Arabs, have contributed to the worsening situation and driven the Jewish majority and the Arab minority to open confrontation.

THE DISPUTE UNFOLDS

At the beginning of the 1990s during Zayyad's term as mayor of Nazareth, the idea was raised to undertake a wide-ranging development programme for the city for the end of the century and the millennium. Central to the Nazareth 2000 project was the construction of a plaza at the foot of the Basilica of the Annunciation, known as the City Square project. Back in 1994, Salman Abu-Ahmed, the head of the as yet unobtrusive Islamist opposition group on the Nazareth city council, had proposed that a new city hall building be erected on the land at the foot of the Basilica. The city council rejected Abu-Ahmed's motion at the time on the grounds that such a teeming public structure at that critically clogged location would further hamper the already impossible traffic conditions at the spot.

In January 1997, the city council adopted a resolution, with Abu Ahmed present and with no opposition, to construct the City Square in line with the Nazareth 2000 project. However, another council member did ask for an inquiry about whether the land belonged to the *waqf*, and his request was recorded in the minutes. Customarily, *waqf* lands in towns settled continuously over centuries are well-known and well-demarcated. Their trustees watch them and use them and make sure that no one trespasses onto them, while the local Muslim courts ensure that their management is in accordance with *shari'a* law. This is all the more in a town which had been under Muslim rule for most of its history, and where Islamic jurisdiction had been applied all along.

On 19 December 1997, as the construction on the plaza gathered momentum, the head of the Nazareth Waqf Board, Abu Nawwaf, demanded to see the mayor and presented him with a plan to erect an enormous mosque in the city square, a plan which obviously had been concocted long before it was revealed to the public. The mosque project would have dwarfed the entire Nazareth 2000 project and indeed contained an 86-metre-high minaret, topped by a glass panoramic observatory, and, more importantly, would have surpassed in stature the adjacent Basilica. Horrified, but composed, Mayor Jeraisi suggested that the plan be submitted, as required, to the city, and then the District and National Urban Planning Commissions for review.

Abu Nawwaf and his group were faced with the prospect of a lengthy bureaucratic process that would allow the construction of the City Square in front of the Basilica to become a *fait accompli*. So, two days later, Abu Nawwaf and a group of followers constructed a huge tent in the square, lined it with carpets, and declared it a temporary mosque pending the construction of the permanent one. The move transformed the Nazareth City Square from the focal location of millennium celebrations in front of the splendid Basilica, into a disputed patch of land where a new mosque had an equal right to be built.

The authorities were slow to respond in light of the unfolding Ramadan and the approaching Christmas holidays, for fear from the eruption of violence, as indeed the Islamists threatened should any attempt be made to remove them by force. This allowed the tent to become a permanent structure, frequented day and night by Muslim vigilantes, over the objection of the city and the national government, which demanded their removal. However, intrusion became possession as the months went by. And it was only through a court order that anything could be done legally to oust the intruders. Having become the main bone of contention and the pivot of the city politics, eruptions of violence constantly threatened the peace, with the Israeli police standing in between, attempting desperately to avert blood-letting between Christians, who were incensed by this illegal take-over, and the Muslims who felt that their majority in the city allowed them to take any decision palatable to them. The Islamists led the Muslims of Nazareth and the adjoining villages in the Galilee to rally in their support, in their drive to win the local elections in 1998, and capture a majority of seats on the city council. Now Abu Nawwaf and his people, backed by the vast support of the general population, maintained a round-the-clock watch to physically protect their new acquisition. Threats of bloodshed mounted if the squatters were evacuated by force, hence the interest of all concerned to resolve the issue peacefully.

Legal suits were initiated by the Israeli government, the legal owner of the plot, but it was clear that a court ruling would take a long time, and in the meantime the Muslims reinforced the walls of the tent with bricks and concrete to withstand the vagaries of winter. With daily prayers, the newly functioning mosque became a regular feature of the city centre, and work on the plaza in preparation for the millennium was frozen. The affair now became known as the 'Shihab a-Din controversy', since Shihab a-Din, a nephew of the glorious Saladin, was said to have been buried adjacent to the grounds under dispute. His tomb, which was indeed part of *waqf* property, had existed since the Middle Ages on that spot, but it had never attracted much attention nor had it been a centre of worship. Now the Islamists claimed that the entire area, including the tomb and the plaza, were part of the same *waqf* property, and they applied the powerful mobilizing symbol of Saladin (via his nephew) to raise passions and enlist the support of Muslims in Nazareth and elsewhere.

THE INFLUENCE OF LOCAL AND NATIONAL ELECTIONS

The Shihab a-Din controversy became the focal point of the local election campaign in November 1998. Six different Islamist splinter groups coalesced to run as one faction for the city council, with Salman Abu-Ahmed as their candidate for mayor to displace Jeraisi, the Christian incumbent. Indeed, while Jeraisi barely retained his position as mayor, a tribute to his personal merit, the Islamists won the majority of the seats on the city council (eleven out of twenty-one). This result paralysed the city, where the mayor's executive power was countered by the majority vote of the Islamists on anything he attempted to do, until he acceded to their demands regarding Shihab a-Din. No governing coalition could be formed to manage the city, no deputies were elected to help the mayor carry out his tasks, no personnel could be appointed, no budget was approved, and the Nazareth 2000 project ground to a standstill. In April 1999, Minister of Interior Eli Swissa appointed a commission of inquiry to recommend either the appointment of a public board to manage the city or new local elections if mediation between the parties could not solve the dispute. However, the commission soon realized that the main obstacle to the functioning of the city was the Shihab a-Din dispute, whose lack of resolution blocked the formation of a city council coalition.

Matters became further complicated with the announcement of general elections in Israel to be held in May 1999. The prime ministerial campaigns of both major parties sought the votes of the Islamists in Nazareth. Emboldened by their new position of power, the Islamists refused several compromise solutions offered to them by the Netanyahu government and the commission of inquiry which would have allowed them to build a mosque on the grounds, although smaller than they had requested. At the same time, the Ministry of Tourism and Nazareth Municipality officials watched their dreams of the Nazareth 2000 project dissipate before their eyes. In the May 1999 elections, opposition leader Ehud Barak, together with his Labour party, made a considerable impact on the Arab community. Prior to the elections, far-reaching demands had been negotiated between the Labour party and the United Arab List, of which the moderate Islamists were part, which were to allow the Muslims of Israel to be recognized as a separate community and also, by implication, for a solution of the Shihab a-Din controversy to the Islamists' liking. The authors of the Arab list of demands, Knesset member Talib a-Sani' and Islamist candidate Tawfiq al-Khatib, wrote to Barak on 12 April 1999 demanding, inter alia, that:

- A new state constitution should be written to recognize the Arabs as a national minority, in fact turning Israel into a bi-national state.
- Education imparted to Israeli Arabs ought to reflect their values and be administered separately.
- The Arabs should be represented on urban planning boards (local and national) in proportion to their numbers. This would give Nazareth a local urban planning board composed overwhelmingly of Muslims to decide about the building of new mosques, for example.
- Muslims should be recognized as an official community and their religious judges (the *qadis*) should function and operate according to their religious worldview. That meant that in the Shihab a-Din dispute, for example, it should be left to the discretion of the *qadis* to declare the land as *waqf* property (as indeed they did), and that all such questions should be removed from the jurisdiction of the Israeli court system.
- Muslims should be exempt from the law, which requires the demolition of illegally built houses. This would allow the illegally built tent mosque in Basilica Square in Nazareth to remain, in direct disregard of urban planning laws and regulations and any eventual verdict expected in the courts of law.

It is not known to what extent Labour and/or Barak responded to these demands, but it was assumed that massive Arab support for the Labour candidate would generate openness and understanding on the part of a new Labour led government.

Attempts to resolve the dispute were also made within the Arab community itself. Muslim religious leaders in Israel, soliciting support from religious authorities in the Palestinian Authority, Jordan and Syria, claimed that the disputed land was *waqf* property and that a mosque should be built there, again threatening bloodshed if their demand is not acceded to. The Islamist *Sawt al-Haqq wa-l-Huriyya* further explained their objection to the construction of the plaza as part of the Nazareth 2000 project, seeing it as 'issuing a definitive [Christian] identity card to the city of Nazareth'.[4] All the while, the Islamists in Nazareth and their supporters throughout the country let it be understood that if the matter is not resolved to their liking, or if any attempt is made to alter the new status quo by force, blood would flow.

CHRISTIAN COUNTER-PRESSURES

Counter-pressure began to build from Christian quarters inside and outside of Israel against the building of the mosque. Within Israel, Christians were torn between their loyalty to their fellow Arabs and a wish to resolve the conflict 'within the family', and their horror at the spectre of being crushed by the Muslim majority and the mounting aggressiveness of the Islamists. This might explain the willingness of the Christian leadership to join the appeal of the notables of the Arab community in Nazareth on 5 April 1998 to go along with the Islamists' demands. At the same time, the Christians in Israel understood the need to appear to their foreign benefactors as being committed to the cause of Christianity in the Holy Land. Israeli government offices soon became busy reporting international Christian concerns and contacting Christian organizations, trying to explain and mitigate their fears:

- The Israeli Embassy in London reported that the Head of the Church of Scotland, the Reverend Alain Main, had decided to cancel his visit to Nazareth, and wrote a letter to the Israeli prime minister urging him to safeguard Christian pilgrims and the Christian population of Nazareth.
- The Embassy of Israel in Washington was contacted by Father Drew Christiansen on behalf of the American Council of Bishops, to express concern about the construction of the

mosque in Nazareth. He singled out statements made by the Israeli Minister of Interior and the Deputy Minister of Education (both from the ultra-Orthodox Shas party, an ally of the Islamists), who sided with the Islamists during their visits to Nazareth as part of their election campaign, and had pledged the government to act in favour of the mosque.

*   On 15 April 1999, the Prime Minister's Advisor on Arab Affairs wrote to Minister of Tourism Moshe Katsav and Minister of Interior Swissa regarding the concerns of the Vatican over the dispute in Nazareth.

Unexpectedly, Knesset member 'Azmi Bishara, an outspoken Arab-Christian nationalist, came to the help of the Christians, stating in *al-Sinara*:

A place, which had no particular historical significance [for Muslims], was made a pivot of solidarity and of the growth of a new collective [Islamic] identity that had never been known in Nazareth, where relations of communal fraternity had always prevailed ... The Nazareth 2000 project aimed at simply underlining the major tourist sites in the city, and it was not to blame if there were no Islamic sites at that location. A similar situation exists in Bethlehem, where the Holy Places are all Christian despite the Muslim majority of the population ... This is as if voices are raised to build holy places for the Muslims in Nazareth [to rival the Christians].[5]

DENOUEMENT OR DEBACLE?

After the May 1999 elections, the new government set up a ministerial committee on Arab affairs whose mandate included the resolution of the Nazareth dispute. The government yielded to the Islamists' demand and acceded to their mosque project, knowing full well that it would scuttle the Nazareth 2000 project, but their decision was not unprecedented. On 15 April 1999, the outgoing government had appointed a commission of inquiry to deal with the Nazareth crisis, but before it had a chance to convene, the cabinet resolved on 18 April to respond partially to the Islamists' request and allow a mosque to be built on an area of 504 square metres, half of it true *waqf* land on which the tomb of Shihab a-Din stood, and the rest taken from the planned 1,905 square metre City Plaza. The cabinet resolution did not mention the Basilica of the Annunciation by name, and claimed that the government had decided to build the mosque in order 'to alleviate tensions' in Nazareth.

At the same time, the commission of inquiry was completing its report. The commission recognized the lack of foundation of the Islamist claim to the disputed land as *waqf* property, but was split in its recommendations. The three members who had led the efforts towards a negotiated resolution and had offered the compromise to the outgoing government as a basis for a settlement, were in favour of continuing those efforts, in the belief that through appeasement they could avert a head-on collision between the Israeli government and the entire Arab population of Israel. They ultimately expanded the original government offer from 500 to 750 square metres, and recommended that the new government adopt it, which it did. The fourth member of the commission submitted a minority report that warned against the far-reaching implications of any compromise in light of the anticipated Christian reaction.

On the day in November when the Islamists laid the cornerstone for their mosque, the Christians in Israel closed the doors of their churches in protest. The Vatican issued a strong reprimand of Israel, accusing it of causing the tensions between the various communities. The Christians in Israel were devastated by the decision of the Israeli government, especially after the October 1999 Nazareth District Court ruling which rejected all the claims of the Islamists and, in fact, vindicated both the Christian counter-claims and the commission of inquiry's minority report. The State of Israel ended up being condemned by the Christians, despised by the Islamists, criticized by the court for not having waited for the termination of the legal proceedings before acting, and the paralysis of the Nazareth municipality continued. A few days later the Tiberias District Court, which reviewed other aspects of the same dispute, also reprimanded the Islamists for their false claims regarding the *waqf*, and blasted the government and its reasoning.

After Israel ceded Bethlehem and Ramallah to the Palestinian Authority in late 1995, the influence of Islam in those cities grew stronger and the Christians continued to emigrate after outbursts of violence against them. In light of this, the Christians look with horror at the present Islamization of Nazareth, presenting the nightmare that the third most important Christian holy place in the Holy Land might also be turned over to the Muslims. In Nazareth, the Shihab a-Din mosque would have been (finally it was not) erected under the watching eyes of Israel, as a new holy shrine for the Muslims that dwarfed the Basilica of the Annunciation and obscured the Christian nature of the city. In fact, one year after the agreement of the government to acquiesce in the Muslim demands, and in spite of the interim solution achieved for the functioning of the city apparatus, tensions persisted, the Islamists continued their vigil in the Shihab a-Din Square and they did not relent from their pressure to begin immediately with the construction of the mosque, urban planning considerations notwithstanding. Only under the Sharon government, and after massive intervention from the American President and the Pope, did Israel reverse its decision, and also obtain a court order in 2003 to destroy the illegal foundations of the mosque. But the disappointed Muslims vow that this is not the end of the story. In support of their quest to defy the Basilica rather than build a mosque – alternative locations for which were offered by the government – the Islamists hung a slogan on the premises of the tent until removed, citing the verse of the Qur'an which says that 'Allah did not beget, nor was He begotten', of course a direct challenge to the relations between the Father and the Son.

The Arabs in Israel in general, and the Islamists in particular, have learned from the Nazareth experience that if they are persistent enough and aggressive enough, they will have their way since they can rally the Muslim majority among the Arabs in Israel for any showdown with the government, and certainly with the Christians in the country. They have also learned that they hold the key in any future election for the Labour candidate for prime minister. They have also internalized the methods of the Jewish ultra-Orthodox parties, which support whichever side satisfies their particular sectorial needs.

The Arabs of Israel would have even greater leverage if they acted in a unified bloc (like the Shas party). However, being bitterly divided between Islamists and communists, Muslims and Christians, modern secularists and new-age traditionalists, and

Arab nationalists and malleable integrationists, the political impact of the Arabs in Israel is much diluted. However, the explosive potential of violence in their midst far from diminishing, on the contrary exploded in October 2000, when many of them joined the Palestinian *intifada* against Israel. Those violent events, where some Arabs lost their lives in battles against the police, demonstrated that when the Arab-Muslim minority in Israel faces the choice between their people/faith and their country, they join the former. Jewish furore also burst violently against the Muslim Arabs for the disruption of life they caused in the Galilee, notably in Nazareth. This means that the watershed of October 2000, where Muslims in Israel crossed the lines over to what the Jews consider the enemy lines, has added to the untenable nature of their existence in Israel. The Arab victims of those outbursts, who are already hailed as martyrs, can only create new potentially explosive Shihab a-Din memorials which in due course will erupt in Israel's face.

NOTES

This was first published in the *Journal of Israel Affairs* (2003), pp. 49–63.

1. *Dhimmi* is the judicial, political, economic and social status accorded under Islam to the Scriptuaries, that is the 'People of the Book' (Jews and Christians) which prescribed their protected but inferior status, in return for which they had to pay a special poll-tax and submit to all kinds of abuses and humiliations.
2. See R. Israeli, *Green Crescent over Nazareth: The Displacement of Christians by Muslims in the Holy Land* (London: Frank Cass, 2002), p.60.
3. For details, see Daphna Tsimhoni, 'Christians in Israel Between Religion and Politics', in Elie Rekhes (ed.), *Arabs in Israeli Politics* (Tel Aviv: Tel Aviv University, 1998).
4. Israeli, *Green Crescent over Nazareth*, p.60.
5. *Fasl al-maqal* (a local Arabic magazine), 22 January 1998. Cited in ibid., p.155.

PART IV

SUMMING UP

CHAPTER ELEVEN

Squaring the Palestinian Triangle

ONE PALESTINIAN PEOPLE AND ONE PALESTINE

Many solutions have been floated around during the past twenty years regarding the problems of the Palestinian people and of the territories in Palestine where they constitute a majority. For this purpose, conventional wisdom has differentiated between the Palestinians living in Israel Proper, the so-called 'Israeli-Arabs', as if this were not a contradiction in terms, and the rest of the Palestinians who either have another nationality (Jordanian, Lebanese, and so forth) or are stateless altogether. The former, who used to be considered members of an ethnic-religious-linguistic-cultural minority, have meanwhile turned into a vocal national minority, which, by demanding 'equal rights', is claiming joint ownership of Israel by its two constituent peoples and is actually striving to turn Israel into a bi-national state. The latter have been clamouring for self-determination, for an end to Israeli occupation, and for their own statehood under the leadership of the PLO, which purports to be the sole legitimate representative of all the Palestinians – namely, those under occupation, but also those who maintain Jordanian, Israeli, and other citizenships.

The question of territory has also been confused by the very fact that the territories presently under Israeli administration have been disconnected in Israeli and world public opinion from the eastern part of Palestine now called Jordan. Thus, on the one hand, Israel has been insistent on treating the 'Israeli Arabs' as full-fledged citizens in a Jewish-Zionist state with which they cannot identify, and on the other hand, it has been disregarding the natural and historical link of all the Palestinians, including those dwelling in Israel, to the land of Greater Palestine. No wonder, then, that all the solutions attempted so far, which detached the Palestinians of the West Bank of the Jordan River (including Israel) from those of the East Bank, fell short of coming into fruition. For with one-half of the Palestinian people in Jordan and one-sixth in Israel, how could anyone produce a comprehensive solution to the Palestinian problem in the West Bank and Gaza alone?

Approximately ten models of solutions have been created since the 1967 war, and the failure of all of them to gain currency only shows how dismal they were in coming to terms with the Palestinian problem in 'all its aspects', as promised by the Camp David Accords. If we do not revert to the basic premises of historical Palestine as one unified arena, and of the Palestinian people in all its dispersions as one national unit, neither the Palestinian problem nor the 'territories' issue can be laid to rest. That is, there will not be peace and tranquillity in the Middle East, now and in the generations to come, unless the conventional wisdom and the accepted norms and notions are challenged, and a less static and more imaginative approach is found.

PERILS OF THE STATUS QUO

Upon the establishment of the State of Israel, a small minority of Palestinian Arabs was 'trapped' in what became Israel's sovereign territory and has since had to reconcile with its new status as a minority. Those Arabs, who were cut off from the rest of the Palestinians for nineteen years (1948–67), were supposed to be loyal to Israel, in return for which they would benefit from all the rights and services that the state affords all its citizens. But neither half of the equation was fulfilled. Moreover, in 1967, when the boundaries of Israel melted, and more Palestinians came under Israeli rule, the combined bloc of Palestinians, now numbering over four million, posed a new challenge for Israel.

Israel's failure to integrate its Arab citizens became apparent at that time. For, instead of providing them with incentives to become part of the mainstream, by joining the state educational system in Hebrew, by recruiting them into Israel's armed forces, and making them partners to Israel's fate, everything was done to reinforce their separate Arab education in Arabic. They were never asked to pledge allegiance to Israel's flag, and they were excluded from serving in its army, which is the most exciting and integrating experience for all Israeli youth. The consequence is obvious – two separate, not to say antagonistic, societies grew in Israel: one Israeli-Jewish, the other Palestinian-Arab, which is only technically 'Israeli'. The failure to educate the minority to conform with the ideals and the objectives of the majority has created a distinct sub-society, or anti-society, which cultivated its own desires, norms, and aspirations, feeding upon large and deep strata of frustration and bitterness emanating from unequal opportunities in education, services, economic and political positions of power, and employment in military and security-related industries.

The 1967 war, which eliminated in one stroke the borders between 'Israeli Arabs' and their brethren across the 'Green Line', has further compounded this already difficult situation and driven it to the point of no return. For although the Arabs in Israel could derive encouragement and pride from their vastly superior economic, educational, and political development, compared with their relatives who were under Jordanian rule until 1967, they were equally boosted by the revelation that they actually were not a minority in the Jewish State, but rather part of an Arab majority that surrounded Israel, and an integral component of the Palestinian people that aspired to its own national independence and territorial integrity. Paradoxically, it was precisely their relatively improved economic and educational position, and the democratic norms that they had internalized within Israeli society, which impelled them to ask for more, and to feel self-confident enough to identify with their Palestinian kin. Thus, they turned from a diffident and self-effacing minority into a vocal and assertive national group. When they demand equal rights, they do it as Israelis who were educated and permitted to clamour for equality, but when it comes to duties involving identification with the Jewish-Zionist state, whose aspirations they cannot share, they invoke their Arab-Palestinian and sometimes Muslim, identity.

Figures have also resounded loudly in this escalation, for the small and marginal minority of 160,000 in 1949 has now grown to encompass more than a million people (in 2005 – approximately 18 per cent of the total population of Israel), and demographic projections predict that within 20 years, it will attain a figure of two million (approximately 23 per cent of the population) This large bloc, which constitutes local majorities in the Triangle and the Western Galilee, has now voiced the seemingly reasonable claim that the 'state belongs to all its inhabitants', which means that Israel is no longer a State of the Jews or a Jewish State, but in fact a Jewish-Arab entity, by virtue of the two national groups living within its confines and holding its passports. The nightmare of a bi-national state begins to lurk on the horizon, even before we added to the equation the Arabs of the territories. Indeed, the Land Days, which have been observed by Israeli Arabs since 1976, the emergence of the 'Committee of Arab Mayors' that purports to represent all Arabs of Israel, the support that the latter lend to the *intifada*, and their sporadic acts of sabotage and subversion that are occasionally made public by the Israeli authorities (more than 300 in 1988), ought to ring resounding alarms throughout Israel.

The result is that the 'Israeli Arabs' are first of all Arabs and Palestinians, and they identify themselves as such. Those Israelis who believe that those Arabs are loyal to their country simply take loyalty to mean non-participation in acts of sabotage. But this is not the case, for loyal Arabs (and there are certainly and fortunately some of those, too) are not only those who enjoy Israel's democracy and its educational, economic, and health services, but those who are also eager to celebrate its Independence Day, to educate their children in its language and culture, to identify with its Jewish-Zionist goals, and to fight for its security. An Arab student who studies at Hebrew University, and operates within the perimeters of law and order, cannot be considered loyal unless he is also prepared to stand nightwatch at the student dormitories just as his Jewish friend would. Arabs in Israel could be considered loyal only if their justified demands for rights and equality of opportunities were coupled with equally fervent demands for equality in national duties.

Yet, another phenomenon makes the status quo untenable, and that is the revival of Islam among the Israeli Arabs, as part of the rising tide of Islamic fundamentalism, some of whose manifestations we see in Iran, Lebanon, the West Bank and Gaza, or even the Rushdie affair and its ramifications. In the recent elections to the local councils in Israel (February 1989), the Islamic Movement in the Arab villages in Israel made impressive gains and became an institutionalized political power that can no longer be ignored (six Arab Councils are headed by Muslim fundamentalists and many other Council members were elected in other towns and villages). Admittedly, the leaders of this movement, who had been arrested in 1980–81 because of their active participation in sabotage and subversive activities, have learned their lesson and are now operating only within the limitations of law, playing brinkmanship with the farthest boundaries of legality. But there is no doubt that the Islamic state of mind, which is spreading among the Muslims of Israel under the guise of innocent and constructive socio-religious activities, bears the seeds of a potential irredentist claim vis-à-vis Israel. They have been preparing the grounds for that eventuality by setting up 'anti-state' institutions of welfare, health, education, and the like.

All these alarming characteristics of the Arabs in Israel pale in comparison with the much more frightening issue of the more numerous and less submissive Palestinians in the territories. Their numbers (over 3 million in 2005), their formal foreign affiliation (all of them hold non-Israeli passports), and their national consciousness, which is at a much higher pitch, are all expressed in the *intifada*. They have taken full advantage of the presence of Israel, under whose occupation they have enjoyed newly established universities, a dramatic rise in technological development and in living standards, new norms of democracy and freedom, the breakdown of archaic social structures, and the adoption of new socio-political forms of organization. At the same time, however, they wished to preserve and cultivate their own identity, they developed their own local and national leadership which, as a whole, identified with the PLO, and never lost sight of their occupied status, and its corollaries of resistance and struggle. Those Arabs, who have continued to educate their children according to Jordanian curriculi and to resort to the Jordanian-style administrative and judicial systems, are, expectedly, even less loyal to Israel than the 'Israeli Arabs'. Moreover, the *intifada*, which burst out in December 1987, has become enough of a continuous, sustained, and wide-scale movement to spell out their irresistible ambition to independence and to rid themselves of what they regard as Israeli occupation. These aspirations are, naturally, fed by the sweeping tide of Palestinian nationalism, and to no less an extent by the overbearing enthusiasm of the fundamentalist Hamas movement, which regards as its ultimate goal the establishment of an Islamic state over the entire area of Palestine.

The Israeli Arabs who do not belong to the Islamic Movement are likely to demand secession from Israel in the long run, based on the right of self-determination of the Palestinian people of which they are a part. This claim would be reinforced if Israel maintained its rule over the territories, for then the combined population of Arabs under Israeli rule would amount to 40 per cent – that is, Israel would become a de facto bi-national state. The proponents of the Islamic movement on both sides of the 'Green Line' have already begun preparing for their Islamic state and have set up the necessary machineries to take over when they are afforded the opportunity. In the West Bank and Gaza, Hamas has unabashedly launched a challenge to the PLO and stated its plan to establish no less than a full-fledged Islamic state under its aegis. All this means that anyone who advocates the maintenance of the status quo is dreaming. All those who believed that the Arabs of Israel and of the territories could be held, indefinitely, under Israeli control, have been proved wrong. The situation is worsening almost daily, although there is an occasional respite. At times, it is possible to reduce the level of violence or to reduce the riots in the West Bank from a menace to a nuisance level, but the general trend seems inexorable. Therefore, there is no merit to seeking interim solutions that could only postpone the day of reckoning. One needs to devise a fundamental solution that would encompass all, or most, Palestinian Arabs, and finally bring about peace and tranquillity to all.

PALESTINIZATION OF JORDAN

The not unfounded allegation was advanced that the territory east of the Jordan River, now called Jordan, is part of historical Palestine. The fact that the British mandatory power decided to sever that territory, which constitutes three-quarters of Palestine, and give it another name, does not diminish one iota of its historical and geographical belonging to Palestine. Moreover, viewed in present-day practical terms, and not only in historical terms, the so-called Jordanians are actually Palestinians, not only because they live in part of Palestine but principally because two-thirds of them identify themselves as Palestinians. True, the UN Partition Resolution of 1947, which lent international legitimacy to the State of Israel, applied to the territory west of the river, but if we tackle the problem today on the fashionable basis of 'self-determination', there is no denying that the people of Jordan are Palestinians, in their majority at the very least. Prime ministers, such as Zaid Rifa'i, were Palestinians, many cabinet ministers are Palestinians, and the majority of Amman, the capital, defines itself as Palestinian. Because the PLO purports to represent all Palestinians, and most Palestinians accept it as their sole representative, it can easily claim, on the basis of 'self-determination', that Jordan is, actually, Palestine. All that needs to be done, according to this view, is to dub Jordan 'Palestine', and the problem would, thereby, be resolved.

But the issue is more complicated than that, because Jordan is home to only one-half of the Palestinian people (more than 3.5 million out of six million), while most of them reside under Israeli rule (3.5 million in the territories and more than one million in Israel proper). As long as this large mass of Palestinians identifies itself as such and recognizes the PLO as its leader, it will remain the centre of gravity of Palestinian national life without which no Palestinian state can be established or survive. 'Israeli Arabs' often claim that the PLO does not represent them, and that they regard themselves as the inhabitants of Israel even if there should be a Palestinian state. But, at the same time, they also claim that the PLO is the 'sole representative of the Palestinians'; if they recognize the PLO and its platform, they, by necessity, also accept it as their representative.

Those who support Palestinization of Jordan hope that if the PLO should take over in Amman, as they were close to doing during 'Black September' in 1970, then the allegation that it is Israel that prevents self-determination from the Palestinian people would be dispelled. But this is not the case, for even in such an eventuality, Israel would continue to rule most of the 'unliberated' Palestinians, and, far from laying the problem to rest, the Palestinian case would gain more impetus, using the Jordanian territory as a precedent, in order to demand self-determination not only in the West Bank and Gaza, but also in the Triangle and the Galilee in Israel proper. Thus, this solution holds no promise for Israel.

Others support the mirror-image of the first solution – namely returning to the status quo ante bellum of 1967 by returning the West Bank, or most of it, to Jordan. Some Israeli politicians have raised the notion of functional partition between Israel and Jordan, with the former maintaining security control and the latter assuming domestic affairs of the Palestinians to rid them of Israeli occupation and to satisfy their yearning to be ruled by Arabs. At the basis of this concept is the assumption that the King is moderate, pro-Western, and that he would control the Palestinians better and more effectively than Israel without, however, posing a threat to Israel.

A variation of this thinking spoke about a territorial compromise, as part of the Jordanian option. The Allon Plan, for example, is considered a manifestation par excellence of this approach – that is, to return to Jordan the non-vital and thickly populated areas of the West Bank, while Israel retains the strategic grounds that are also thinly populated by Palestinians. Everyone knows, however, that such an option never existed in the world of reality, except for three weeks between 8 June 1967, when Israel took over East Jerusalem and 28 June, when Israel annexed it. For since that date, and during all the dialogues, meetings, and exchanges of messages between Israeli leaders and King Hussein, the Jordanians have adamantly refused any peace settlement that would not encompass all 'occupied territories, including East Jerusalem'. Where was that 'Jordanian option' then, except in the world of illusion of some Israeli statesmen?

Even had King Hussein accepted the Israeli view of territorial compromise, that would not have resolved the thorny issue of self-determination, which is paramount in the eyes of Palestinians and without which no permanent solution can be envisaged. At most, this approach could have resolved Hussein's problems, but that should not be Israel's concern, because that 'moderate' and 'pro-Western' ruler, none other, did not hesitate to use American tanks and guns to attack western Jerusalem in June 1967, despite Israel's supplications that he should keep out of the war. But he thought that he could ride the Egyptian bandwagon to victory and thus triggered the disaster that befell him. After that war, when the Americans refused to supply him with Hawk missiles, he did not hesitate to turn to the Soviet Union and to acquire batteries of their SAMs.

For years the government of Israel, like the rest of the world, except for Britain and Pakistan, had insisted that Hussein's rule in the West Bank was illegal. How could Israel, then, negotiate the fate of those territories with someone who had never gained legitimacy for his annexation of those lands? Moreover, Hussein himself had accepted the notion of the PLO as the sole representative of the Palestinians, and he has undertaken to submit to Palestinian rule any 'liberated' part of their territory. In June 1988, when Hussein finally recognized the inconsistency of his own policy and announced the severance of Jordan from the West Bank, he thereby confirmed that any territories he would receive from Israel would be turned over to the Palestinians. Thus, the 'Jordanian option' has become a 'PLO option'. Is this what Israel wanted to achieve? Hussein himself was facing serious problems of legitimacy for his autocratic rule in Jordan over a Palestinian majority. Why should Israel lend a hand to that outdated and undemocratic government that is tottering on the brink of collapse under the weight of its own inconsistencies and illegitimacy? Why should Israel conclude a deal with a proprietor who has long ago forfeited his right and possession over the asset Israel wants to negotiate away?

THE PLO STATE

The Palestinian state, which was declared on 15 November 1988, in Algiers, might appear to be a satisfactory attempt to resolve the Palestinian problem. However, judging by their insistence on the right of return, their continued commitment to 'armed struggle', their persistent negation of Zionism, and their inability or unwillingness to abrogate the offensive and subversive items (to Israel) of the Palestinian Charter, it is clear that the PLO has not reconciled yet to the idea of an independent Jewish State of the Jewish people, by the Jewish people, and for the Jewish people. Therefore, a PLO-dominated state in the West Bank and Gaza would be a recipe for instability, *irridenta*, and subversion against Israel. Moreover, with Arab rejection-front backing, the PLO is bound to seek to gain control over all of West Palestine and then

East Palestine, to 'liberate' all components of the scattered Palestinian people, and to set up a greater Palestinian state that would encompass most Palestinians. Palestinian ambition to use the incremental policy of stages, adopted in 1974, and spelling out the plan to use any 'liberated' part of Palestine as a launching pad to liberate the rest, has never been abrogated or amended, neither explicitly nor implicitly. But this is not the point, for even if the PLO meant every word and pledge it undertook, and even if it should content itself with a mini-Palestinian state, its very claim to represent all Palestinians, while its state encompasses only one-third of them, would signify that two-thirds of the problem would remain unresolved. This would, in turn, imply that acts of terror, bitterness against truncated Palestine, and dreams of eliminating Israel in the long run would militate against such a settlement. It is necessary to reject the PLO claim that asserts that the mini-state would only constitute a refuge to some of the Palestinians while the others, like the Jewish Diaspora, would continue to live outside it. This comparison has no leg to stand on, because the Jewish Diaspora live, for the most part, in open, democratic, and prosperous countries and do not wish, for the moment, to move to Israel, which is eager to accept them in its midst. Most Palestinians, on the contrary, live in refugee camps or under autocratic regimes in the Middle East, and they would continue to knock on the doors of a Palestinian state, which would be unable to absorb them. Palestinians would be all the more impelled to seek Palestinian citizenship because many of them are stateless in Arab countries, except for Jordan (which is part of Palestine in any case). Thus, a mini-state would constitute a mini-solution and no more.

There are other crucial considerations militating against a shrunken Palestinian state in the West Bank and Gaza, such as the unrealistic Palestinian demand that Israeli settlements be dismantled and removed. For, in principle, exactly as there are many Arab settlements within Israel proper, there is no reason that Jewish settlements cannot exist within the densely populated Arab areas of Palestine. Another problem is demilitarization which, for many Israelis, looks as a matter of course. There is no assurance, however, that the Palestinians could reconcile to remaining powerless and to give up any of their military force in view of the prominence of armed forces everywhere as one of the major paraphernalia of independence. (See, for example, post-war Japan, which already maintains a strong 'self-defence force' despite its commitment to renounce, 'forever', military power.) And what if any independent Palestinian state should invite foreign troops to its soil, Arab or otherwise? Could Israel resist or go to war? And what if such troops are marched into the Palestinian state under the auspices of a major power? Would anyone come to Israel's succour or condone an Israeli act of war to scuttle such a danger?

AUTONOMY AND FEDERATION

In 1972, King Hussein proposed the idea of autonomy for the Palestinians in the West Bank, within his reputed 'Federation Plan'. The king's intent then was to regain control of the territories he lost in 1967 by paying lip-service to some sort of Palestinian 'independence'. In fact, that plan was geared to make the Palestinians masters of their domestic affairs while the source of authority and sovereignty would lay with the Hashemite Crown, so that Jordanians would legitimize Palestinians, not the other way around, despite the overwhelming majority of Palestinians (over 80 per cent) in such a federated state. Foreign and security matters would remain the domain of the central government in Amman. This solution, if implemented, could have enormous advantages, for it would have ensured a stable government in the long run and would have guaranteed the participation of Palestinians in the federal government. No wonder, then, that the Reagan Plan of 1 September 1982, and then the Shultz Initiative of 1988, devised variations of that same theme.

The Israeli government suggested the mirror-image of the Federation Plan, that is autonomy, as an interim settlement, but deriving its authority from the Israeli legislature. But the Autonomy Plan of Camp David, which followed this pattern of thought, did not offer quite the same advantages of the Federation Plan. On the one hand, it was to be a temporary agreement, not a permanent one; and it did not provide the Palestinians with any place in the determination of Greater Israel's affairs. It did determine that Israel would retain control of foreign and security affairs while the Palestinians would manage their own domestic domain. On the other hand, the Israeli Plan was more generous inasmuch as it left open the possibility of a Palestinian state following the interim period of autonomy, which would last from three to five years, while the Jordanian Federation Plan was to exclude terminally the question of Palestinian independence. The appeal of this Israeli Plan is what resuscitated it in the form of mayorial elections in the West Bank and Gaza, as spelled out by the Israel government in 1989.

But both of these alternatives for autonomy were rejected by the Palestinians because neither of them responds to their basic aspiration for self-determination and for an independent Palestinian state. These substitutes seemed, perhaps, a good solution to Jordan's or to Israel's problems, but not to the Palestinian plight. The Palestinians still remember the trauma of September 1970, when King Hussein massacred thousands of them, and they are not likely to throw in their lot with him. This is all the more so since the king himself has accepted the 1974 Rabat decision to recognize the PLO as the sole representative of the Palestinians and has detached himself from the heartland of Palestine in 1988, as a result of the *intifada*. The Israeli Autonomy Plan was agreed upon only by Israel, Egypt, and the United States, but the last two partners have disassociated themselves from it in the meantime. Europeans and the rest of the Arabs have never accepted this plan of Israel's because they did not believe that it was either feasible or desirable.

And, most important, the 'Declaration of Independence' of the Palestinians on 15 November 1988, has foreclosed the road before the Palestinians to accept anything short of their independence. Any attempt by Israel to enforce one-sided autonomy, as Moshe Dayan had suggested, would not bring about peace and tranquillity, exactly as a forced marriage cannot produce conjugal harmony. Therefore, if marriage by love is impossible, one could at the very least aspire for a marriage of expediency, based on the mutual interests of both parties. No peace is possible between Israel and the local leadership of the Palestinians in the territories because of the inherent contradiction between the nationalists and ultra-religious factions on the one hand, and those who are likely to embrace the Autonomy Plan, while the majority reject it, on the other.

ANNEXATION AND TRANSFER OF POPULATION

The above options have discussed 'Jordanization' and 'Palestinization', but there is also an 'Israelization' one. Contrary to the maximalist and intransigent image that was attached to this alternative, which would involve outright annexation of the territories by Israel, one could defend it as precisely responding to the Israeli Left's slogan of 'territory for peace'. But the departure point of the proponents of this plan is totally different: they are prepared to renounce three-quarters of the land of historical Palestine east of the Jordan in return for peace, but they seek to retain that one-quarter of the land west of the river, without which, in their mind, Israel could not ensure its national existence and security.

But this approach has not been adopted by the majority of Israelis despite its seemingly conciliatory approach. The reason is demographic: most Israelis would retain the territories if they were not populated by the 3.5 million Palestinians who reject Israel's rule. But even if they had accepted Israel's government (as Dr Nusseibeh has suggested in recent years, provided the one-man one-vote principle is maintained), the Israelis would be faced with an intractable dilemma: either a democratic and egalitarian Israel with rights for all, with the corollaries of a bi-national state immediately and an Arab majority state in the future; or a Jewish Israel where the Jews would maintain rights and rule and the Arabs would be devoid of both. No Israeli government could face that dilemma and resolve it in any acceptable way.

In this regard, one may observe one of the most fascinating paradoxes in the Israeli political culture: the Israeli Liberal Left and the Civil Rights watchers are precisely those who fear that they could not envisage a bi-national state and, therefore, press for disengaging from the territories and maintaining the Jewish nature of the state; conversely, the adamant right-wing nationalists view with disdain the pessimistic outlook of the Left and can envisage a Greater Israel where Jews and Arabs can coexist in full equality. In this momentous debate there are unstated arguments as well: those who want to relinquish the territories view the question of Jewish majority as so overbearing that they elect to be dubbed 'defeatists' by some, 'racists' by others, rather than face the prospects of oppressing civil rights in a country where Arabs might jeopardize the Jewish majority. The Right is prepared to swallow the accusation that it accepts diluting the Jewish majority and ruling another people, rather than to imply that it would give up any part of Eretz Israel or have to restrict Arab civil rights when the Jewish majority is threatened.

Thus, regardless of whether or not the arguments are stated, the overwhelming consideration bearing on annexation is demography. No one can control or even predict the rate of population growth of the Palestinian Arabs, especially as the Palestinians, both in Israel and in the territories, have become aware of the 'demographic war' and are pinning their hopes on it for deciding the future of Palestine. Therefore, the idea of 'transfer' was evoked by some ultra-rightist Israelis as the only solution to Israel's dilemma and to the Palestinian demographic menace. Transfer of Palestinian populations to neighbouring Arab countries, they reason, is necessary to maintain Israel's rule on the territories without endangering either the Jewish or the democratic character of the country.

Much of the outrage of the Israeli public against such a solution emanates from moral sensitivity to the horrifying prospect of uprooting a civilian population from its land and moving it elsewhere. But people remain oblivious to the idea of transfer that is inherent in the Palestinian National Charter, which envisages that only the Jews who were in Palestine before 1917 ('the beginning of the Zionist onslaught') would be allowed to remain. This means that the rest – that is, everyone except for those 80,000 pioneering Zionists, most of whom are dead by now in any case, would have if not somehow to evaporate, then to be transferred back to their countries of origin, if they should survive the 'armed struggle' that the Charter pledges in order to regain Palestine. Compared with this sinister prospect, the Israeli transfer plan would be much more humane if carried out, and at the very least would constitute an ideological counteract to the Palestinian ambitions, if it is not. To this argument one could add, of course, that several hundreds of thousands of Jews have already been transferred from the Arab countries into Israel in the 1950s and the 1960s. Since the Palestinians are claiming that they are part of the Arab homeland, one could interpret the two transfers as an exchange of population, not as a one-sided, forced transfer by Israel.

Joseph Schechtman, the greatest authority on population

transfers, who researched the exchanges of populations in Europe after World War II, has set standards for the morality of this otherwise abhorrent measure. All the criteria he determined to justify the transfer are handily applicable to the Israeli–Arab situation, and they can be summarized in the following rule: if there are no prospects for reconciliation and harmony between the ruling majority and the ruled minority, and if there is no practical way to separate territorially the minority from the majority, it is far more moral to uproot the minority and transfer it elsewhere, despite the terrible suffering and injustice caused to this generation in the process, than to cause suffering and injustice to both the majority and the minority in all generations to come.

The problem is not moral, but political and practical. In order to transfer large populations from one country to another with a minimum of suffering, one needs two prerequisites: that the population in question agrees to move and that a host country be prepared to absorb them (for example, Turks of Bulgaria these days). Those two conditions were met when 800,000 Jews, including the present writer, were transferred from the Arab countries to Israel. But with Palestinians the situation is different: they have been cultivating the value of *sumud* (steadfastness) in their clinging to the soil, and there is no Arab state ready or willing to absorb them. Therefore, short of war or of a blood bath of untold proportions, transfer as a solution is simply a pipe dream with no relation to reality.

SQUARING THE TRIANGLE

It is evident, then, that a novel option is needed that could weave some of the positive elements of the other options into a strong fabric that would respond to the most vital interest of the three entities where Palestinians dwell today: Israel, Jordan, and the territories. A novel solution is needed not because of the *intifada* or because of outside pressures on Israel, but simply because all other options, some of which have been negotiated for years, have failed to produce even the beginning of a permanent settlement. From Israel's point of view, instead of facing world opinion defensively, in an attempt to thwart the image of rejection that is associated with its policy, it could turn things around by seizing the initiative and proclaiming a daring and generous new plan that would not diminish Israel's security. Its principal components could be:

The Palestinian People's Right to Self-Determination
The Palestinians, whose absolute majority are in Jordan (3.5 million), in the territories (3.5 million), and in Israel (over a million), with the rest in refugee camps or in near and far diasporas, are entitled to Israel's recognition and aid to realize their basic aspirations. In return, they ought to recognize a parallel right of the Jewish people to self-determination in their Jewish state. This is a crucial element that Israel ought to insist on, because this is precisely what the Palestinian National Charter denies. That Palestinian constitutional document, which was never abrogated, in fact states that Judaism is a faith, and, therefore, Jews are not a nation, implying that they do not deserve a state. Recognizing the State of Israel's right to exist, in this context, would not be sufficient, because, according to the PLO logic, which is supported by the majority of Palestinians everywhere, the State of Israel, which belongs to all of its inhabitants, would become another Palestinian state in the long run after Israel retreats to the 1947 Partition boundaries, and the Right of Return of the Palestinians would be implemented.

There is, of course, a different problem facing Israel, regarding the representatives of the Palestinians with whom it has to negotiate. The Palestinians have arguably chosen the PLO, and it is certainly their right because they consider it as their movement of national liberation. But Israel can refuse to talk with such an interlocutor as long as it continues to condemn and denigrate the movement of national liberation of the Jewish people – Zionism – as 'racist', and continues to discredit and delegitimize it in its unaltered Charter as in the Algiers Declaration. The rhetorical advances uttered toward Israel in recent months do not include even a hint reversing that direction. If anything, the Fatah Conference held in Tunis in August 1989 even reinforced the old clichés. As long as this is the case, Israel can offer to talk to the 4.5 million Palestinians under its rule (in Israel and the territories), about the peace plan outlined below. If they concur, they would thereby signify a break with the Charter. If they do not, the burden of proof shifts to them.

The Palestinians' Right over Palestine

The Palestinians claim a right over all Palestine, exactly as the Israelis do. Therefore, the only feasible solution is a mutual recognition of that right, from which derives the necessity to partition the land. In other words, Greater Palestine (or Eretz Israel) will have to be divided by agreement between its two proprietors into an Israeli-Jewish state in the West and a Palestinian-Arab state in the East. It does not stand to reason that three-quarters of the land be severed from it and called by another name (Jordan) while the remaining quarter should become the object of a new partition. We have seen that this approach is anchored in both history and demography. If the Palestinians today want a state, they ought to demand it from the autocratic king from the Hijaz who has been ruling three-quarters of their land and one-half of their people who constitute the majority of the population there. If they want to be loyal to the king and keep him, it is their affair; if the king wishes to test his long-standing claim that he is beloved of his subjects and is popular with them, they would certainly consent to turn their state into the 'Hashemite Kingdom of Palestine' and their king into a constitutional monarch, while the Palestinian majority retains the actual governmental authority.

This is the government, whatever its composition, that Israel would have to deal with on the implementation of this peace plan. The negotiations will then be protracted, difficult, and tortuous regarding the final boundaries between them. This argument, however, would be a quantitative one about territory and assets that can be agreed upon in the process of give-and-take as a means and compromise as an end. It would no longer be a qualitative conflict – a Palestinian state regardless – between Israel and the rest of the world. Such a Palestinian state would not, by nature, be any stronger than present-day Jordan. And if this 'moderate' Jordan could attack Israel in 1967, and is now able to bring into its borders Iraqi, Saudi, and Syrian divisions to battle Israel, there is no reason for Israel to fear that a Palestinian state would be any worse threat. The fate of the territories now held by Israel will then be discussed not with the King, a proposition to which all Israeli governments have committed themselves, but with the Palestinian government based in Amman, which is Israel's true co-owner of the land. In the past, Israel has denied the king's right to claim sovereignty over the territories. What gives him more of a right today after he has detached himself from that claim?

When such a state is established, the PLO will become redundant, even if its present leaders should be elected to lead its government. The Palestinian government would then become, with or without the Hashemite king, Israel's partner for negotiation not only about the territories but also about the permanent status of the Palestinian population presently under Israel. This government would be recognized by Israel provided that it drops its ideology of pursuing 'armed struggle' (those are the terms of the Charter) not only 'renounces terrorism', recognizes the right of self-determination of the Jewish people, Zionism as the movement of national liberation of the Jews, and the principle of partition of Greater Palestine. Until such a Palestinian state evolves, Israel can cultivate the idea among the 4.5 million Palestinians under its rule today and even assist them in attaining hegemony in Amman, should the king refuse to compromise with them by giving up some of his absolute authority in favour of the majority in his country.

A Novel Definition of Sovereignty
This necessity would establish a distinction between ownership of territory and the personal status of the inhabitants, to respond to the contradictory desires of the Palestinians for self-determination and statehood for the Palestinians on the one hand, and the acute security needs of Israel which would make a major withdrawal impractical on the other. In other words, regardless of the contours of the permanent boundaries agreed upon between Israel and Palestine, many Palestinians would remain under Israeli rule – all 'Israeli Arabs' of today and probably most inhabitants of the territories. They could choose among three options:

- To sell their property and move east into the Palestinian state, where they can rebuild their future out of their own choice;
- To acquire Israeli citizenship by a series of symbolic and practical acts that would put their loyalty to the state beyond doubt: oath of allegiance to the flag, identification with the Jewish-Zionist state, educating their children in Hebrew in the state mixed school systems, and military service in its armed

forces. In this case, they should be guaranteed all the rights accruing to Israel's Jewish nationals; or

- To stay as alien residents in Israel and enjoy its advantages: freedom, democracy, prosperity, services, as long as they abide by the law and pay their taxes, but they would owe their political loyalty to the neighbouring Palestinian state where they could also express their personal political ambitions by electing and running for office. In a situation of peace and open boundaries between Israel and Palestine, the Arabs who would opt for this alternative (presumably the majority, including Israeli Arabs) would move freely to and fro, similar to Canadians in the United States, with minimal checking procedures on the border check-points. They would have realized their ambitions for freedom, independence, and statehood, but they would not have to vacate their present towns and villages. It is likely that in the far future, when the Palestinian state is well established, peaceful, and prosperous, many Palestinian Arabs still under Israeli rule would opt to move there. But even if they do not, the distances are small enough to make practical the cleavage between the country of residence and the country of allegiance. Those who would remain in Israel as foreign aliens, but would opt, at the same time, to pursue acts of terror or of disturbing public order, can be 'repatriated' (not 'expelled').

In principle, Israel must recognize the reciprocity of this arrangement, under the theoretical assumption that during the negotiations upon the final status of the territory, the present day Israeli settlements there might come under discussion. Under the principle of reciprocity, it can be agreed that the inhabitants of the settlements that might fall within Palestinian sovereignty would enjoy the same choice between the three options offered to the Palestinians. The principle of reciprocity would also allow Israel to check the pace of settlements in the West Bank and Gaza, as an added incentive to peace. For in a situation where over a million Palestinians live in Israel proper, prior to the permanent settlement, and many more would stay under Israel subsequent to the settlement, the present-day 250,000 Israeli settlers in the territories claimed by the Palestinians are only a small fraction of the Palestinians in Israel. Thus, the closer Israel comes to parity with

Palestine in the pattern of settlement within the population of the other side, the higher the stakes and the more pressing the interest that both parties would have to maintain peace after the settlement is signed. Perhaps, then, Israel would have also to revise its Law of Return to signify that Israeli citizenship is acquired, universally, by those who perform symbolic acts of identification and practical acts of service to the state, and not automatically granted to any Jew who arrives in Israel.

BALANCE OF GAINS AND DRAWBACKS

This sort of solution cannot satisfy all desires of all parties. Each party would be distressed by the disadvantages inherent in such a settlement, but it could also cheer at the prospects that it promises. Each party will find that it pays a price (a heavy one at that) for achieving its ambitions, but also that most of its vital ambitions would be achieved. Perhaps this is the most promising formula for a permanent peace treaty between Israelis and Palestinians. For peace, as with any commodity, bears a price tag, and it is apparent that the other options, which have been proposed in the international exchange of ideas, carry far too expensive price tags. Let us consider the goods accruing to every party as well as the required price.

1. *Israel,* at the price of totally and finally renouncing eastern Palestine, and even negotiating the fate of the territories it now holds west of the Jordan River, would achieve most of its desires: it would keep most of the strategic areas west of the river to satisfy its security needs, while the demographic menace against the constitution of the state would be neutralized; the Palestinian Arabs under Israeli rule, once they are assured of statehood, nationhood, and freedom of choice as to their future, would calm down and desist from violence; the problem of Israeli Arabs, who are torn between their country and their people, would be resolved and each individual would be the master of his or her own fate; Israel could then regain the image of a peace-loving and generous country, once its crucial contribution to Palestinian independence is proven; Israel's eastern border would be secure and peaceful; it would be able

to remain a Jewish and democratic state, free from the demographic menace; Israel's improved image and peaceful boundaries would render it an attractive place for other Jews around
the world; and Israeli settlements in the territories would not
only be maintained, but they could even be reinforced under
the reciprocity rule invoked above.

2. *The Palestinians*, who also claim the right to all Palestine, would
   have to compromise by ceding to Israel most of the territory
   west of Jordan. They would likewise have to abrogate or alter
   the Charter, so that the 'Right of Return' and 'armed struggle'
   are amended and an accommodation of the Jewish-Zionist state
   is adopted. In return, they would get three-quarters of historical Palestine, where plenty of territory is available for resettling
   refugees who have been languishing in tepid camps for the past
   sixty years. They would finally have a state of their own, and
   gain Israel's recognition and safe boundaries with her. They
   would control the fate of most Palestinians, either directly
   through Palestinian rule over them, or indirectly, via citizenship
   to those dwelling in Israel and elsewhere. They could enjoy
   Israeli technical and economic aid, and Israel's collaboration in
   trade, labour markets, ports to the Mediterranean, and help
   against common enemies who would not reconcile with the
   Israeli–Palestinian peace. They would, in short, be able to channel their enormous energies, talent, manpower, and creativity
   to developing their country, resettling their refugees, and cultivating their heritage and culture. They would also be able to
   enjoy a large and strong army posted east of the Jordan River,
   which would pose no threat to Israel.

3. *The Jordanian Royal House* would have to renounce a large
   part of its ruling authority and become a constitutional
   monarchy, in recognition that 'popular will' in today's Jordan
   is expressed by the Palestinian population that constitutes the
   majority there. Certainly, no ruler has ever relinquished
   power out of his own volition, but this would be a much smaller sacrifice than the territorial and ideological concessions
   that both Israel and the Palestinians would be called upon to
   make. In return, the king would, perhaps, be able to regain
   some lost parts of his kingdom; he would increase the number
   of his subjects, enjoy full legitimacy as head of a 'Hashemite

Palestinian' state whose government represents the preponderance of the Palestinians within and outside the kingdom.
He would enjoy peace with Israel and stability for his crown,
and would be able to devote his energies to government, culture, and economic matters as a reigning but not governing
head of state. He could, perhaps, even retain some authority
as Supreme Commander of the armed forces; he could dissolve the Parliament, nominate the government, and the like.
If he is so sure of his popularity among his subjects, he could
even abdicate his throne and run for election as the head of
state or the prime minister thereof.

It is evident that if such a plan were announced by Israel, it would
immediately be rejected as a non-starter by the Palestinians and
the king. Therefore, it is vital that the United States and such
Arab countries such as Saudi Arabia and Egypt, who carry much
influence in Jordan and control much of its livelihood, should
first adopt the plan or a variation of it as a basis for negotiations,
before it is presented to the world. When the king is then faced
with the painful choice of either losing everything or compromis-
ing with the Palestinians and Israel, he might consider this
option. So might the Palestinians, who can only gain from a settlement of this sort, and so might Israel who can be talked into
such a solution. The most vital interests of all parties are served
and, therefore, they are likely to make the necessary concessions.
This proposal would then create the necessary ambiance to produce other similar solutions along the other borders with Israel
after the Palestinian powder keg had been defused and the
Palestinian settlement is alive, breathing, and kicking (gently and
creatively). Then, all sorts of other regional arrangements could
be dreamt of, such as federations, confederations, common markets, and even security pacts. This can be done only after the
Palestinians have savoured the taste of freedom and independence. Only then would they be sufficiently self-confident to consider sacrificing part of it for the sake of establishing larger supra-
state organizations. Only then could the Middle East march
toward new horizons that are unimaginable today.

It is possible that the present solution is far from perfect, but
the others are even worse. Great statesmanship consists of

seizing the imperfect, the difficult, and the uncomfortable before it becomes infeasible and impossible. Otherwise, we are all bound to embark on an impasse that could only lead to more war and bloodshed. Perhaps the *intifada*, which has rendered Palestinian suffering even more unbearable, would be the turning point that could prove to everyone that the tragic Palestinian Triangle could be finally squared.

NOTE

This was first publshed in *Terrorism*, 13 (1990), pp. 337–51.

CHAPTER TWELVE

Is Stability Necessary or Advisable for Peace?

There is nothing stable in the world;
uproar's your only music
(John Keats, Letters, 13 January 1818)

There is an atavistic human quest for stability. The fear to lose what one has, the suspicion from uncertainty and what it may hold, the need for repetition of the known and the rehearsed, are stronger than the curiosity to explore new avenues, and more overwhelming than the daring it takes to change the familiar. Therefore, change and turmoil have been the domain of the outstanding few, while conservatism and stability are the region of the many. Not surprisingly, conservatism and stability have been safeguarded by those who could lose from change, while the impulse for change has been the motivating force behind the have-nots, revolutionaries or 'progressives', who could only gain from it.

In politics, national and international, the catch-word is 'stability'; namely, regardless of the nature of a domestic regime, and of the uneasy coexistence between various powers on the international arena, everyone craves stability. In other words, better to have a stable evil government somewhere, than have a more benevolent administration collapse every now and then unpredictably throwing the country into instability. With a stable regime, one asserts, one could do business and rely on continuity, expectability and accountability, while with a chaotic system one is afraid and reluctant to deal, lest investments are wiped out, alliances collapse, regional security compromised and trade halted.

But one has to pause for a moment to ask whether stability is always desirable, possible or necessary; and whether change, especially if it is for the better, is not preferable even when it generates chaos, disorder and unpredictability, at least in the transition phase. Hence, instead of taking stability as a paradigmatic axiom and as a prerequisite for peace and prosperity, that one has to pursue at any cost and under all circumstances, one ought to take a look at the necessary differentiation between desirable and undesirable stability; a stability one ought to encourage and another that one must undo; a good stability and a bad one.

POSITIVE STABILITY AND NEGATIVE STABILITY

For decades, the Cold War was an element of stability between the two superpowers: each of them could destroy the other many times over; each dominated its system of alliances that were pitted against the other's (NATO versus the Warsaw Pact); each undermined the other in overt and covert activities; each operated under the assumption that it ought to win over new allies and subtract them from the other; each competed with the other on the international scene in economics, ethics, politics, sports, propaganda, the military and the production of weapons of mass destruction. And yet, that stability, which translated from the 1960s onwards into 'peaceful co-existence' and later into the various SALT talks, contained an element of instability inasmuch as each side proclaimed its upcoming victory by peaceful means over its rival. By definition, if you compete with your rival and wish to undo it, or change it to your liking, you introduce instability into the equation.

This exercise in unstable stability climaxed under the Reagan Administration of the 1980s, when on the one hand, frequent summitry with Gorbachev was proclaimed to be diminishing world tensions and eradicating the dangers of Armageddon; but on the other hand, Star Wars was initiated by the Americans to stretch the Soviet economy to its limit and push it to abandon the arms race. This process, in retrospect, triggered the changes in the Soviet Bloc and brought about its demise and the dismantling of communist regimes everywhere thereafter. So, as long as the seeming inter-power parity prevailed, there was a similitude of stability that was constantly undermined by American ambitions to bring to an end the 'Evil Empire', and the Soviets' desperate attempt to hold their own while they were aware that the hollow structure of communism was well on its way to crumbling and creating a new instability of world proportions.

That American endeavour to create an instability that would bring down communism, while at the same time clamouring for stability, was eventually replaced by a new quest for stability once the new post-Soviet Yeltsin regime of the 1990s proved more to the liking of America, insofar as it signalled and herald-ed the triumph of capitalism. This new shift in American policy was also predicated on the assumption that being the only remaining superpower, the US could henceforth single-handedly run the new world of *Pax Americana*, in which it would play the predominant role, hence its vested interest in perpetuating it through stability and economic prosperity. But there are already signs that, a forceful and nationalist post-Yeltsin regime having taken over, it is by no means certain that Russia will toe the Western line, and it will probably try to reassert, in competition with the US, a more dominant role in the world. The first indica-tions of this have already been seen in the provision of Russian nuclear technology to Iran, and in Russian support for Saddam's regime in Iraq. Again, this might turn into a new stability for the Russian regime which generates regional and world instability.

These varying American choices and responses go a long way to show that stability as a flat and general proposition has little meaning unless it is qualified as positive or negative, and for whom. This dilemma of striving to attain a positive stability, while seeking to undermine a negative one, has had many antecedents in world history and in world affairs today, not only as part and parcel of foreign policy made by the major powers, but also in the day-to-day decisions that every country takes. The seeming contradictions in foreign policy stem from the necessity to relate to other countries not as the product of a preconceived strategy, concocted in armchairs behind the closed doors of some chanceries, but as a response to rising challenges from the out-side. In this sense, it is erroneous to speak of foreign policy, but rather of foreign relations within which every country attempts its best to respond to rising problems not of its own doing. When it is shaken by what lies at its doorstep, it calls the situation 'unstable', but when it responds to the expected and predictable, it dubs the occasion 'stable'.

During the Second World War the US, the Soviet Union and China were allies against Germany and Japan; immediately after the war, the US and Japan became the closest allies in East Asia against the Soviets and the Communist Chinese. The alliances forged during the war, in a period of turmoil and instability, which came in response to German and Japanese aggression in Europe and the Pacific, were reversed immediately after the war with a view of establishing a new era of stability. But why were the alliances shifted so radically? It was thought that while wartimes were inherently unstable, the post-war era could afford new alignments that would create stability. But once again it was proved that competition was antithetical to stability.

The Cold War, which pitted one half of the world against another, with the Third World striving to play a role in the middle, was a case in point. In Europe competition brought about the escalation of the arms race – hardly a component of stability, the Berlin crisis and then the Ulbricht Wall, the Hungarian revolt, the Prague Spring and then the Brezhnev Doctrine; in the Americas, it was the Castro takeover in Havana, with the attending urban guerrilla warfare in Central and South America, the Guevarist movement and then the Cuban crisis, the anti-Allende Coup and the rise of Pinochet, with the Liberation Theology and the American intervention in Panama and Granada; in the Middle East, several wars between Israel and the Arabs, then the nationalist coups in Egypt, Syria, Iraq and the Yemen, followed by Islamic revolutions in Libya, Iran and the Sudan; in Asia, two India–Pakistan wars, one China–India war, the Korean War, the Vietnam War, the Taiwan Crisis, the Afghanistan War and any number of less visible conflicts in the jungles of Thailand, Burma, Malaysia and Indonesia. All these were illustrations of instability in the putatively 'stable' world of the Cold War, which was supposed to be sustained by the infamous 'balance of fear'.

Predictably, the contenders in all those conflicts accused each other of destabilizing local, regional and world peace and security, claiming that if they could only be left alone to their devices without outside interference, peace and stability would reign. But the question is what exactly disturbs that stability: a communist takeover in Korea and Vietnam, or American intervention to avert it; China asserting its sovereignty in the Taiwan Straits, or the 7th Fleet's attempt to block it; India's hold on Kashmir and Ladakh, or the Chinese and Pakistani attempts to dislodge it; a Prague Spring and a Solidarity Uprising in Gdansk, or a Soviet move to smash them; the lawful election of a Socialist government in Santiago, or the unlawful move to crush it and replace it with dictatorship; Israel's holding on to territories claimed by the Arabs, or the latter's repeated attempts to retrieve them? Stability, then, like beauty and wisdom, is in the eye of the beholder. This observation, in itself, already puts into doubt any sweeping definition of 'stability', much more so any value judgement about the worth of stability.

It seems, then, that what we call 'stability' can hardly be evaluated with objective tools of logic, or with fair scales of equity. For example, Suharto's Indonesia was described as 'stable' for thirty years, and then it turned out that the brutality, corruption, nepotism, oppression, discrimination and violence which held that stability together were precisely the elements which prompted its demise. Admittedly, that regime, like Pinochet's and like the Shah's in Iran or the King's in Saudi Arabia, had also generated prosperity, if compared with previous and following regimes; but one wonders whether the same economic achievements could not be attained by more benevolent rulers, even at the cost of less 'stability', in the short run, and a longer-lasting stability in the final analysis (like in Italy). The reverse is also true: can economic prosperity and temporary stability be achieved within a relatively tight but benevolent regime, though ultimately that stability may prove hollow and untenable? (See Tito's Yugoslavia, Kuwait, Singapore, Taiwan, to cite but a few cases.)

The major powers value stability. But what sort of stability do they envisage? How do they propose to settle the contradictions between value and asset, ideological versus perceived national interest? Is 'stability' in Saudi Arabia valuable at any price, even with its dismal record of human rights and absolute monarchical rule? In other words, does possession of oil reserves absolve one from the need to respect the rudiments of democratic rule and of human rights? Or, is the ideological commitment to those lofty ideals so flexible as to apply only when it is materially convenient? That means that the quest for 'stability' follows perceived interests even when it is evil, and that the values of democracy and human rights are only paid lip-service when it is possible.

Take the case of North Korea. The West has proclaimed that its putative possession of a nuclear capability contributes to instability. Why? Because only the Western powers' possession of the same contributes to world stability – an axiom which needs no proof. One cannot aspire to replace what it perceives as a bad regime and at the same time clamour for stability. Where does one want to seek stability? In the existing evil (in its eyes) order or in its replacement and by what? The very fact that the US and South Korea are alerting the world to the famine in the North, and their generous demarche to send in food, is in itself an element of instability, inasmuch as it signals that the northern regime is unable to feed its people, and therefore the population has to be encouraged to replace it. If you want to replace regimes you cause instability.

Now why is it that in North Korea, in Allende's Chile, in Castro's Cuba and in Saddam's Iraq, there was need to change the regime in order to achieve 'stability', while in Saudi Arabia, in Pinochet's Chile, in Suharto's Indonesia and in the Shah's Iran, 'stability' was supposedly achieved by the governments in place, and therefore they ought to be protected rather than overthrown? Is it because this sort of 'stability' is best achieved via democracy? Not necessarily, as the removed Allende's democratically elected regime, and, conversely, the protected autocratic rule in Riyadh, would attest. There is no escaping the conclusion that a good or positive stability, namely one that caters to one's interests, must be preserved, even if, paradoxically, it creates havoc and death (South Vietnam), oppression and obscurantism (Saudi Arabia), violence and misery (Indonesia) and so on. Conversely, stability must be eliminated when it does (perceived) disservice to the beholder even when it is democratically based (Allende's Chile) or provides continuity and stability (Saddam's Iraq). Moreover, a flip-flop policy can be adopted towards the very same regime: think about American courtship of the same Saddam, as expressed in Ambassador April Gillespie's approval of the Iraqi dictator and his policy, and the American reversal of that policy when Saddam dared to threaten American interests in Kuwait.

STABILITY AND PEACE

Is stability a prerequisite for peace? Does stability necessarily lead to peace? We have seen that the stable governments of Nasser in Egypt in the 1950s and 1960s, and Saudi Arabia's, Syria's, Iraq's and Jordan's continuous and seemingly stable systems, far from producing peace in the Middle East, on the contrary spawned war and conflict. Conversely, it was Sadat's transitory government, lasting one decade between Nasser and Mubarak, which produced the initiative that continues to nurture the peace process to this day. This means that peace (namely, regional or world stability) is not necessarily the product of local or national stability, nor is the contrary right either: it was the stable regime of North Korea which triggered the Korean War in the 1950, and it was the stable regimes of Nasser and Assad, and for that matter of Israel, which triggered the many conflicts in the Middle East; it was the seemingly stable Soviet Union and its clients which generated the East European (Hungary in 1956, Czechoslovakia in 1968) and the Central Asian (Afghanistan in 1979) crises. Or might one say that those conflicts were boosted by the inherent instability of those regimes?

It would seem that the reasons for peace and conflict have to be sought elsewhere than in stability/instability which, as we have seen, cannot be defined by an objective yardstick. For while everyone speaks of the need for stability and pays lip-service to it, everyone means a different kind of stability. Maybe the entire world would be remarkably stable if it was permitted to fall under Hitler's or Stalin's aegis. Without inner or outer opposition to counter them, those totalitarian regimes would have achieved stability and world peace. But this is not the kind of peace or stability that most people in the West have in mind. Negative stability, as evidenced in the great empires in history, as in the modern Nazi and Soviet empires that were based on force, conquest, coercion and pluralistic societies and cultures which could not be held together indefinitely, is then transitory by nature. The negativity of this stability, which by definition needs to be improved upon, is defined by ideological outlook (e.g. liberal democracies looking upon totalitarian or theocratic regimes; or socialist countries looking upon crude capitalism, or theocracies looking upon loose and permissive societies). If its opponents regard this stability as negative and are therefore bent on rocking it, this in itself defines it as unstable in the long run.

It is, then, the positive kind of stability which is analytically problematic for achieving peace, because, paradoxically, it is not predicated on a constant ideological rift but on shifting perceptions of self-interest. For instance, the Bosnia and Kosovo crises and the Kurdish and Chechnyan counter-examples: in Bosnia and in Kosovo it was imperative for the West to intervene, in order to rescue those underdogs from the claws of the 'evil' and 'rapacious' Serbs, in order to achieve stability in the Balkans. But the much more numerous Kurds, who have been fighting in vain for their liberty for a much longer period of time, deserve neither the sympathy nor the intervention of the West on their behalf, even when their continued repression in Turkey, Iraq, Iran and Syria causes instability in their regions. What is even more stupefying is that the Bosnian and Kosovar Muslims have been aided by Iranian and other Muslim fundamentalists who do not hide their contempt and enmity towards the West and they were nevertheless aided for the sake of stability, while the Kurds were left to their fate, in spite of the fact that they are oppressed by authoritarian regimes of the worst kind, for fear of causing instability.

It turns out, then, that the argument of stability/instability, which is advanced to justify a policy, is more a pretext to rationalize the protection of one's perceived immediate interests than a well-grounded long-term policy calculated to attain well-defined goals. When one so wishes, stability is at stake, and when one is otherwise inclined, then instability is invoked. Take the first and second Gulf Wars for example: when the 'island of stability' that was the Shah's Iran was swept by revolution, the US and others thought that the Islamic revolutionaries introduced an element of instability in the Gulf. But when Khomeini took over and evinced signs of resilience and stability, the US and other powers did not hesitate to pit Iraq against it, as if by creating a new instability stability could be restored. The war between those two powers in the Gulf lasted for eight years (longer than the Second World War!), and no one seemed preoccupied by the instability it caused. Quite the contrary, the oil market adjusted to the new situation, and Saddam's 'moderation' was lauded in the West, so much so that America's best Arab friends in the Middle East (Egypt and Jordan) were prodded to join the four-party 'union' with Iraq and Yemen, which legitimized the Iraqi regime in the eyes of the West, as long as Saddam was waging his murderous war against the Iranians. Normally, war is certainly not a measure sought by those who profess stability, but here it seemed to preoccupy no one.

In that first Gulf War, the West failed to comprehend Saddam's designs which undermined stability, when they imputed to him the moderation he did not possess and overlooked his invasion of the Iranian shoreline which would have assured him (and them, they thought) Iraqi control of much of the Iranian oil and a coast line that would enable him to deploy a strong navy in the Gulf without incurring Iranian threats on his clogged 25-mile wide access to the ocean from the Shatt-al-Arab waterway. But when he failed against the Iranians, who now became the element of stability against the whims of the Iraqi ruler, he turned to the opposite shore of the Gulf, Kuwait, in order precisely to achieve those two same strategic goals: a seashore and more oil reserves. But now, the same Saddam became a devil who plotted to overthrow stability and bring a reign of chaos into the Gulf. With Saddam reigning over Kuwait, and possibly the northern Saudi coast, thus laying his hand on much of the oil reserves of the world, a remarkable stability would have prevailed in that region, if the US had opted to regard it that way. After all, he could not have drunk his oil and was depending on Western markets to sell it.

But the US reasoned differently: if a dictator takes over Kuwait and menaces Saudi Arabia, in both of which there was no great democracy in any case, then stability is menaced and the US is compelled to act, even to go to war, in order to restore stability at the cost of creating more instability. Of course, rationalizations were churned out very busily: America had to rescue those 'friends' from the tyrant (who exactly ruled them before the Iraqis, illustrious democrats?); democratization would be boosted in those countries after America's intervention, but in fact after Saddam was defeated, the Americans were urged to leave the Saudi shores and all the Gulf states reverted to their strict monarchical rule of 'dancing sheikh to sheikh'; Saddam was to be dethroned, but he remained solidly on his base, now humiliated and seeking revenge, not exactly a recipe for stability; the Shi'ites and the Kurds were to be rescued from the claws of the dictator, but both were left to his mercy; the Iraqi military backbone was to be broken, but it endured. No stability was served, the oil was subtracted from one dominion and subjected to the other, both as unstable as could be.

CONCLUSIONS

Like John Stuart Mill's memorable saying in another context, it would seem that 'a party of order or stability and a party of progress or reform, are both necessary elements of a healthy state of political life' (*On Liberty*, II). Translated to the international scene, one is bound to recognize that stability and instability must dwell together like the lamb and the wolf in Isaiah's prophecy. For stability, when evil, must and will be gnawed at by its opponents until it is eroded and destroyed, as was the case with Hitler's and Stalin's. To attain this, one must support the necessary instability which, alone, can undermine that sort of stability. When instability is evil in the eye of the beholder, then one must and will deploy efforts to stabilize the situation in a way acceptable to liberal democracies, which will render it a positive stability.

Bibliography

ARABIC AND ISLAMIC MEDIA

Much of the Arabic materials cited here is extracted from Memri (Middle East Media Research Institute)

Afaq 'Arabiya (Egypt)
Akhbar al-Yaum (Cairo)
Akher Sa'a (Egypt)
Al-Ahram (Cairo)
Al Akhbar (Cairo)
Al-'Arabi (Cairo)
Al-'Awda (Palestinian Authority)
Al-Ayyam (Yemen and Palestinian Authority)
Al-Hayat (London)
Al-Dustour (Jordan)
Al-'ilm (Cairo)
Al-Islam wa-Filastin
Al-Gumhuriya (Egypt)
Al-Jazeera TV (Qatar)
Al Manar TV (Hizbullah, Lebanon)
Al-Mustaqbal (Lebanon)
Al-Qahira (Cairo)
Al-Quds (Palestinian Authority)
Al Quds al-'Arabi (London)
Al-Ra'y
Al-Raya (Qatar)
Al-Risala (Palestinian Authority)
Al-Riyad (Saudi Arabia)

Al-Sha'b (Egypt)
Al-Sharq al Awsat (London)
Al-Sirat (Umm al-Fahm)
Al-'Ukadh (Saudi Arabia)
Al-Usbu' (Cairo)
Al-Wafd (Egypt)
Al-Watan (Kuwait)
Fasl al-Maqal (Nazareth)
Hadith al-Madina (Egypt)
Iqra' TV (Saudi Arabia and Egypt)
Kul-al-Arab (Israel)
October (Cairo)
Palestine TV (Palestinian Authority)
Sawt al-Umma (Egypt)

NON-ARABIC MEDIA

Agence France Press (AFP)
Egyptian Gazette (Egypt)
Guardian (London)
Haaretz (Tel Aviv)
IMRA (Independent Media Review and Analysis, Israel)
IRNA (Iranian News Agency)
Jerusalem Post (Jerusalem)
Le Monde (Paris)
Liberation (Paris)
Ma'ariv (Tel Aviv)
Mercury
Middle East Digest
Middle East News On line
New York Post (New York)
Philadelphia Inquirer (Philadelphia)
Revue des Deux Mondes (Paris)
The Times (London)
Washington Post (Washington DC)
Xinhua News Agency (China)

BOOKS

Alexander, Yonah, *The 1988–9 Annual of Terrorism* (The Netherlands: Martinus Nijhof, 1990).

Bat Ye'or, *The Decline of Eastern Christianity under Islam: From Jihad to Dhimmitude* (Madison, NJ: Fairleigh Dickinson University Press, 1996).

Bodzemir, M., *Islam et Laicite: Approches Globales et Regionales* (Paris: 1996).

Canak, Jovan (ed.), *Greater Albania: Concepts and Possible Consequences* (Belgrade: Institute of Geo-Political Studies, 1998).

Craig-Harris, Lillian, *China Considers the Middle East* (London: Tauris, 1993).

Haim, Sylvia, *Arab Nationalism* (Berkeley, CA: University of California Press, 1962).

Israeli, Raphael, *Muslims in China: a Study in Cultural Confrontation* (London: Curzon Press, 1980).

Israeli, Raphael, *Man of Defiance: A Political Biography of Anwar Sadat* (London: Weidenfeld and Nicolson, 1985).

Israeli, Raphael, *Peace is in the Eye of the Beholder* (Berlin and New York: Mouton, 1985).

Israeli, Raphael, *Muslim Fundamentalism in Israel* (London: Brassey's, 1993).

Israeli, Raphael, *Fundamentalist Islam and Israel: Essays in Interpretation* (New York: University Press of America, 1993).

Israeli, Raphael, *Poison: Manifestations of a Blood Libel* (New York and Oxford: Lexington Books, 2002).

Israeli, Raphael, *Green Crescent Over Nazareth: The Displacement of Christians by Muslims in the Holy Land* (London: Frank Cass, 2002).

Israeli, Raphael, *Islamikaze: Manifestations of Islamic Martyrology* (London: Frank Cass, 2003).

Johnson, Nelson, *Islam and Politics of Meaning in Palestinian Nationalism* (London: Kegan Paul, 1982).

Kepel, Gilles, *A l'Ouest d'Allah* (Paris: Seuil, 1994).

Lapidus, Ira, *Contemporary Islamic Movements in Historical Perspectives* (Berkeley, CA: University of California Press, 1983).

Linton, R. (ed.), *The Science of Man in the World Crisis* (New York: Columbia University Press, 1957).

Mayer, Ann, *Islam and Human Rights: Traditions and Politics* (Boulder, CO: Westview Press, 1991).

Naveh, Danny (compiler), *The Involvement of Arafat, Palestinian Authority Senior Officials and Apparatuses in Terrorism Against Israel, Corruption and Crime,* released by Israel's government in April 2002.

Nuseibeh, Sary and Mark Heller, *No Trumpets, No Drums* (New York: Hill and Wang, 1993).

Patterns of Global Terrorism, US Department of State, April 1998

Peroncel-Hugoz, J.P., *The Raft of Muhammed* (New York: Paragon, 1988).

Post, Jerrald, *The Qa'eda Training Manual: Military Studies in the Jihad Against the Tyrants* (London: Frank Cass, 2002). Also published as a special issue of *Terrorism and Political Violence,* 14, 1 (Spring 2002).

Qut'b, Sayyid, *Ma'rakatuna ma'a al-Yahud* (Our Battle Against the Jews) (Beirut, 1986).

Report on Law Enforcement among Minorities in Israel in the 21st Century (Hebrew) (Jerusalem: Jerusalem Center for Public Affairs, 1993).

Rekhes, Elie, *Arabs in Israeli Politics* (Tel Aviv: Tel Aviv University, 1998).

Sela, Abraham (ed.), *Poiltical Encyclopedia of the Middle East* (Jerusalem: Jerusalem Publishing House, 1999).

Sivan, Emanuel, *Radical Islam* (New Haven, CT: Yale University Press, 1985).

Terzic, Slavenko (ed.), *Islam, the Balkans and the Great Powers (xiv–xx Centuries)* (Belgrade: Serbian Academy of Science, Vol 14, 1997).

The Secret Ties Between the Nazis and the Zionist Movement Leadership (Amman: Dar ibn-Rushd, 1984) (Arabic)

Toubia, Nahid (ed.), *Women in the Arab World: the Coming Challenge* (London: Zed Books, 1990).

Warraq, Ibn, *Why I am not a Muslim* (New York: Prometheus, 1995).

Watt, Montgomery, *Muhammad at Medina* (Oxford: Clarendon Press, 1956.

Weissbrod, Amir (ed.), *Turabi: Spokesman of Radical Islam* (Tel Aviv: Dayan Center of Middle Eastern and African Studies, Tel Aviv University, 1999) (Hebrew),

ARTICLES

Amir, Menachem, 'Political Crime and Common Criminality: Some Preliminary Considerations', *Violence, Aggression and Terrorism,* 1, 4 (1981).

Batakovic, Dusan, 'La Bosnie-Hercegovine: le Systeme des Alliances', in Slavenko Terzic (ed.), *Islam, the Balkans and the Great Powers (xiv–xx Centuries)* (Belgrade: Serbian Academy of Science, Vol. 14, 1997).

Bled, Jean-Paul, 'La Question de Bosnie-Hercegovine dand la Revue des Deux Mondes', in Slavenko Terzic (ed.), *Islam, the Balkans and the Great Powers (xiv–xx Centuries)* (Belgrade: Serbian Academy of Science, Vol. 14, 1997).

Bruinessen, Martin van, 'Islam, Women's Rights and Islamic Feminism', ISIM (September 2001).

Burdman, Daphne, 'Education, Indoctrination and Incitement: Palestinian Children on their Way to Martyrdom', *Journal of Terrorism and Political Violence,* 15, 1 (Spring 2003), pp.96–123.

Busset, H. 'Omar's Image as the Conqueror of Jerusalem', *Jerusalem Studies of Arabic and Islam,* 8, (1986), pp.153–4.

Elad, Amikam, 'Why did Abd-al-Malik build the Dome of the Rock?', in J. Raby and J. Johns (eds), *Bayt al-Maqdas* (Oxford: Oxford University Press, 1992), pp.33–57.

Fuletic, Duro, 'Consequences of a Possible Creation of Greater Albania', *Review of International Affairs,* L, 1085–6 (October–November 1999).

Hadzivukovic, Vesna, 'The Future Saints', *Chronicle of Announced Death* (Belgrade, 1993).

Hawting, Gerald, 'Al-Hudaybiyya and the Conquest of Mecca', *Jerusalem Studies of Arabic and Islam,* 8 (1986), pp.1–23

Israeli, Raphael, 'Sadat Between Arabism and Africanism', *Middle East Review,* 2 (Spring 1979), pp.39–48

Israeli, Raphael, 'On the Identity Problem of Israeli Arabs', in A. Hareven (ed.), *One out of Six Israelis* (Jerusalem: Van Leer, 1981) (Hebrew).

Israeli, Raphael, 'The Charter of Allah: The Platform of the Islamic Resistance Movement (Hamas)', in Y. Alexander, *The Annual of Terrorism, 1988–9* (The Netherlands: Nijhoff, 1990), pp.99–134

Israeli, Raphael, 'Muslim Fundamentalists as Social Revolutionaries: the Case of Israel', *Terrorism and Political Violence*, 6, 4, (1994), pp.462–75.

Israeli, Raphael, 'Islamikaze and their Significance', *Journal of Terrorism and Political Violence*, 9, 3 (Autumn 1997), pp.96–121.

Israeli, Raphael, 'Education, State-Building and the Peace Process: Educating Palestinian Children in the Post-Oslo Era', *Journal of Terrorism and Political Violence*, 12, 1 (Spring 2000), pp.79–84.

Israeli, Raphael, 'State and Religion in the Emerging Palestinian Entity', *Journal of Church and State*, 4 (Spring 2002).

Kister, Meir, 'Al-Hira', *Arabica*, 15 (1968).

Kister, Meir, 'The Massacre of Banu Qurayza', *Jerusalem Studies of Arabic and Islam*, 8 (1986), pp.61–96

Lecker, Michael, 'The Hudaybiyya Treaty and the Expedition against Khaybar', *Jerusalem Studies in Arabic and Islam*, 5 (1984), pp.1–11.

Lewis, Bernard, 'The Return of Islam', *Commentary* (Winter 1976).

Litvak, Meir, 'The Islamization of Palestinian Identity: the Case of Hamas', *Data Analysis* (Tel Aviv: Moshe Dayan Center, Tel Aviv University, August 1996).

Majer, Hans, 'The Functioning of a Multi-ethnic and Multi-religious State: The Ottoman Empire', in Slavenko Terzic (ed.), *Islam, the Balkans and the Great Powers (xiv–xx Centuries)* (Belgrade: Serbian Academy of Science, Vol. 14, 1997).

Minces, Juliette, 'Women in Algeria', in L. Beck and N. Keddie (eds), *Women in the Muslim World* (Cambridge, MA: Harvard University Press, 1978).

'Policy Watch', 296 (1998), No 3, Washington, DC: Washington Institute.

Popovic, Alexander, 'La Politiqye Titist envers les Religions et ses Consequences', in M. Bodzemir, *Islam et Laicite: Approches Globales et Regionales* (Paris: 1996), pp.98–102.

Reuter, Jens, 'From Religious Community to Nation: The Ethnogenesis of the Bosnian Muslims', in Slavenko Terzic (ed.), *Islam, the Balkans and the Great Powers (xiv–xx Centuries)* (Belgrade: Serbian Academy of Science, Vol. 14, 1997).

Stowasser, B.F., 'Liberated Equal or Protected Dependent? Contemporary Religious Paradigms on Women's Status in Islam', *Arab Studies Quarterly*, 9, 3 (1987).

Todorov, Vrban, 'The Federalist Idea as a Means for Preserving the Integrity of the Ottoman Empire', in Slavenko Terzic (ed.), *Islam, the Balkans and the Great Powers (xiv–xx Centuries)* (Belgrade: Serbian Academy of Science, Vol. 14, 1997).

Tsimhoni, Daphna, 'Christians in Israel Between Religion and Politics', in Elie Rekhes, *Arabs in Israeli Politics* (Tel Aviv: Tel Aviv University, 1998).

Webman, Esther, 'Antisemitic Motifs in the Ideology of Hizaballah and the Hamas', *Project for the Study of Antisemitism* (Tel Aviv: Tel Aviv University, 1994).

Winkelman, Mareike Jule, 'The Construction of Female Identity in Muslim Modernity', *Newsletter of the International Institute for the Study of Islam in the Modern World* (ISIM), September 2001.

Wirth, Louis, 'The Problem of Minority Groups', in R. Linton (ed.), *The Science of Man in the World Crisis* (New York: Columbia University Press, 1957).

Index